SPIEGEL DER ZEIT

An introduction to current affairs
based on extracts from *Die Zeit*

GERTRUD SEIDMANN

LONGMAN

LONGMAN GROUP LIMITED
London

Associated companies, branches and representatives throughout the world
This edition © Longman Group Ltd (formerly Longmans, Green and Co Ltd) 1969

First published 1969
New impression 1970

SBN 582 36180 X

Printed in Great Britain by Lowe & Brydone (Printers) Ltd., London

Acknowledgements

Grateful thanks are due to the former Editor of **Die Zeit,** Herr Josef
Müller-Marein, for kindly permitting the compilation of this book, and
the use of copyright material, and to the many authors whose work in
some cases has been so ruthlessly abbreviated; to **Die Zeit/Globus** for
the use of the diagrams on pp. 16, 23, 27, 75, to Leonore Mau and
DEFA for the photographs on pp. 38 and 93, to Herr Paul Flora for
permitting the reproduction of the witty drawings with which he continues
to embellish the pages of **Die Zeit** and to R. B. Tilford whose scrutiny
of the notes saved me from several errors and omissions.

Foreword

'**Die Zeit** is one of the world's best newspapers,' wrote Kenneth Ames in the *Spectator*: a graceful tribute from one respected weekly to another, which indeed offers up such riches of information, comment and discussion that each weekly issue might well provide food for a month's serious study.

One could think of few better media to introduce the young student, once he has mastered the basic skills of the German language, to the topics and the language of informed current discussion within Germany—whether about the country itself and the life within it, or about European and world affairs—were it not for the length and density of the articles, the size of the pages, the sheer volume of each copy, which must seem forbidding at first sight.

The compiler of this book has therefore tried to ease the student's first steps into this territory by choosing brief but significant extracts, and in some cases abbreviating longer articles; by providing short notes, and more extended *Sprachübungen*, which will, it is hoped, serve to increase his command of the language both passive and active; and to encourage further thought and discussion by suggesting essay topics relating to each of the ten headings under which the extracts are grouped. The omission of *Sprachübungen* relating to Sections 2 and 10 has been deliberate: matters of tragic seriousness and a humorous *coda* are not suitable pegs for linguistic exercises.

Two more extended notes, on the *Bundesrepublik* and the *DDR*, have been placed before the first section, to provide a contextual glossary of political terms which recur again and again in the texts; a similar extended note on the German school system precedes Section 7.

G.S.

Contents

Notes on Political Terms

Die Bundesrepublik: die Bundesrepublik Deutschland, BRD, or *die Deutsche Bundesrepublik,* official designation since 1949 of the state colloquially known as *Westdeutschland,* formed on the basis of the amalgamation of the three Western Allied zones of military occupation on German territory after the Second World War. It consists of 10 *Bundesländer* and West-Berlin. Its constitution was established by a *Grundgesetz* promulgated in 1949. The Federal Government, *die Bundesregierung,* at the head of which stands the Chancellor, *der Bundeskanzler,* is formed on the basis of party representation in the legislative chamber of parliament, *der Bundestag;* the second chamber, *der Bundesrat,* is nominated by the governments of the *Länder.*

The principal political parties, *Parteien,* at the time to which these extracts refer, were the *CDU (Christlich-Demokratische Union)* and its sister-organisation, the *CSU (Christlich-Soziale Union)* in Bavaria, a party of the centre which had provided successive Chancellors since the first postwar head of government, Dr. Konrad Adenauer; the *SPD (Sozialistische Partei Deutschlands),* the second largest, was in opposition until the formation of the *Große Koalition* in 1966, when it entered into coalition with the *CDU* under the leadership of Dr. G. Kiesinger; and the much smaller *FDP (Freie Demokratische Partei),* until 1966 the *CDU's* coalition partner, which united both liberal and rightist elements.

The *BRD* was one of the six original members of the *Europäische Wirtschafts-Gemeinschaft (EWG),* the European Common Market which grew out of the Coal and Steel Authority of 1952, with its administrative headquarters in Brussels.

Die Deutsche Demokratische Republik, DDR: the official style of the Eastern German state, established mainly on the territory occupied by Russian forces after the war, including East-Berlin and terminating to the East at the Oder-Neisse line. At the time of writing it was not recognized as a sovereign state by either the *BRD,* Great Britain or the United States; in the *BRD* it was officially styled the *sowjetische Besatzungszone (SBZ)* and colloquially known simply as *'die Zone',* the dividing line between the two Germanies as *die Zonengrenze.*

Its controlling political party was the communist *SED, Sozialistische Einheitspartei Deutschlands.*

The sharp political cleavage between the two Germanies inevitably made the question of a possible re-unification in the future—*Wiedervereinigung*—of more than purely German significance.

MUTMASSUNGEN ÜBER DEUTSCHLAND

1

Die Zeit bat 1965 einige Deutschlandkorrespondenten der ausländischen Presse, ihre persönlichen Eindrücke über Deutschland niederzuschreiben. Der Titel der Serie, aus der hier kurze Ausschnitte gebracht werden, spielt auf Uwe Johnsons Roman *Mutmaßungen über Jakob* an.

1. Land ohne Hauptstadt

Es ist aus verschiedenen Gründen nicht leicht, über die Bundesrepublik zu schreiben—sogar dann, wenn man in diesem Land seit mehr als fünf Jahren diplomatischer Korrespondent ist.

Selbst wenn man lange in Westdeutschland ist, kann man nur die Eindrücke summieren, aber es ist nicht möglich, die in jeder Hinsicht komplizierte Situation zu bewältigen.

Will man ein Land kennenlernen, dann beginnt man die Beobachtung in der Regel in seiner Hauptstadt. Westdeutschland jedoch hat im Grunde genommen keine Hauptstadt und hat bisher kein Zentrum geschaffen, das als Ort für eine solche Beobachtung geeignet wäre. Eine Hauptstadt in des Wortes eigentlicher Bedeutung ist Bonn nicht—genausowenig wie Washington oder Ankara oder Brasilia. Die Entstehung einer Hauptstadt kann man nicht anordnen. Daher ist Bonn bestenfalls Sitz der staatlichen Verwaltung und des Bundestages.

Die Beobachtung des Besuchers ist also vom Startort abhängig—davon, ob er die Reise durch Deutschland in Hamburg oder in München beginnt, im Ruhrgebiet oder in Frankfurt am Main. Fast ein Jahrhundert nach dem ersten Versuch, Deutschland von oben zu vereinen,[1] hat der traditionelle Partikularismus keineswegs aufgehört, die charakteristische Eigenschaft der deutschen Landschaft auch in politischer Hinsicht zu sein.

Marian Podkowinski *(Trybuna Ludu, Warschau)*

2. Zwei Völker

Ich bin immer wieder zu derselben Feststellung gekommen: Es gibt zwei deutsche Völker. Das erste Volk hat Bürger, die vierzig Jahre und mehr alt sind, das andere besteht aus den jüngeren Leuten. Das erste „Volk" hat unter dem Nazismus gelebt, den Krieg mitgemacht oder eben noch erlebt und ist von allen diesen Erlebnissen gebrandmarkt. Schon physisch unterscheiden sich die Menschen so sehr, daß man schon optisch den Eindruck hat, man habe es mit zwei verschiedenen Völkern zu tun. Sie reagieren auch, sobald sie vor wichtige Fragen gestellt werden, ganz verschiedenartig.

Die ältere Generation denkt an Prosperität und Sicherheit,

die jüngere an die Wiedervereinigung. Die Älteren sind mißtrauisch, die Jüngeren erwarten trotz aller scheinbaren Skepsis eine bessere Zukunft. Es bleibt zu hoffen, daß die jungen Deutschen ihre Zukunft bekommen werden, bevor sie alt sein werden.

Roland Delcour (Le Monde, Paris)

3. Deutschland ist doch anders

Ich kam im April 1963 in die Bundesrepublik—damals, als in Baden-Württemberg[1] die Welt unterging. Anders konnte man, so wenigstens versicherten die konservativen Zeitungen, die Tatsache nicht interpretieren, daß 400000 Metallarbeiter die Arbeit niedergelegt hatten und für höhere Löhne streikten.

Die Überraschung von damals habe ich nicht vergessen, denn die Reaktion der deutschen Öffentlichkeit auf den Streik der IG-Metall[2] wurde für mich ein Schlüssel zum Verständnis der politischen und wirtschaftlichen Situation in der Bundesrepublik; sie lehrte mich die Einstellung der Deutschen von heute zum Staat und. zur Gesellschaft begreifen. Nachdem ich die ersten Wochen in Deutschland fast daran verzweifelt war, dieses Land jemals zu verstehen—dieses höfliche, aber schwer faßbare Land mit seinen breifarbenen Häusern und wohlinformierten Menschen, brillenbewehrt und alle in Mänteln mit schwarz-weißem Fischgrätenmuster— jetzt war plötzlich etwas Ungewöhnliches passiert, es war geradezu eine Offenbarung.

Wie viele Ausländer, hatte auch ich die Klischeevorstellung von Deutschland akzeptiert: Eine mächtige, maschinenhafte Organisation, von gehorsamen Robotern in Gang gehalten, verteidigt von einer ungeheuer schlagkräftigen Armee und mit einem Knopfdruck von Bonn aus kontrolliert. Mein Erlebnis von damals öffnete mir die Augen, und ich sah ein Land, wo die Arbeiter sogar zu streiken wagen, wo die Soldaten (schlecht ausgebildet und mit ausrangiertem Material ausgerüstet, das ihre Alliierten gerne loswerden wollen) den Tag herbeisehnen, an dem sie wieder zu ihrem bequemen Bürostuhl zurückkehren können.

Neal Asherson (The Observer, London)

4. Die öffentliche Meinung

Ich möchte etwas näher auf ein Gebiet eingehen, das mich aus mehreren Gründen interessiert. Ich meine ‚die öffentliche Meinung‘ und denke an Presse, Funk, Fernsehen und die öffentlichen Debatten.

Ich habe den Eindruck gewonnen, daß das Fernsehen oft am schnellsten und wachsten ist, wenn es darum geht, Mißverhältnisse zu beleuchten und kontroverse Fragen zu debattieren. Die seltsamen Methoden, Post aus der DDR zu sortieren, wurden am eindringlichsten im Fernsehen geschildert.

An zweiter Stelle möchte ich die politischen Wochenzeitungen[1] nennen, von denen dieses Blatt hier mir ganz unentbehrlich geworden ist.

Die Tagespresse[2] ist vielfältig, reichhaltig und oft achtenswert, aber ich bin nun in eine mehr angelsächsisch gefärbte Schule gegangen und finde, daß Nachrichten, und besonders Nachrichten über Menschen und menschliche Belange zu kurz kommen. Dagegen ist in den großen Tageszeitungen[3] an prinzipiellen Analysen, vor allem der hohen Politik, kein Mangel. Es ist mir klar, daß die Zeitungen im Wettbewerb mit dem Fernsehen mehr Zusammenfassungen und Analysen bringen müssen, um die Leser in einer komplizierten Welt zu orientieren, aber ich glaube nicht, daß das eine das andere ausschließt. Eines allerdings suche ich vergeblich in den deutschen Zeitungen: eine Debatte. Ich glaube, es wäre sehr förderlich, wenn sie manchmal richtig böse gegeneinander zu Felde zögen.

Wenn ich nun die Tageszeitungen mit der höchsten Auflage[3] und ‚die Illustrierten‘[3] in einem Atemzug nenne, so deshalb, weil sie nach den gleichen Prinzipien redigiert werden. Ein Jahr lang waren die Illustrierten relativ politisiert, aber mit den Bundestagswahlen scheint diese Episode zu Ende zu gehen. Da ich wöchentlich drei Illustrierte nach Hause schleppe, sind meine beiden Söhne in Fragen der Anatomie erheblich versierter, als ich es in ihrem Alter war: der härteste Wettbewerb findet eben doch auf diesem Gebiet statt. Das mag kein Schaden sein, aber das ist sicherlich auch kein Nutzen.

Ich habe eigentlich von ‚der veröffentlichten Meinung‘ gesprochen und nicht von der ‚öffentlichen‘. In jeder funktionierenden Demokratie gibt es wohl eine Differenz zwischen diesen beiden. Die ‚veröffentlichte Meinung‘ ist der

4

‚öffentlichen Meinung', so scheint mir, ein gutes Stück voraus, und der Abstand zwischen den beiden ist hierzulande ungewöhnlich groß.

Per Sjögren (*Dagens Nyheter*, Kopenhagen)

Aufsätze und Aufsatzübungen

1. Versuchen Sie sich vorzustellen, welchen Eindruck ein Ausländer von Ihrem Heimatlande bekommen würde, wenn er seinen Besuch
(a) in der Hauptstadt,
(b) an einem anderen, von Ihnen gewählten Orte antreten würde.
2. Schreiben Sie eine kurze, markante ‚Klischeevorstellung' von
(a) England   (b) den USA   (c) Frankreich   (d) Schottland.
3. Schreiben Sie eine kurze Übersicht über die Presse Ihres Heimatlandes.

DEUTSCHLAND GESTERN

2

Eines der wichtigsten Probleme, dem Deutschland am Ende des zweiten Weltkrieges gegenüberstand, war die sogenannte ‚Auseinandersetzung mit der Vergangenheit‘—d.h. die Notwendigkeit, die zwölf Jahre des Nationalsozialismus, Krieg, Niederlage und militärische Besatzung objektiv zu betrachten und zu verstehen zu lernen.

5. Der Streit über die Vergangenheit

Der an Schizophrenie erinnernde Streit über die deutsche Vergangenheit fällt dem Ausländer sofort auf. Jedes Gespräch beschäftigt sich unweigerlich mit der Vergangenheit and läßt entweder ein Gefühl von Schuld oder Trotz verspüren. Die physischen Narben sind weitgehend verschwunden. Die seelischen Narben dagegen ganz und gar nicht. Das ganze Volk setzt sich immer noch mit dieser einen Frage auseinander. In dieser Beziehung, so muß der Beobachter feststellen, lebt die Bundesrepublik noch in der Nachkriegszeit.

L. Bruce van Voorst (Newsweek)

6. Hitler und seine Zeit: Eine Fernsehdokumentation als Buch

Heinz Huber und Arthur Müller unter Mitwirkung von Waldemar Besson (Herausgeber): *Das Dritte Reich.*[1] *Seine Geschichte in Texten, Bildern und Dokumenten.* Verlag Kurt Desch, München, 2 Bände, 854 Seiten, 175,—DM.

Das Dritte Reich, eine Sendereihe in vierzehn Folgen, wurde vom Deutschen Fernsehen vor vier Jahren zum ersten Male ausgestrahlt. Zweimal wurde die Reihe seither wiederholt. Offenbar hat ihr Erfolg den Desch-Verlag ermuntert, das einmal zusammengetragene Material als Buch herauszubringen. Das Ergebnis ist die bisher fraglos wertvollste Bildgeschichte der Hitler-Zeit.

Etwa 1 500 Photographien, Schaubilder, photokopierte Dokumente, Zeitungsausschnitte und Plakate geben dieser Geschichte des Dritten Reiches ihr eigenes Gepräge. Kaum hätte ein Verlag im Alleingang dieses Material sammeln können, dazu gehört wohl das Arbeitspotential— und natürlich auch das Geld—bundesdeutscher[2] Rundfunkanstalten.

Bei der Darstellung der Vorgeschichte des Dritten Reiches holen die Autoren ungewöhnlich weit aus. Sie gehen zurück bis zur Revolution von 1848,[3] der ersten verpaßten Chance einer deutschen Demokratie. Über Kaiserreich und Weltkrieg führen sie zur zweiten—allerdings viel schwächeren—Chance nach Weimar.[4] Wer dem historischen Determinismus anhängt, mag zuweilen glauben, es habe so kommen

7

müssen, wie es schließlich kam. Eine falsch oder falsch verstandene Tradition, gemischt aus Nationalismus, Militarismus und Untertanengeist, wird hier deutlich. Man sieht kaum ein Bild, auf dem keine Uniformen erscheinen. Das kann manches erklären, zumal wenn die politische Unvernunft des Auslandes hinzukommt, wie nach dem Ersten Weltkrieg.

Dennoch haftet der Wendung ins ‚weltanschaulich‘ sanktionierte Verbrechen, wie es 1933 in Deutschland begann, Rätselhaftes und Unheimliches an, das vielleicht Bilder eher darstellen als Worte. Da posieren die Hauptakteure des Hitler-Putsches[5] 1923 in der trotzigen Haltung biederer Märtyrer, da demonstriert der Kronprinz neben Röhm[6] gegen das Verbot der SA, und da verneigt sich schließlich Hitler vor dem Präsidenten der gestorbenen Republik,[7] der in Uniform und Ordensschmuck des toten Kaiserreiches steif vor ihm steht.

Und plötzlich ist alles anders: Mädchen schwingen fröhlich die Keule, Arbeitskolonnen[8] mit geschultertem Spaten, Richter[9] erheben die Arme zum Hitler–Gruß, alles ‚im gleichen Schritt und Tritt‘.[10] Wohin?—Zunächst brennen nur Bücher, aber in den Fabriken montiert man vorwiegend Kanonen, Panzer, Flugzeuge. In Österreich und im Sudetenland[11] mischt sich Hitler als Befreier unter die jubelnde Menge, in Prag[11] tritt er nur noch an ein Fenster im zweiten Stockwerk der Burg, in den Gesichtern der Tschechen spiegeln sich Verzweiflung und Haß, Ribbentrop[12] und Molotow unterschreiben lächelnd.

Dann brennt Europa. Über Rotterdam[13] hängt eine einzige Rauchglocke, ein jüdischer Junge im Warschauer Getto[13] beißt weinend in ein Stück Brot. Eintönig ist die Fratze des Krieges, die Marschierenden auf verschneiten und verschlammten Wegen, die Toten am Wegrand. Das letzte Bild zeigt einen Mann, eine Frau, ein Kind—und ein Trümmerfeld.

Wohl noch zu keiner Zeit haben scheinbarer Glanz und wirkliches Grauen so nahe beieinander gewohnt wie in diesen zwölf Jahren. Die harten Kontraste haben denn auch die Auswahl und Anordnung der Bilder entscheidend mitbestimmt. Dennoch entdeckt man keine Widersprüche, keine Kehrseiten. Zwischen Macht und Leid verschwimmen die Grenzen. Himmlers[14] Lachen geht über in die Tränen zusammengetriebener Juden, und die vierspurige Autobahn mündet ein in die endlosen Straßen Rußlands, über die sich

Soldaten schleppen. Diese Szenen sind gestellt von einem Mann, der—unabhängig von allem Zwang historischer Kausalität—mit einem Volke Tragödie spielte. ‚Noch keinem Sterblichen‘, so meinte er in seinem Testament, seien so viele ‚schwerste Entschlüsse‘ abverlangt worden wie ihm. Daß er diese Entschlüsse herausgefordert hatte, bestritt er, daß er ihnen nicht gewachsen war, verschwieg er, wenn er es überhaupt ahnte.

Die Aufgabe einer Bildgeschichte des Dritten Reiches kann es nur sein, das Unheimliche jener Zeit einzufangen. Das ist in beiden Bänden beispielhaft gelungen. Das Rätsel Hitler freilich konnten sie auch nicht lösen.

Dieter Ross

7. Auch die Gerechtigkeit braucht ihre Zeit

Nach 165 Tagen: Zwischenbilanz im Frankfurter Auschwitz-Prozeß[1]

Die Zahlen sprechen für sich. Die Zahlen jener vier Jahre, in denen das Feuer in den Krematorien nicht erlosch, in denen die Gaskammern niemals leer blieben. Über zwei Millionen Menschen starben in Auschwitz, wurden vergast, erschossen, erschlagen, zertreten, ausgehungert. Vierzig Quadratkilometer groß war das Gelände der Massenmordmaschinerie, mit seinen Lagern, Baracken, Krematorien und Gaskammern. 6000 SS-Männer[2] hielten die Todesfabrik in Gang, Offiziere, Ärzte, Sanitäter, Gestapomänner,[2] Bewacher.

Auschwitz und kein Ende? Der Prozeß begann vor 18 Monaten, zum Weihnachtsfest 1963. Er dauert nun schon über 165 Verhandlungstage, das ist zusammengerechnet fast ein halbes Jahr Tag für Tag Auschwitz-Prozeß, von früh morgens bis zum späten Nachmittag.

Die Zuhörerbänke haben sich gelichtet, die Spannung hat nachgelassen, die Szene des Tribunals hat sich gewandelt. Keine Zeugen mehr, die den Tränen nahe sind, die unter der Erinnerung fast zusammenbrechen. Auch kein lärmender Auftritt mehr zwischen Kaul, dem Staranwalt aus Ostberlin, und seinem Widerpart Laternser, der schon in Nürnberg[3] verteidigte. Keine zornige Unterbrechung der Sitzung durch den Vorsitzenden. Es ist ruhig geworden im Auschwitz-Prozeß. Das Schrecken verschwindet hinter Paragraphen, Verordnungen, Befehlen. Es wird zu einer Sache nüchterner Interpretation. Leer ist der Zeugenstuhl vor der Richterrampe, auf dem jene saßen, gebeugt, zitternd, die wie durch ein Wunder davongekommen waren. In den mit stahlblauen Vorhängen drapierten, von der Junisonne hell erleuchteten Verhandlungssaal ist die Sachlichkeit eingezogen. Zu Ende das Frage– und Antwortspiel über das Entsetzliche, zu Ende der Streit um Aussagen und Meinungen. Die Advokaten haben nun das Wort.

Auschwitz dauerte rund 1 500 Tage. Wieviel zählen da die 165 Tage des Auschwitz-Prozesses? Und die weiteren zwanzig bis zur Verkündung des Urteils?

Dietrich Strohmann

8. Suche nach den unbesungenen Helden

Auch das gab es in Deutschland: Hunderte von Judenrettern

„Das habe ich getan." Die Antwort des Arztes kam zögernd. Die Antwort auf die Frage, wie er damals sein Leben einsetzte, um das Leben anderer zu retten, den Verfolgten zu helfen—den Juden, die in jenen Jahren des Terrors zu ihm in die Frankfurter Praxis kamen.

„Das habe ich getan." Auch das tat der Arzt. Er gab denen, die wußten, daß sie in den nächsten Tagen abtransportiert wurden, Gift. Erst war er voller Zweifel gewesen: „Darf ich als Arzt, der verpflichtet ist, Menschenleben zu retten und zu heilen, so etwas tun?" Der Arzt Dr. L. tat es. Er gab denen, die den Gaskammern nicht mehr entrinnen konnten, das Gift.

Dr. L. zählt zu der großen, doch unbekannten Schar der ‚unbesungenen Helden'. Er ist einer von jenen Deutschen, die viel riskierten, um denen zu helfen, die den gelben Stern[1] tragen mußten.

Die meisten, die wie dieser Arzt Juden zur Seite standen, bleiben anonym. Sie weigern sich, heute von etwas zu sprechen, was sie für eine Selbstverständlichkeit hielten, für ihre Christenpflicht oder einfach für eine humane Forderung. Sie leben als die unbekannten ‚unbesungenen Helden' unter uns und weisen es weit von sich, als ‚Helden' gefeiert zu werden.

Dieses Kapitel aus der Geschichte des Dritten Reiches ist noch nicht geschrieben—das Kapitel eines stillen Ruhmes. Das gab es in jenen finsteren Jahren eben auch: die heimliche ‚Konspiration des Wohltuns‘. Sie sollte, gerade für die jüngere Generation, ans Tageslicht gehoben werden.

Dietrich Strothmann

9. Fünfundvierzig Milliarden Wiedergutmachung

Die Bundesrepublik hat für die Wiedergutmachung[1] national-sozialistischen Unrechts bisher rund 27 Milliarden Mark ausgegeben, und sie wird nach den nun vorliegenden Gesetzen insgesamt ungefähr 45 Milliarden Mark dafür aufbringen. Über 35 Milliarden davon sind für das Bundesentschädigungsgesetz auszugeben, das in erster Linie jüdischen Verfolgten zugute kommt. 4,3 Milliarden entfallen auf das Bundesrückerstattungsgesetz, das die Entschädigung für beschlagnahmtes Eigentum regelt. Die bereits voll bezahlten Wiedergutmachungsleistungen an Israel machen 3,45 Milliarden aus. Der Rest verteilt sich auf andere Wiedergutmachungen.

Aufsätze und Aufsatzübungen

1. Beschreiben Sie in großen Zügen
(a) den Verlauf des Zweiten Weltkriegs in Europa und Nordafrika
(b) die Zustände in Deutschland unmittelbar nach Kriegsende.
2. Erzählen Sie kurz die Geschichte des ‚Dritten Reiches‘.

VON
ZEIT
ZU
ZEIT

3

Als politisches Wochenblatt legt **Die Zeit** hauptsächlich Nachdruck auf Kommentar und Diskussion über politische Ereignisse und Gestalten, denen lange Spalten im ersten Teil des Blattes gewidmet sind; die letzte Seite dieses Teiles bringt jedoch, unter dem Wortspiel-Titel *Von Zeit zu Zeit*, eine kurze Übersicht über die Nachrichten der Woche, sowie auch etwas längere Berichte über die jüngsten Entwicklungen in der Politik.

10. Von Zeit zu Zeit 1

Nach dem Rücktritt des Freien Demokraten[1] Ewald Bucher wurde der Christ-Demokrat[1] Karl Weber zum Bundesjustizminister ernannt.—Mit einer Mahn-Rede an Bonn und Paris eröffnete Konrad Adenauer[2] den Düsseldorfer CDU-Parteitag.—Trotz einer fiebrigen Erkältung analysierte der Bundesaußenminister die gegenwärtigen Schwierigkeiten der deutschen Außenpolitik.

Israel bat Großbritannien um die Initiative für ein kontrolliertes Waffen-Embargo für den gesamten Nahen Osten.—Präsident Gamal Abdel Nasser erlaubte die Beisetzung Ex-König Faruks in Ägypten.—Der chinesische Parteichef Mao Tse-Tung hat sich nach einer Meldung aus Hongkong für 100 000 DM einen Mercedes 600 in Spezialausführung erworben.—Die indische Regierung verhütete durch Auflösung des Landtags von Kerala eine kommunistische Machtübernahme.

Ein Vietkong-Kommandotrupp zündete eine 100-Kilo-Bombe vor der US-Botschaft in Saigon. —US-Hubschraubern wurde das Überfliegen schwedischen Hoheitsgebietes nicht gestattet. —Zum Schluß seiner Deutschland-Reise lud der norwegische Ministerpräsident Einar Gerhardsen seinen Gastgeber Ludwig Erhard zu einem Gegenbesuch ein. —Zu Verhandlungen mit der EWG-Kommission traf eine polnische Regierungsdelegation in Brüssel ein.

In Noten an die drei Westmächte protestierte die Sowjetunion gegen die nächste Bundestagssitzung in Westberlin.[3] —Sowohl die sowjetischen als auch die amerikanischen Astronauten bestätigten Schwierigkeiten bei der Landung ihrer Fahrzeuge.—Die von Ranger IX übermittelten Mond-Photos zeigen mehrere für Raumschiffe geeignete Landestellen. —Unter dem Verdacht des Mordes an einer amerikanischen Bürgerrechtlerin wurden vier Ku-Klux-Klan-Mitglieder verhaftet. —In Köln wurde ein Autofahrer nach einem Unfall Opfer der Lynchjustiz.

Zur Abwehr der parteipolitischen Opposition drohte Premierminister Harold Wilson mit Neuwahlen. —Bei einer Nachwahl in Schottland schlug der liberale Kandidat den Konservativen und den Labour–Rivalen. —Im Londoner Claridge's nahm Königin Elizabeth den Tee mit dem Herzog und der Herzogin von Windsor. —Seine 40 jährige Zugehörigkeit zur Gewerkschaftsbewegung feierte der DGB-[4] Vorsitzende Ludwig Rosenberg. —Mit der Schließung der

Grube ‚Füsseberg‘ erreichte der Siegerländer[5] Erzbergbau seine Ende.

Den Bau von Hotels im Zusammenhang mit Tankstellen kündigte die Esso AG[6] in Hamburg an. —Ein schweres Erdbeben hat Santiago und Valparaiso in Chile heimgesucht. —Protestierende Studenten der Universität Madrid beantworteten ihre Exmatrikulation[7] mit einem Sitzstreik. — Truppen unterdrückten einen Aufruhr marokkanischer Studenten. —Dem Schriftsteller Ernst Jünger[8] gratulierte der Bundespräsident telegraphisch zum 70. Geburtstag. — Im Alter von 75 Jahren starb in Hollywood Stummfilm-Star May Murray.   2. April 1965

11. Blitzkrieg im Nahen Osten

Nach drei Wochen der Spannung brach am Montag Krieg zwischen Israel und seinen arabischen Nachbarn aus. Bis Mittwoch waren Israelis in einem Blitzfeldzug bis zum Suez-Kanal vorgedrungen und hatten Scharm el Scheich an der Meerenge von Tiran erobert.

Beide Seiten beschuldigen sich gegenseitig der Aggression. Ägypten behauptet, israelische Flugzeuge hätten die Feindseligkeiten mit Luftangriffen auf Flugplätze im Gazastreifen, am Suezkanal und in die Umgebung von Kairo eröffnet. Israel gibt an, ägyptische Panzer hätten sich im Anmarsch auf die israelische Grenze befunden, ägyptische Luftwaffenverbände seien auf den Radarschirmen im Anflug geortet worden; daraufhin seien die Kampfhandlungen eröffnet worden.

Der UN-Sicherheitsrat hörte sich am Montag die gegenseitigen Beschuldigungen Israels und Ägyptens an und ging nach elfstündigen Konsultationen auseinander.

12. Zwanzig Jahre UN

Vor zwanzig Jahren, am 25. April 1945, versammelten sich in San Franzisko die Vertreter von 51 Nationen zur Gründungskonferenz der Vereinten Nationen (UN). Inzwischen hat sich die Zahl der Mitglieder mehr als verdoppelt (115). Bei der Gründung waren die afroasiatischen Staaten nur zwölfmal vertreten, Afrika allein sogar nur viermal (Ägypten,

Aethiopien, Liberia und Südafrikanische Union). Heute stammen 60 der Mitglieder aus Asien oder Afrika. Der Block der lateinamerikanischen Staaten blieb mit 21 unverändert.

Nach wie vor verfügt die Sowjetunion als einziges Land in der UN-Vollversammlung über drei Sitze, da 1945 auch die Ukraine und Weißrußland als vollwertige Mitglieder zugelassen wurden. Im Sicherheitsrat sitzt als ständiges Mitglied immer noch Nationalchina, obwohl das chinesische Festland bereits 1949 unter kommunistische Herrschaft geriet.

Fast eine Milliarde Menschen (Gesamtweltbevölkerung 3283 Milliarden) leben außerhalb der UN, da die Regierungen ihrer Länder den Vereinten Nationen auf eigenen Wunsch (Schweiz, Indonesien) oder unfreiwillig fernbleiben. Auch die europäischen Zwergstaaten Monaco, San Marino, Andorra und Liechtenstein gehören der Weltorganisation nicht an.

Trotz der lebensgefährlichen Finanzkrise des letzten Winters, trotz der Unkenrufe Chruschtschows, Sukarnos, Tschu En-lais und de Gaulles, ist die UN bisher noch leidlich über die Runden gekommen. Eine kranke UN ist den meisten Staaten immer noch lieber als eine Welt ohne UN. An der Waffenstillstandslinie in Kaschmir, auf der Sinai-Halbinsel, in Palästina und auf Zypern sind ihre Dienste zur Zeit weniger denn je entbehrlich. Und die UN ist das Forum, wo sich in dieser Woche, wieder einmal, groß und klein mit einem der wichtigsten Weltprobleme auseinandersetzen: der Abrüstung.

13. Die Einfuhren stiegen schneller

Der Außenhandel der Bundesrepublik mit den übrigen EWG-Ländern belief sich im vergangenen Jahr in beiden Richtungen auf 44 Milliarden Mark. Die Zunahme gegenüber 1963 betrug 12,6 Prozent. Die Einfuhr stieg um 17,6 Prozent auf 20,4 Milliarden Mark, während die Ausfuhr um 8,6 Prozent auf 23,6 Milliarden Mark zunahm. An der Gesamteinfuhr der Bundesrepublik waren die EWG-Länder 1964 mit 34,7 Prozent (Vorjahr = 33,2 Prozent) beteiligt, an der Gesamtausfuhr mit 36,4 Prozent (Vorjahr = 36,3 Prozent). An der Spitze des deutschen Warenaustausches mit EWG-Ländern steht nach wie vor Frankreich.

14. Wandel im Außenhandel

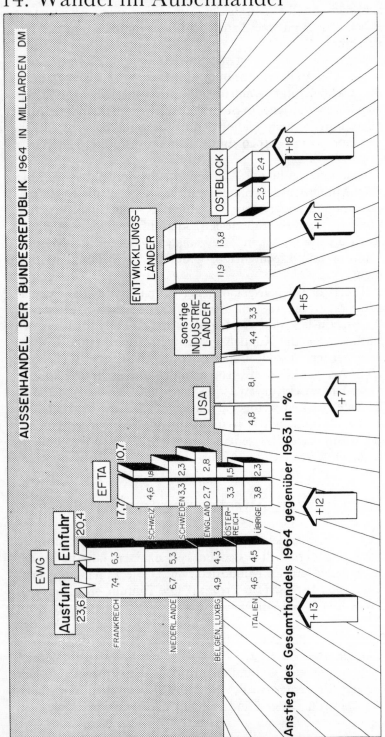

AUSSENHANDEL DER BUNDESREPUBLIK 1964 IN MILLIARDEN DM

EWG

Einfuhr 20,4
Ausfuhr 23,6

	Ausfuhr	Einfuhr
FRANKREICH	7,4	6,3
NIEDERLANDE	6,7	5,3
BELGIEN, LUXBG.	4,9	4,3
ITALIEN	4,6	4,5

EFTA 17,7 / 10,7

	Ausfuhr	Einfuhr
SCHWEIZ	4,6	1,8
SCHWEDEN	3,3	2,3
ENGLAND	2,7	2,8
ÖSTERREICH	3,3	1,5
ÜBRIGE	3,8	2,3

USA 4,8 / 8,1

sonstige INDUSTRIE-LÄNDER 4,4 / 3,3

ENTWICKLUNGS-LÄNDER 11,9 / 13,8

OSTBLOCK 2,3 / 2,4

Anstieg des Gesamthandels 1964 gegenüber 1963 in %

+13   +12   +7   +15   +12   +18

15. Bonn in der Finanzklemme

Die Devise heißt : Mehr Steuern, weniger Ausgaben

Die Konsolidierung der Bundesfinanzen wird über Wohl oder Wehe der Großen Koalition entscheiden. Diese Meinung vertrat Bundesfinanzminister Strauß[1] bei der Verabschiedung des Bundeshaushalts für das Jahr 1967 vor dem Bundestag. Einzelheiten dieses Etats, der mit einem Volumen von 77,2 Milliarden Mark um 7,2 Milliarden seinen Vorgänger übertrifft, interessierten die Abgeordneten weit weniger als der Überblick, den Strauß über die Finanzlage gab.

In diesem Jahr werden die Schulden des Bundes voraussichtlich um 12,5 Milliarden Mark steigen; das ist ein Drittel der Ende vergangenen Jahres vorhandenen Schuldenlast.

Nicht nur deswegen bedarf es einer sorgfältigen mittelfristigen Finanzplanung. Die durch Gesetze und sonstige Verpflichtungen festgelegten Dauerausgaben sind weit höher als die veranschlagten Steuereinnahmen. Nach den Plänen von Strauß ist daher vorgesehen, im Etat 1968 Dauerausgaben von 7,2 Milliarden Mark zu streichen und 2,5 Milliarden Mark durch Steuervergünstigungen zu gewinnen.

Im Finanzkabinett konnten sich die Minister noch nicht über die Ausgabenkürzungen einigen. 2,7 Milliarden Mark sollten beim Sozialhaushalt eingespart werden. Daneben sind vor allem die Ausgaben für Verteidigung, Landwirtschaft, Verkehr und Wohnungsbau betroffen.

Diese Meinungsverschiedenheiten im Finanzkabinett gingen den Ausführungen von Strauß vor dem Bundestag voran. Auf dem Spiel steht darüber hinaus das Ansehen der Großen Koalition in der Bevölkerung. Alle Sachverständigen sind sich darüber einig, daß die Große Koalition die Sanierung der Bundesfinanzen nicht länger aufschieben darf, wenn sie die Voraussetzung für eine stabile Innenpolitik nicht aus der Hand geben will.

16. Tod für Taximörder[1]?

Wieder einmal fordern Abgeordnete der bürgerlichen Parteien die Todesstrafe für bestimmte Gewaltverbrechen (Taximord, Kindesentführung, Sittlichkeitsverbrechen an Kindern, Polizistenmord). Anlaß war diesmal die Ermordung eines Taxifahrers in Bonn. Nach dem Henker riefen die CDU-Spitzenpolitiker Adenauer,[2] Dufhues, Brentano[3]

und Rasner, und der FDR-Politiker Zoglmann. Im Bundes-
kabinett waren die Meinungen geteilt. Bundesjustizminister
Bucher glaubt nicht an die abschreckende Wirkung der
Todesstrafe. Bundeskanzler Erhard[4]: „Ich bin dagegen."
Die SPD-Meinung gab Carlo Schmid[5] wieder: „Ein Staat,
in dem der Henker so gewütet hat wie im Deutschland der
Nazi-Zeit, sollte dem Menschengebaren archaischer Zeiten
eine entschiedenere Absage erteilen als weniger Befleckte."
Der Bundestag hat seit 1950 schon einige Male über die
Todesstrafe diskutiert, meistens nach aufsehenerregenden
Mordtaten. 1958 verlangte der damalige Innenminister
Schröder[6] sogar die Hinrichtung von Landesverrätern. Im
selben Jahr ergab eine Umfrage in der Bundesrepublik 75
Prozent für die Todesstrafe. Ihre Gegner haben sich jedoch
stets über den Volkswillen hinweggesetzt: „Die Demokratie
muß die im Emotionellen urteilende Masse aufklären, und
das Parlament muß im Bereich des Moralischen fort-
schrittlicher sein als die Masse." (Carlo Schmid 1955)

17. Von Zeit zu Zeit 2

An der Schwelle des Wahlkampfes[1] sprach sich Ludwig
Erhard[2] gegen eine Große Koalition aus. — Kanzlerkandidat Willy Brandt[3] verkündete die Wahlkampflosung
seiner Partei: „Sicher ist sicher—darum SPD."
Der Bonner US-Botschafter George McGhee forderte
von der Welt die volle Anerkennung des ‚von Grund auf
gewandelten' deutschen Volkes. — Mit der Verabschiedung
einer Novelle zum Bundesentschädigungsgesetz setzte der
Bundestag einen Schlußpunkt unter die Wiedergutmachung.
Der Bundeskanzler flog am Wochenanfang zu Gesprächen nach Washington. — Berlins Regierender Bürgermeister[4] wurde vom französischen Staatspräsidenten
Charles de Gaulle empfangen.
Zur Pariser Konferenz der NATO-Verteidigungsminister
kam der Amerikaner Robert McNamara mit dem Vorschlag
eines gemeinsamen atlantischen Rüstungsmarktes und einer
erweiterten automaren Mitbestimmung der Bündnispartner.
— Der jugoslawische Parlamentspräsident Edvard Kardelj
lobte die Haltung der Franzosen in der Deutschland-
Frage.
Die Spannung im Nahen Osten verschärfte sich durch
Zwischenfälle an der israelisch-jordanischen Grenze. — Die

Hauptgruppe der Beamten der ehemaligen deutschen Botschaft in Kairo verließ die ägyptische Hauptstadt.

Peking dementierte Gerüchte über einen Schlaganfall Mao Tse-tungs und ließ die neuen Kreml-Führer als eine ‚Handvoll Lumpen‘ bezeichnen. — In der chinesischen Volksarmee wurden alle Rangabzeichen abgeschafft. — Begünstigt durch schwere Regenfälle unternahmen die Vietcong in Südvietnam massive Angriffe.

Mit Wochenbeginn öffnete sich die Berliner Mauer[5] über die Pfingsttage zum vierten und letztenmal im Zuge der bisher beschlossenen Passierscheinregelung.[6] —Der Deutsche Jugendherbergs-Verband erhöhte die Übernachtungsgebühren. —Der bisher uk[7] -gestellte Eiskunstläufer und Schlagersänger Hans-Jürgen Bäumler braucht wegen einer Wirbelsäulenverletzung vorerst noch nicht zu den Gebirgsjägern einzurücken.[8] — In der ersten Runde schlug Weltmeister Cassius Clay seinen Herausforderer Sonny Liston unter tumultuösen Umständen k.o. — Nach einem dürftigen Festival erhielt ein englischer Film die ‚Goldene Palme‘ von Cannes. — Eine von Winston Churchill gemalte Darstellung des Comer Sees wurde von einem Amerikaner für 155 000 DM ersteigert. — Auf eine Brüsseler Fernsehansagerin wurde im Studio ein Schuß abgegeben. — Versuchsweise wurden 50 Hamburger Ärzten Sonderparkplätze zugeteilt.   4. Juni 1965

Aufsätze und Aufsatzübungen

1. Geben Sie eine kurze Übersicht über die wichigsten Nachrichten (a) des Tages   (b) der Woche.

2. Berichten Sie in größeren Zügen über eine aktuelle Frage des Tages; versuchen Sie dabei, die größtmögliche Anzahl von Argumenten für und wider anzuführen.

MODERNES
LEBEN

In den über vierzig Seiten einer einzigen Ausgabe der **Zeit** sind unter
den Titeln *Länderspiegel, Wirtschaft, Wissenschaft* und *Modernes Leben*
die vielfältigsten Berichte über das Leben in Deutschland und im
Ausland zu finden.

18. Sind die Deutschen noch zu erkennen?

Es ist schwierig, heute über Deutschland zu schreiben, weil die Jugend lieber Coca-Cola als Bier trinkt und auf den Straßen der Großstädte die sprichwörtliche ‚dicke Bertha‘ sowie das vielbesungene ‚Gretchen‘ nicht mehr zu finden sind, wogegen die Mädchen und Frauen, die man überall sieht, keineswegs an das traditionelle deutsche Fräulein oder die würdige Matrone erinnern. Die Passanten, die man in Düsseldorf, Hamburg oder Frankfurt am Main trifft, könnte man ebenso in Rom, London oder New York sehen— sie haben nichts mehr gemein mit dem sprichwörtlich schlecht angezogenen Deutschen, der Filzhut, Lodenmantel[1] und Stiefel trug.

Marian Podkowinski

19. Ein Student unter Berliner Arbeitern

I

Als Untermieter zog ich in eine Berliner Arbeiterwohnung ein. Mein Zimmer lag zum Hinterhof hinaus, was immerhin Schutz vor dem Verkehrslärm bot, nicht jedoch gleichzeitig Schutz vor Radio, Fernsehen oder lauten familiären Unstimmigkeiten. Und doch muß ich das höfliche Bemühen der Leute anerkennen, mir, dem Studenten, Ruhe zu gönnen und manchmal auch zu gewähren.

Der Arbeitstag meiner Hausleute ist gewöhnlich hart. Wenn man nach Hause kommt, bietet das Fernsehen die nötige Unterhaltung. Oder man geht ‚kurz ’ne Molle zischen‘ —ein Bier trinken— liest die Bild-Zeitung[1] und erhitzt sich manchmal an einem sensationellen Thema (Rentnermord, Taximörder, Sexualverbrechen).

Am Wochenende aber will man ‚leben‘. Am Samstagabend besuchen sich ehemalige Schulkameraden, Kriegskameraden oder Arbeitskollegen, Bekannte aus der Umgebung oder Verwandte. Man feiert in der Wohnung ein bißchen, man geht mal ins Kino oder irgendwohin, wo was los ist. Gern ‚versackt‘ man auch mal: Mit hundert oder mehr Mark aus der Lohntüte verschwindet der Verdiener am Freitag und taucht erst am nächsten Morgen wieder auf, wenn die ersten

Verkehrsmittel gerade wieder fahren. Der Sonntagmorgen wird allgemein verschlafen; das Sonntagessen ist immer ein Festmahl. Aber am Abend wird nichts mehr unternommen. Die Arbeitswoche wirft ihren Schatten voraus.

II

Die Wohnung enthielt nur das allernötigste: Betten, Doppelbettcouch, Schränke, Sessel, aber hier und da auch ein paar schmückende Dinge: Nippfiguren, einen künstlichen Blumenstrauß, Topfblumen, ein Porzellanreh, bunte Ansichtskarten, Andenken von einer Kirmes, Souvenirs vom Urlaub. Ein hübscher und kräftig singender Wellensittich sei nicht vergessen.

Einen Tisch, auf den man Bücher legen und etwas schreiben kann, gab es in der ganzen Wohnung nicht. Ich erhielt von meiner Wirtin ein zusammenklappbares, kleines kreisrundes Sommertischchen. Außerdem stand noch im Wohnzimmer, das durch die Doppelbettcouch gleichzeitig Schlafzimmer für die Erwachsenen war, und allgemeines Eßzimmer, ein länglicher, kniehoher Tisch.

Ich fragte mich, wo die elfjährige Tochter und der fünfzehnjährige Sohn eigentlich Schularbeiten machen. Zufällig sah ich dann das Mädchen beim Schreiben, sie saß am Rand eines Sessels am kniehohen Tisch. Sie widmete ihre Aufmerksamkeit abwechselnd dem eingeschalteten Fernsehapparat und ihrem Schulheft. Aber ihr Gesicht habe ich nie aufmerksam oder verträumt gesehen, eher teilnahmslos. Ich habe sie selten etwas sagen hören; ein verlegenes Kichern war ihre Reaktion, wenn ich sie ansprach. Die größte Sorge der Mutter ist, daß ihre Tochter immer noch nicht—nach der Ganzheitsmethode—lesen kann, und daß ihr Sohn ein ‚anständiger Kerl‘ wird. Seine Mutter will aus ihm einen Werkzeugschlosser machen; das einzige, was er machen will, ist ‚Kies‘,[2] wie er mit lässig maulendem Slang kommentierte.

Klaus D. Frank

20. Der Index der Lebenshaltungskosten

Als Modellfamilie gilt der vierköpfige städtische Arbeitnehmerhaushalt[1] mit zwei Kindern, von denen mindestens eines unter 15 Jahren ist. Der alleinverdienende Haushaltsvorstand bezieht das statistisch ermittelte mittlere Einkommen von 905,40 Mark.

Monatliche Verbrauchsausgaben der Index-Haushalte

2.Viertelj. 1964 durchschnittlich 872 DM

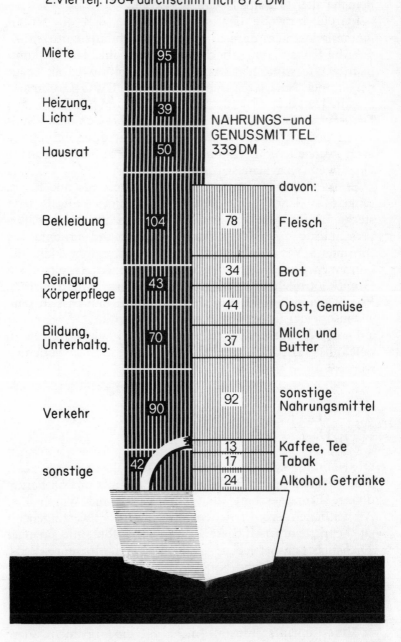

Miete — 95

Heizung, Licht — 39

Hausrat — 50

NAHRUNGS-und GENUSSMITTEL 339 DM

davon:

Bekleidung — 104

Reinigung Körperpflege — 43

Bildung, Unterhaltg. — 70

Verkehr — 90

sonstige — 42

Fleisch — 78

Brot — 34

Obst, Gemüse — 44

Milch und Butter — 37

sonstige Nahrungsmittel — 92

Kaffee, Tee — 13

Tabak — 17

Alkohol. Getränke — 24

21. Was stimmt?

Die EWG nützt dem Verbraucher, frohlockt und beweist Professor Hallsteins Brüsseler Kommission.[1] Die EWG verteuert alles, schimpfen Hausfrauen und Familienväter beinahe aller Gehaltsklassen. Was stimmt?

Erfreulicherweise läßt sich feststellen, daß die EWG-Kommission nicht unrecht hat, wenn auch hinzuzufügen ist, daß die Konsumenten noch nicht so auf ihre Kosten kommen, wie es wünschenswert wäre. Einmal sanken als Folge der immer schärferen Konkurrenz im EWG-Großmarkt u.a. die Händlerpreise für Autos, Radio- und Fernsehgeräte, Damenstrümpfe, Kühlschränke, Waschmaschinen, Süßwaren und Schokolade. Zum anderen wurden im Drang nach rationellerer Fertigung durch größere Serien manche Qualitäten (aber keineswegs alle) besser.

Es ist aber zu konstatieren, daß keineswegs alle Preise sanken, in denen heute 70 Prozent weniger Zoll als 1957 steckt. Dafür gibt es zwei Gründe; in manchen Fällen verschluckte der Handel den Gewinn und erhöhte die Spannen.[2] Vor allem aber setzen noch immer Handelsschranken dem freien Wettbewerb Grenzen: es gibt noch Grenzkontrollen, Umsatzausgleichssteuern und Zollreste. Psychologisch realisiert noch nicht jeder, daß es sich bald genauso leicht in Metz wie in Köln einkauft.

Die EWG für den ungenügenden Verbrauchernutzen zu tadeln, ist verfrüht. Damit sie allen nutzt, muß sie vollendet werden.

B.

22. Marktplatz für Mütter und Kinder

Die Hamburger handelten nach dem amerikanischen Rezept: Man nehme viele Parkplätze (2000), pflanze um sie herum diverse Einzelgeschäfte und Kaufhäuser, die Waren aller Art feilbieten—vom frischen Spargel aus Schwetzingen bis zu Teppichen aus Teheran. Vermische alles mit ein paar Dienstleistungsbetrieben: Autowäscherei, Friseur, Bank, Eisdiele, Bierecke und Kindergarten und nenne das Ganze ‚Einkaufszentrum‘. Als pikantes Gewürz hole man für die Eröffnung eine bekannte Persönlichkeit, die mit einer Schere das blauweiße Eröffnungsband zu durchschneiden hat.

‚Elbe-Einkaufszentrum‘—nicht auf einer grünen Wiese

gebaut, sondern im Schnittpunkt vieler Straßen und inmitten eines neuen Wohnviertels, erreichbar nicht nur für Autofahrer, sondern auch für Fußgänger und Busfahrer. So präsentieren sich unweit der Elbe an der Osdorfer Landstraße große Autoparkplätze mit der Möglichkeit, in 45 Geschäften und Kaufhäusern einzukaufen—oder auch 45 Geschäfte und Kaufhäuser mit der Möglichkeit, sein Auto abzustellen. Elbe-Einkaufszentrum heißt das bisher in der Bundesrepublik größte *Shopping-Center,* das nicht auf freiem Gelände abseits der Stadt gebaut ist, sondern mitten in ein städtisches Wohngebiet. 35 Millionen Mark hat das Unternehmen gekostet, die Bauzeit betrug 20 Monate, und die Kaufleute versprechen sich einen Umsatz von 80 bis 100 Millionen Mark jährlich.

In Amerika und Schweden mauserten sich die ursprünglich als Supermärkte geplanten Einkaufszentren zu regelrechten ,Kulturzentren' mit Kino, Kirche, Tanzcafés, Schwimmbädern und Lesehallen, abendlichem Feuerwerk und Tierpark für die Kinder. Das Hamburger Zentrum wirkt dagegen noch konservativ, und auch die unermüdlich rieselnde Unterhaltungsmusik aus den Lautsprechern vermag keine Tivoli-Atmosphäre[1] zu zaubern. Dem Käufer oder Bummler bietet sich ein modern-biederer Marktplatz. Seinen Haushaltbedarf kann er hier decken. Güter des ,gehobenen Bedarfs'—das *Pierre-Cardin*-Modell, das Herrenhemd nach dem allerletzten Schnitt oder eine Flasche Pommery[2]—sucht er hier vergebens. Das findet er nur in der City, dort allerdings keinen Parkplatz und auch keinen Kindergarten.

H.K.

23. Fünfundsiebzig Jahre deutsche Gewerkschaften

Im Juli des Jahres 1889 proklamierte ein internationaler Gewerkschaftskongreß in Paris den 1. Mai zum alljährlichen ,Kampftag der Arbeit'. Als im darauffolgenden Jahr an diesem Tag zum erstenmal auch in den größeren Städten des Reiches Arbeiter zu Tausenden dem Ruf ihrer Funktionäre folgten und mit roten Fahnen durch die Straßen zogen, um für den Achtstundentag zu demonstrieren—damals wurde in den Fabriken noch täglich bis zu 14 Stunden gearbeitet— sprach man von Aufruhr und Landesverrat; die Polizei stand in höchster Alarmbereitschaft.

Seither ist ein dreiviertel Jahrhundert vergangen; und in diesem dreiviertel Jahrhundert ist aus dem rechtlosen und um seine primitivsten Rechte kämpfenden Proletarier von einst der mit Rechten wohl ausgestattete und sich dieser Rechte auch wohl bewußte Wirtschafts-und Staatsbürger von heute geworden.

Der Deutsche Gewerkschaftsbund hat besonders in den letzten zehn Jahren große Erfolge erzielt; Arbeitszeiten von 45 Stunden und weniger, doppelt so hohe Einkommen wie 1950, Urlaub von drei Wochen und mehr, zusätzliches Urlaubsgeld für fünf Millionen, verbesserte Renten-, Kranken-, und Unfallversicherung. So ist es in dem neuen Aktionsprogramm des DGB zu lesen, das am 1. Mai dieses Jahres offiziell verkündet wird.

Wolfgang Krüger

24. Die Deutschen sind friedlich

Die Bundesrepublik rechnet zu den streikärmsten Ländern. In den zehn Jahren von 1954 bis 1963 fielen im Jahresdurchschnitt je hundert Beschäftigte noch nicht ganz fünf Arbeitstage durch Streik aus. In Frankreich und Großbritannien waren es dagegen rund zwanzig Tage, in Belgien über dreißig und in den USA fast fünfzig Tage. Am streikfreudigsten waren die Italiener: Auf je hundert Beschäftigte gerechnet wurde wegen Streiks an etwa siebzig Tagen im Jahr nicht gearbeitet.

25. Handwerk auf goldenem Boden

(Seite 27)

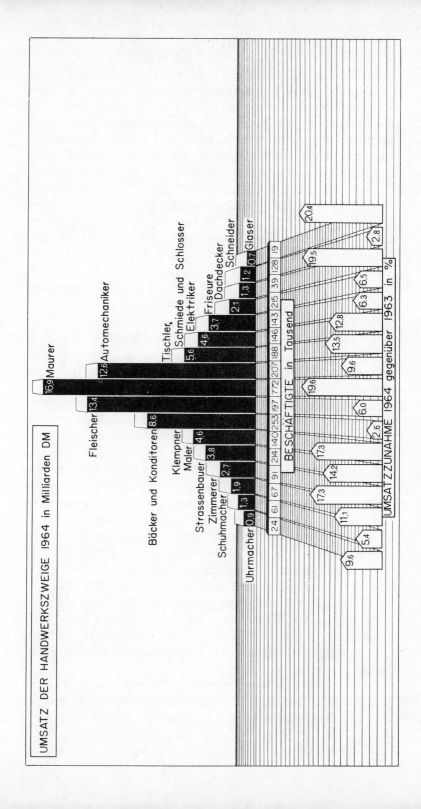

UMSATZ DER HANDWERKSZWEIGE 1964 in Milliarden DM

Maurer 16,9
Automechaniker 12,6
Fleischer 13,4
Bäcker und Konditoren 8,6
Tischler 5,6
Schmiede und Schlosser 4,6
Elektriker 3,7
Friseure 2,1
Dachdecker 1,3
Schneider 1,2
Glaser 0,7
Klempner 4,6
Maler 3,8
Strassenbauer 2,7
Zimmerer 1,9
Schuhmacher 1,3
Uhrmacher 0,9

BESCHÄFTIGTE in Tausend

24 | 61 | 67 | 91 | 214 | 140 | 253 | 197 | 772 | 207 | 188 | 146 | 143 | 215 | 39 | 128 | 19

UMSATZZUNAHME 1964 gegenüber 1963 in %

20,4
2,8
19,5
6,5
6,3
12,8
13,5
9,6
19,6
6,0
2,6
17,3
14,2
17,3
11,1
5,4
9,6

26. Kastenmerkmale

Jedes flüchtige Gespräch mit einem Deutschen, den man zufällig in einem Restaurant, im Wartesaal oder in einer Raststätte an der Autobahn trifft, beginnt mit Klagen über die Teuerung und endet mit Bemerkungen über Autos oder über den im Ausland verbrachten Urlaub. Inzwischen hat sich bereits eine spezifische Einteilung ergeben—man unterscheidet zwischen denjenigen, die kein Auto haben, denen, die einen VW fahren und schließlich denjenigen, die sich einen ‚Mercedes‘ leisten können. Es genügt, vor einem Laden mit einem ‚Mercedes 300‘ vorzufahren, um sich einen Kredit zu sichern. Im Sinne der neuen gesellschaftlichen Konvention gelten Firma und Modell des Autos, das man fährt, als Kastenmerkmal.

Marian Podkowinski

27. Autofahrer-Partei in Hamburg

Deutschlands jüngste Partei wurde am Stammtisch[1] gegründet. Sie nennt sich *Apollonia* und tagt im Hamburger Ratsweinkeller.[2] Der Zahnarzt Wolfgang Dwenger, Mitglied eines Automobilklubs, hatte die Idee, und seine rund 20 Stammtischbrüder, ebenfalls Zahnärzte, waren begeistert. Die Herren am Stammtisch dauert das beschwerliche Los der Autofahrer. Die Autofahrer-Partei (AFP) wird künftig ihre Interessen vertreten. Wenn in vier Jahren Deutschlands Straßennetz um 18 Prozent erweitert wird, die Automobile sich jedoch um 80 Prozent vermehren, dann, so rechnet Dwenger, wird auf Deutschlands Straßen kein Verkehr mehr möglich sein. Mit sieben Getreuen—so viele braucht man, wie erinnerlich, wenn man eine Partei gründen will— zog der Zahnarzt zum Hamburger Amtsgericht und ließ seine Partei ins Vereinsregister eintragen.[3]

Sein nächster Weg führte zur Annoncenabteilung einer Tageszeitung. Schließlich fehlten der Partei noch die Mitgliederscharen. In wenigen Tagen meldeten sich 30 unzufriedene Autofahrer.

„Wir sind politisch unabhängig!" sagt Dwenger, ein politischer Autodidakt. „Unsere einzige Weltanschauung: Die Straßen müssen besser werden." Ihm schweben achtspurige Autobahnen vor, auf denen der deutsche Automobilist alle seine PS[4] ausspielen kann. Sein großes Vorbild:

die amerikanischen Highways. Auf die Frage, wie er sich die Finanzierung vorstellt, antwortet er schlicht: „Ich bin kein Experte." Aber dann fällt ihm doch so die übliche Lösung ein: Jeder Steuergroschen, den ein Autofahrer an den Staat abführt, soll dem Straßenbau zugute kommen.

Das Budget der Autofahrer-Partei bestreitet Dwenger zunächst noch aus eigener Tasche. Später werde man dann weitersehen. Später, wenn die Autofahrer-Partei auf Bundesebene operiere. Das Fernziel Dwengers ist Einzug der Stammtischbrüder in den Bundestag.

Koalitionsgespräche mit der Fußgänger-Liga in Berlin werden noch auf sich warten lassen. Die Liga hält naturgemäß nicht viel von Dwengers Neugründung. Vorerst quälen Parteiboß Dwenger jedoch andere Sorgen: „Wir müssen zusehen, daß unsere Partei die Fünf-Prozent-Kurve[5] kriegt."

Wolfgang Bombosch

28. Perpetuum Automobile

Seit nunmehr sieben Jahren schon bin ich kein Mensch mehr für Freund und Feind, und auch nicht fürs Finanzamt, sondern ein Pendler. Ich pendle täglich sechzig Kilometer, hin und zurück, notabene; aber mich plagen nicht Baustellen und Frostaufbrüche, nicht die Trunkenheit von anderen Menschen am Steuer: Ich pendle nämlich mit der Bundesbahn, zweiter Klasse.

In diesen sieben Jahren hat sich einiges geändert: Ich habe doppelt soviele Züge wie vor sieben Jahren und fahre elektrisch sieben Minuten schneller. Verspätungen kommen nicht mal mehr im Winter vor—aber ich bin vollkommen vereinsamt. Vor sieben Jahren noch habe ich meine Frau im Zug kennengelernt—und wenn ich mich nun auf meinem kunst-rot-ledernen Eckplatz niedergelassen habe und meine wohlbesockten Füße auf dem Platz gegenüber, wenn ich neben mir meine Akten ausgebreitet und den Rest des Abteils mit Tasche und Mantel belegt habe, dann sehne ich mich bisweilen nach einem Menschen, womöglich weiblichen Geschlechtes.

Ich habe zwar einen Pendelkollegen auf meiner Strecke, aber das ist einer mit Abschreibemöglichkeiten,[1] der fährt aus diesen Gründen nicht mit meinem Zügle, sonder nur mit dem TEE.[2] Wenn ich also so hinausschaue ins bukolische

Land am Oberrhein, dann bin ich allein wie niemand sonst. Und wenn die Autobahn, blockiert bis zum Horizont mit Produkten deutscher Wertarbeit, vorüberhuscht, dann weiß ich, was es heißt, fahnenflüchtig zu sein. Verbissenen Gesichtes stehe ich dabei, wenn im Geschäft von Parkplätzen die Rede ist und wenn meine Freunde am Sonntag zur Kirchzeit ihren Fetisch in die Schwemme fahren im Stadtwald: Noch immer ist mein Angebot an die Bundesbahn, am Wochenende Waggons zu waschen, unbeantwortet!

Den letzten Stoß aber gab man mir diese Woche: sieben Jahre mal 52 Wochenkarten treu gedient, und nun bin ich nicht einmal rentabel! Leute wie mich will man auf die Straße setzen, zu meinem eigenen Heil, denn wenn ich täglich 120 Kilometer mit dem Auto zur Arbeit fahre, brauche ich keine Steuern mehr zu zahlen bei meinem Gehalt, und die Bahn macht weniger Defizit!

Ich kann es schon verstehen: Da haben wir einen solchen Bedarf an Autobahnen, daß wir nächstens vierzehn Stockwerke tief in die Erde gehen müssen, um Platz zu schaffen, und statt ans Werk zu gehen, subventioniert man den hartnäckigsten Schmarotzer im Staate, der Wolfsburg[3] nicht gibt, was Wolfsburgs ist, den Bundesbahnpendler. Aber jetzt wird es ein Ende haben damit, ein Ende mit den subventionierten Müßiggängern der Schienen, ein Ende mit mir.

Erst wenn ganz Deutschland ein einziges Parkhaus[4] ist, wird Friede sein.

Peter Mörser

29. Der Mann am Mast: Unfall auf der Straße

Bei Grün fuhren die Wagen an, rollten über die Kreuzung, geradeaus, über einen Zebrastreifen; dort fuhr der Wagen vor uns einen Mann um, leicht, geräuschlos und ohne Aufhebens. Der Mann ging zu Boden wie in einem Boxring, und fiel—fast elegant—mit dem Gesicht aufs Pflaster.

„Den hat's erwischt", sagte der Fahrer des Autobusses, in dem ich saß, und setzte hinzu: „O mein Gott, warum hat er auch nicht aufgepaßt . . ." Der Wagen vor uns hatte gestoppt. Der Fahrer war herausgesprungen. Jetzt stand er über dem Mann, in der Pose eines verzweifelten Ringrichters, und schien zu zählen: Eins, zwei, drei . . .

Der Mann am Boden bewegte sich, rutschte auf Knie und Hände, kam langsam in die Höhe, ohne daß der Mann, der ihn umgefahren hatte, ihm half, und schwankte weiter über den Zebrastreifen zum Bordstein, der Fahrer hinter ihm her.

„Der ist hart im Nehmen", sagte unser Busfahrer hinter der Scheibe und schüttelte den Kopf, „tut doch so, als ob nichts gewesen wäre . . ." Auf dem Bordstein breitete der Mann die Arme aus, und fiel so heftig um einen Mast, daß oben das Schild ‚Vorfahrt beachten' wackelte. Und dann drehte sich der Verunglückte um den Mast wie ein Kind auf dem Spielplatz im Laufkarussell. Wir im Bus konnten nicht hören, was draußen gesprochen wurde. Wir sahen nur, wie der Autofahrer plötzlich zugriff, den Mann am Mast ordentlich hinstellte und schließlich den Zeigefinger hob: Komisch sah das aus, wie eine Illustration zum Struwwelpeter.[1] Der Fahrer gab dem Mann offensichtlich eine gute Lehre mit auf den Weg: Daß ich dich umgefahren habe, ist deine eigene Schuld. Wenn ich nicht gleich gebremst hätte, wärst du jetzt tot. Dudududud.— Aber der Mann hörte nicht hin, wie Konrad aus dem Struwwelpeter[1]. Statt dessen lächelte er wie ein Betrunkener, der die Engel schon singen gehört hat, über den erhobenen Zeigefinger hinweg, griff sich an die Kehle, setzt die Brille automatisch wieder gerade und begriff noch nicht, daß er ja weiterleben und weitergehen durfte. Der Fahrer gab sich alle Mühe, ihm das einzubläuen: Er zeigte dem Mann am Mast immer noch den Zeigefinger, als unser Bus schon weiterrollte . . .

Übrigens: So klar wie der erhobene Zeigefinger ihn machen wollte, war der Unfall eben gerade nicht gewesen. Denn schließlich war er auf einem Zebrastreifen passiert . . .

Nina Grunenberg

30. Farbe bekennen

Informationen und Visionen zum europäischen Farbfernsehen

Es lebe der Fortschritt! Das ist der Schlachtruf der Progressisten aller Zeiten und Zonen.

Das Fernsehen ist da—schwarz-weiß. Das Farbfernsehen kommt, gewollt oder ungewollt. Denn alles, was für Fortschritt gehalten oder ausgegeben wird, ist unaufhaltsam. In Amerika ist das Farbfernsehen zwar noch nicht auf einem Siegeszug, aber immerhin im Vormarsch. In Europa wird allenthalben über das Farbfernsehen diskutiert, mit dem Farbfernsehen experimentiert. Auch in der Bundesrepublik gibt es Menschen, die nur noch rot oder blau oder grün sehen, wenn sie an Fernsehen denken. Einer von ihnen ist *Horst A.C. Krieger*, Leiter der Fernsehtechnik beim Westdeutschen Rundfunk.

„Man sagt, Herr Krieger, in der Bundesrepublik würde 1967 das Farbfernsehen eingeführt. Ist diese Terminfestlegung realistisch?"

„Durchaus, was die technischen Möglichkeiten angeht."

„Werden von der einschlägigen Industrie bereits Vorbereitungen für den Bau von Farbfernsehempfängern unternommen? Und wie unterscheiden sich diese Geräte von den Schwarz-Weiß-Apparaten?"

„Um den zweiten Teil der Frage zuerst zu beantworten: Genau wie in Amerika werden die Farbfernsehgeräte die Bedingung der Kompatibilität und der Rekompatibilität erfüllen müssen—das heißt: Mit einem Gerät der Zukunft müssen Farbsendungen farbig *und* Schwarz-Weiß-Sendungen schwarz-weiß empfangen werden können."

„Das muß wohl auch so sein, denn die neue Farbepoche des Fernsehens wird im Anfang und innerhalb einer übersehbaren Zukunft nicht nur Farbprogramme bringen können."

„Natürlich nicht. In der Bundesrepublik wird man bescheiden anfangen, etwa mit einer Stunde täglich."

„Die Geräte der Zukunft werden vermutlich größer und teurer sein?"

„Der Bildschirm wird nur unwesentlich größer sein als der bisherige. Die Preise werden im Anfang erheblich höher liegen, schätzungsweise bei 2 500 Mark."

„Gibt es irgendwo in Europa jetzt schon Menschen, die regelmäßig Farbfernsehsendungen ausstrahlen und auffangen?"

„Natürlich. Das Kölner Farbstudio verbreitet Testsendungen, die in den Labors der Industrie empfangen und ausgewertet werden."

Werner Höfer

31. Bücherliste aus dem Computer

In Frankfurt am Main entsteht die erste elektronisch hergestellte National-Bibliographie der Welt.

Notwendig ist mehr Mut zum Einsatz der Technik, verkündete Bundesinnenminister Paul Lücke Anfang des Jahres vor Beamtenvertretern. Daß es ihr an solchem Mut nicht fehle, bewies vor kurzem die Deutsche Bibliothek in Frankfurt am Main: Sie präsentierte die erste elektronisch hergestellte National-Bibliographie der Welt.

Mehr als ein Jahr hatten Techniker und Bibliothekare an der Entwicklung und Programmierung einer neuen Computer-Anlage gearbeitet. Es galt ein System zu finden, das technische Gegebenheiten und bibliothekarische Erfordernisse gleichermaßen berücksichtigte.

Nur mit Hilfe der Technik, das wußten Bibliothekare wie Computer-Spezialisten, konnte es gelingen, das ‚Archiv des deutschen Schrifttums' aus der Misere zu befreien, in die es sich in den letzten Jahren immer weiter verstrickt hatte.

Seit 1945 sammelt die Deutsche Bibliothek in Frankfurt am Main alle deutschen Neuerscheinungen und Veröffentlichungen aus deutschsprachigen Ländern. Aber die Flut der Buch- und Zeitschriftenzugänge steigt unablässig.

Im November 1964 begann deshalb die damals neu gegründete Zentralstelle für maschinelle Dokumentation (ZMD) der Minerva GmbH[1] mit den Arbeiten am ‚Projekt Deutsche Bibliographie'.

Mit derzeit 32 ausgeklügelten Programmen hat das neu erdachte System bereits einen wesentlichen Teil der Probleme gelöst, die bei der maschinellen Herstellung der Bibliographie auftauchen.

Sascha Friedrichs

32. Weltraumrausch

Millionen Menschen in der Welt durften am Fernsehschirm den Start zur viertägigen Weltraumreise des US-Raumschiffes Gemini IV miterleben. Mit einem außergewöhnlichen Aufwand an Publizität hatte die US-Weltraumfahrtbehörde NASA den abenteuerlichen Versuch des Majors Edward White angekündigt, das erste Rendezvous-Manöver im Weltall auszuprobieren. Wäre es gelungen, hätte Amerika im Wettlauf zum Mond die Sowjets erstmals hinter sich gelassen.

Ursprünglich wollten die Wissenschaftler bei diesem Flug nur feststellen, wie der menschliche Organismus auf einen längeren Zustand der Schwerelosigkeit reagiert. Einer der Astronauten sollte lediglich eine Luke öffnen und seinen Kopf ins All hinausstecken. Nach dem spektakulären Zehn-Minuten-Spaziergang des Sowjetastronauten Leonow im Weltall jedoch packte die Verantwortlichen der NASA der Ehrgeiz, sobald wie möglich diese Scharte auszuwetzen.

Ihr Unterfangen glückte nur halbwegs. Pilot James

McDivitt verfehlte das Rendezvous mit der zweiten Raketenstufe. Dafür konnte sich aber Co-Pilot Edward White noch zehn Minuten länger als Leonow wandernd zwischen Himmel und Erde aufhalten. White beim Wiedereinstieg in die Kapsel: „Dies ist der traurigste Augenblick meines Lebens." Das Rauschgefühl, das ihn außerhalb der Kapsel überkam, übertrug sich auf die Nation, die seine flachsige[1] Unterhaltung mit McDivitt mitanhören (wenn auch nicht verstehen) konnte. Der Sputnik-Komplex ist überwunden. Präsident Johnson an die Astronauten: „Jeder Amerikaner fühlt sich in eurer Schuld."

Selbst im Ostblock geizte man nicht mit Anerkennung. Radio Prag: „Ein rekord-brechendes Ereignis." Radio Budapest unterbrach sogar seine Kurzwellensendungen für Nordvietnam, um während der Landung von Gemini IV den Funkverkehr mit der Bodenstation nicht zu stören. Ungewöhnlich war auch der nachdenkliche Kommentar einer tschechoslowakischen Zeitung, ob denn diese kostspielige, überflüssige Rivalität zwischen Amerikanern und Sowjets noch weitergehen müsse.

33. Nur auf den falschen Knopf gedrückt . . .

Der bemerkenswerteste Berliner des Monats Mai blieb anonym. Er lieferte zwar Schlagzeilen, er wurde zum Tagesgespräch, er beeinflußte anderthalb Mittagsstunden lang den Alltag von einer Million Bürger (bei mir fiel der Rasensprenger aus und die Platte von Nancy Sinatra); aber seinen Namen? Seinen Namen kennt man nicht.

Weltstädte werden nicht nur an ihren Erfolgen, sie werden auch an ihren Pannen gemessen. Nach New York also brach im Mai nun das Stromnetz Berlins zusammen. Rouladen warteten vergeblich darauf, gar zu werden, Fahrstühle taten zwischen den Stockwerken Seufzer der Erleichterung, und Rasensprenger, wie meiner, versiegten müde, wie erschöpft von pausenlosem Rotieren.

Der Mann hatte einen falschen Knopf gedrückt, und sieben Bezirken mit Großstadtformat ging die Puste aus.

So leicht geht das?

PS: Nicht zu fassen—nur einen falschen Knopf gedrückt . . .

Hans-Jürgen Usko

Aufsätze und Aufsatzübungen

1. Beschreiben Sie die Eindrücke eines armen Studenten, der den Sommer als Hauslehrer bei einer sehr reichen Familie verbringt.

2. Ein Zwischenfall auf der Straße.

3. Machen Sie eine Aufstellung Ihrer Ausgaben

(a) während der letzten Woche

(b) für das vergangene Jahr.

4. Wie sieht das Fahrzeug der Zukunft aus?

5. Welche Vor- und Nachteile bringen die technischen Entwicklungen der Gegenwart mit sich?

GETEILTES
DEUTSCHLAND

5

Mit den ersten Nachkriegsjahren begann ein Problem im Hintergrund
der politischen Diskussion in und um Deutschland zu stehen: das
seiner *de facto* Teilung in zwei Staaten verschiedener Weltanschauung
und verschiedener Bindungen, voneinander getrennt nicht nur durch
politische Differenzen und Kommunikationsschwierigkeiten, sondern
rein physisch durch bewachte Grenzen und in Berlin durch die von der
DDR 1961 errichtete Mauer. Trotzdem entflohen Millionen von Ost-
deutschen in den Westen, wo man ihnen mit privaten und staatlichen
Mitteln half, Fuß zu fassen. Erst spät und zögernd gelang auch eine
leichte Auflockerung der harten Bestimmungen, die Freunde und
Familienmitglieder auf ewig voneinander zu trennen schienen.

34. Barbara bittet[1]

Die Flüchtlinge, die in unsere Berliner Sprechstunde kommen, stehen alle immer noch sehr unter dem Eindruck der gerade überstandenen Flucht. So auch der junge H.K. Er kam hier buchstäblich nur mit den Sachen an, die er auf dem Leib trug, und die waren auch noch völlig von dem Stacheldraht zerrissen worden. Mit einer staatlichen Beihilfe konnte er sich gleich ein paar neue Dinge anschaffen, es langt allerdings noch nicht so recht für einen wärmeren Mantel. Und da der Winter noch nicht vorbei ist, wollen wir ihm ein solches Stück besorgen. Wenn Sie wieder dazu etwas beitragen werden, H.K. wird Ihnen sehr dankbar sein.

Barbara

35. Das Tor ging auf

Bereits einen Tag nach der Öffnung der Passierscheinstellen[1] durfte eine ältere Frau aus Westberlin zur Beerdigung ihrer Tochter in den Ostteil der Stadt gehen. Die DDR-Postbeamten hatten den Passierschein sofort ausgehändigt. Ohne Passierschein schlüpften am selben Tag 57 Ostberliner durch einen unterirdischen Tunnel in den Westteil der Stadt. Die Schüsse aus der Pistole eines Fluchthelfers,[2] die zum Schluß des Unternehmens einen Unteroffizier der Volksarmee töteten, brachten jedoch den Senat in einige Verlegenheit, da der Zwischenfall das Passierscheinabkommen gefährden könnte.

36. S-Bahnhof Friedrichstraße

Wenn es die Berliner Mauer nicht gäbe, müßte man sie erfinden.[1] Gibt es ein besseres Symbol dafür, wie wir nebeneinander auf der Erde leben, aber entgegen aller Vernunft darauf bestehen, voneinander getrennt zu sein?

Doch die Mauer hat Risse, und auch das ist symbolisch zu verstehen.

Durch einen dieser Risse geht die S-Bahn[2] von Westberlin zum Bahnhof Friedrichstraße. Der Ausländer, der aus dem Zug steigt, findet keinerlei Hinweis darauf, was er tun soll. Blickt man hoch, so sieht man zwei Posten mit Gewehr oder Maschinenpistole über der Schulter auf einer Art Balustrade in halber Höhe des Bahnhofsdaches stehen. Blickt man nach

Warten —am unerfreulichsten aller Grenzübergänge

unten, so sieht man eine Treppe, die westdeutsche Besucher benutzen sollen. Wenn man ihnen in Ermangelung anderer Hinweise folgt, gelangt man an ein Fahrkartenhäuschen und fragt dort, wohin Ausländer sich wenden sollen.

Um mehrere Ecken wird man an einen Punkt geschickt, den man bald als den tatsächlichen Mittelpunkt der Welt betrachten wird. Zu einem früheren Zeitpunkt in der Geschichte war er zweifellos nichts anderes als ein rechtwinkliger Knick in einem Gang auf einem altmodischen Bahnhof. Mit neuen Geländern und bewaffneten Posten versehen, während Lampen und Mobiliar in primitivem Zustand belassen wurden, ist er ein wahrer Alptraum, und der rechtwinklige Knick ist Teil eines diabolischen Plans. Wartesäle auf alten Bahnhöfen hatten etwas von dieser kläglich beleuchteten, schmutzigen Trostlosigkeit; dies ist ein Bahnhof, und man wartet.

Nur wartet man auf keinen Zug. Man wartet darauf, für harmlos befunden zu werden. Ja, man ist doch harmlos, oder? Aber ist das gut so? Sollte man nicht lieber gerade die Person sein, hinter der sie her sind—jemand, der Böses im Schilde führt, darauf sinnt, Tunnels unter der Mauer zu graben oder Menschen mit fremder Leute Pässen durch die Übergänge zu schleusen? Was würde Antigone tun? Was würde Karl Marx denken?

Eric Bentley

37. Meine Tante Else

Hörerpost ist lästig. Jeder, der mal im Radio spricht, kennt das: Briefe der Zustimmung, der Begeisterung, der Empörung, Postkartenwünsche in zitternder Schrift. Man überläßt das am besten der Sekretärin.

Neulich kam ein Brief, der mich mit Du anredete und auf minderem Papier geschrieben war. Er kam aus Brandenburg,[1] ein Ulbrichtkopf[2] schmückte besonnen die Briefmarke. Meine Tante Else hat mich im Radio gehört und erinnert sich deutlicher Blutsbande. Familiäre Rührung auch bei mir. Natürlich: als ich siebzehn war, es war 1936, und Hitler hatte gerade die Völker zum Olympischen Spiel geladen, war auch Tante Else einmal bei uns in Berlin zu Besuch—sie war wohl mit einem Apotheker verheiratet. Dankbares Gefühl: Die gibt es noch nach Hitler und Stalin, die lebt jetzt unter Ulbricht in Brandenburg. Ich schrieb einen netten, persönlichen Brief, einen richtigen Neffenbrief,

familiär mit leicht gesamtdeutschen Untertönen, erinne-
rungswach: Weißt du noch damals 1936? Unser Haus stand
noch so schön, und Tante Alma, die immer Stanniol[3] für die
junge Wehrmacht[4] sammelte—lebt die eigentlich noch?

Seitdem hat sich in meinem Leben etwas verändert. Ich
habe zum erstenmal Verwandte in jenem Deutschland, das
wir Zone nennen, das sich selbst DDR nennt. Mir fehlte das
immer. Das andere Deutschland, um das wir uns immer so
sorgen, wurde mir bisher nur publizistisch vermittelt:
Fernseh-Features, Radionachrichten. Zeitungsreportagen
auf Seite 3, Bildberichte, der Terror in der Zone. So etwas
stumpft ab, macht müde. Wieviel Broschüren des Gesamtdeutschen Ministeriums[5] fliegen bei uns täglich in den
Papierkorb? Der Gesamtdeutsche Etat muß enorm sein.

Tante Elses Briefe fliegen bei mir nicht in den Papierkorb.
Sie sind kostbar, ich lese sie immer wieder. Sie sind für
mich eine Quelle der Information und Umorientierung—
ich lerne täglich zu. Zum erstenmal begreife ich langsam,
was DDR eigentlich ist. In dem Wust gesamtdeutscher
Deklamationen, unabdingbarer Rechtsansprüche, Flücht-
lingsstorys, Mauerbetrachtungen und amtlicher SBZ–
Enthüllungen, der täglich auf uns niedergeht, stehen nun
so leuchtende Sätze, wie sie eben nur Tante Else schreiben
kann: Es geht uns ganz gut, auch unser Haus haben wir
wieder, Uwe studiert schon seit zwei Jahren Pharmazeutik
in Greifswald.[6] Um Deine schönen Reisen beneiden wir
Dich natürlich. 1931 waren wir auch einmal an der Riviera—
und daß Du sogar nach Afrika fahren darfst! Das Reisen
fehlt uns am meisten. Wir haben hier ja das herrliche
Thüringen und die komfortablen Ostseebäder—na ja! Und
dann folgten drei Striche.

Ich bin überrascht, wie offen Tante Else schreibt. Schick
mir bitte nicht Deine Artikel und Bücher—die nehmen sie
raus. Neulich haben sie mir sogar ein einfaches Modeheft
aus dem Westen beschlagnahmt. Schick Deine Sachen an
Onkel Herrmann in Düsseldorf. Wenn der im nächsten
Frühjahr zur Leipziger Messe[7] kommt, bringt er es mit.
Kaufleute aus dem Westen werden mit Gedrucktem ganz
passabel behandelt. Es wird höchstens abgenommen. Wann
sprichst Du denn wieder im Radio? Wir haben hier keine
Programme für das. Lieber Neffe, schick bloß keine Pro-
grammzeitschrift, da kommen wir in Teufels Küche.[8] Auch
unsere Nachbarn sind ja so stolz auf Dich, daß Du im
Radio sprichst. Wenn das Deine Mutter noch erlebt hätte!

Seitdem grüble ich immer noch, wie man von Frankfurt nach Brandenburg die Nachricht durchgibt, wann einer im Radio spricht. Nichts Politisches, nichts Gefährliches—nur so ein bißchen Literatur und Kritik. Schreibe ich: Du kannst mich im Sender Freies Berlin hören, so ist das natürlich eine Provokation für den Arbeiter- und Bauernstaat. Was heißt denn schon Freies Berlin? Sie meinen wohl den Hetzsender des besonderen Territoriums Westberlin? Wie macht man das nur?

Ich umschrieb die Sache ganz feinsinnig: weißt Du, Tante Else, in dem Verlag, wo Du neulich diese Erinnerung von mir gefunden hast, bringe ich jetzt etwas Neues heraus: am 10. Mai, 22.40 Uhr. Und das, was wir damals über unsere Familie besprachen, können wir fortsetzen: Es kommt am gleichen Ort am 2. Juli um 17 Uhr. Die Unterscheidung vom 1. und 2. Programm habe ich lieber weggelassen. Tante Else wird das schon finden. Und ich fügte hinzu: Die Leute machen sich hier mit ihren Paketsendungen lächerlich: Linsen und Kleider für die DDR! Aber wenn du mal wirklich was brauchen solltest, schreib es mir.

Neue Schwierigkeiten beim Kuvertieren. Schreibt man auf dem Umschlag nun SBZ oder DDR? Das letztere würde sicher als eine schleichende Aufwertung der Zone betrachtet. Vielleicht gibt es eine Postorder, solche Briefe nicht zu befördern? Und SBZ ist natürlich drüben ein Beschlagnahmegrund, ich verstehe das. Ich schrieb also gar nichts auf das Kuvert. Dann die Unsicherheit mit der Postleitzahl. Tante Else macht immer eine Null davor: 06—Frankfurt. Wollen die damit andeuten, daß wir eigentlich nicht existieren? Der Postbeamte empfahl, vor die Nummer von Brandenburg ein X zu machen. Liegt darin nicht auch eine verborgene Provokation?

Dann gab mir der Postbeamte eine dieser herrlichen Sonderdruckmarken, die uns die unvergeßliche Schönheit und Weite des deutschen Ostens in Erinnerung rufen. Ich klebte sie ahnungslos auf. Seitdem der Brief im Kasten ist, befallen mich nagende Zweifel. Hätte man nicht lieber eine schlichte Durchschnittsmarke nehmen sollen? Wird man den Brief mit der leuchtenden Marke nicht unter Hunderten herausfischen: Stichprobenkontrolle. Und wenn die dann lesen: wir können unser Gespräch fortsetzen am 2. Juli um 17 Uhr—wird das nicht auffällig sein?

Ist das also Deutschland? Feindesland? Bürgerkriegsland?

Man muß wieder chiffrieren, wie damals im Krieg. Auch der Ort Brandenburg und der Name Tante Else ist natürlich chiffriert. Die Tante ist sicher ein Onkel und wohnt auf Rügen. Also alles nur Schwindel.

Auf jeden Fall wünsche ich jedem eine Tante Else. Die sagt viel mehr als das Ministerium für Gesamtdeutsche Fragen.

Horst Krüger

38. Freiburger Studenten in der DDR

Wir wußten nur, daß wir um fünf Uhr nachmittags in der Invalidenstraße in Ostberlin sein sollten. Und so fuhren wir denn vom Bahnhof Zoo mit der S-Bahn hinüber über Kanal und Mauer zum Bahnhof Friedrichstraße.

Das war der Anfang eines einwöchigen Aufenthaltes in der DDR. Unsere Gruppe bestand aus drei Studentinnen und sieben Studenten der volkswirtschaftlichen, juristischen und philosophischen Fakultäten der Universität Freiburg. Ein in Ostkontakten erfahrener Student hatte uns die Einladung der Gewerkschaft Wissenschaft verschafft, in der DDR über Bildungsprobleme in Ost- und Westdeutschland zu diskutieren.

Von Ostberlin aus fuhren wir mit einem Bus über Potsdam nach Dresden.

Untergebracht im nur für Delegationen bestimmten Hotel ,Dresden-Tourist' an der Elbe, eilten wir nun von Diskussion zu Diskussion, stets geleitet von zwei Begleitern, einem Dozenten der TU[1] und Funktionär der Gewerkschaft und einem nachlässig mit einem alten Armeemantel angetanen Studenten und FDJ[2]-Funktionär.

Wir besichtigten das Pädagogische Institut, diskutierten mit seinen Dozenten, hospitierten in einer bis zur 10. Klasse führenden Oberschule in Radeberg bei Dresden, führten ein Rundgespräch mit FDJ-Vertretern und disputierten mit Hochschulprofessoren. Abends hatten einige von uns meist Gelegenheit zu weniger offiziellen Kontakten mit Studenten.

Bei ihnen fühlte man sich wie zu Hause. Man saß auf irgendeiner Bude oder im Lokal bei einem Glas Bier und redete bis drei Uhr morgens. Beziehungen stellten sich schnell und leicht her. Die Gastgeber waren begierig, etwas aus dem Westen zu hören. Sie waren keine Funktionärstypen, keine Apparatschiks, sondern junge Leute, die sich für Politik interessierten und sich für ihre Gesellschaft verantwortlich fühlten.

Ich lernte dabei zwei Kategorien von Studenten kennen: eine kleinere Gruppe, meist bürgerlicher Herkunft, die grundsätzlich gegen das System eingestellt ist. Viele von ihnen verabscheuten auch die stupide Bevormundung von Kunst und Literatur. Eine Aussicht auf Wiedervereinigung sahen sie nicht. Trotzdem sind sie nicht verzweifelt. Nach dem Druck und dem Terror befragt, dem sie sich durch ihre grundsätzlich oppositionelle Haltung aussetzen, erzählten sie uns, man müsse eben vorsichtig sein.

Eine zweite, meinen Eindrücken nach größere Gruppe der Studenten steht ‚grundsätzlich auf dem Boden des Sozialismus'. Auch von ihnen war kaum jemand mit der offiziellen Politik und mit dem Anspruch der Partei auf absolute Führung willig einverstanden.

Sie kritisierten ihr System und wollen erreichen, es offen kritisieren zu dürfen. Ihr Ziel ist ein demokratischer Sozialismus und ihr Idol Professor Havemann,[3] der ihnen freilich nicht zuletzt deshalb imponiert, weil er die Gelegenheit hatte, in den Westen zu gehen—und doch nicht ging.

Überhaupt werden hier die Flüchtlinge nicht sehr bewundert, da man annimmt, es seien überwiegend materielle Gründe gewesen, die sie zur Flucht bewogen hätten.

Der Eindruck dieses DDR-Besuchs auf jeden von uns war sehr stark. Viele schablonenhafte Vorstellungen wurden korrigiert. Noch sprechen wir die gleiche Sprache. In den nächsten Tagen wollen wir die Dresdner Studenten nach Freiburg einladen.

Dietrich Schwanitz

39. Hochzeit in einer LPG[1]

Eigentlich war es so wie vor dreißig Jahren oder auch wie zu Urgroßmutters Zeiten: Es wurde gut gegessen und viel getrunken, es gab Späße und Verse auf Brautpaar und Gäste, und um Mitternacht wurde ein Umzug mit Musik durch das Dorf gemacht. Wer Licht anzündete, bekam ein Ständchen und mußte auf das Wohl des jungen Paares ein Glas leeren. Auf dem Weg zur Kirche streuten Kinder Blumen, und bei der Rückkehr warf der Bräutigam Geldmünzen und Bonbons unter die Dorfjugend. Nur das gab es früher nicht: Am frühen Morgen fuhren die Neuvermählten zum Flughafen Schönefeld. Sie wollen ihre Flitterwochen am Schwarzen Meer verbringen.

Vor dem Gehöft, in dem die Hochzeit stattfand, steht ein Schild: ‚LPG Heimattreue, Brigade III, Hof 6.‘ Zu diesem Hof gehörten einmal 64 Hektar Acker, Wiesen und Weiden, ‚Minutenboden‘, wie der Brautvater, der frühere Besitzer, sagte. Das heißt, der Boden ist sehr schwer. Wenn man den geeigneten Zeitpunkt verpaßt, an dem er beackert werden muß, schafft man die Feldarbeiten nicht mehr. Seit dem 16. Jahrhundert ist der Hof im Besitz der Familie. Jetzt betreut der alte Bauer mit Hilfskräften die Schweinezucht der LPG, die auf seinem Gehöft eingerichtet ist. Die Braut ist Brigadeabrechnerin, sie hält buchhalterisch das Dorf in Ordnung. Die LPG ‚Heimattreue‘ erstreckt sich über drei Dörfer, von denen jedes eine Brigade bildet. Der Bräutigam betreut die Traktorenwerkstatt der LPG.

Bei den älteren Bauern ist noch der Groll über die Schwierigkeiten und Schikanen aus der Nachkriegszeit zu spüren. Die Jüngeren wurmt das nicht mehr. Sie haben mehr Freizeit als früher. So wie es früher in der Landwirtschaft zuging, konnte es nicht weitergehen. Das wußten sie längst. Da kam die LPG. Sie funktioniert schlecht und recht, hier und da auch gut, manchmal sogar ausgezeichnet. Jedenfalls—sie funktioniert.

40. Die deutsche Frage

Was kann aus der Wiedervereinigung werden?

Wiedervereinigung, wie sie in der Bundesrepublik verstanden wird, heißt Wiedervereinigung Deutschlands auf dem Territorium der vier Besatzungszonen, das aufgeteilt ist in die freiheitlich demokratische Bundesrepublik mit Westberlin und in die sowjetische Besatzungszone, die kommunistische Deutsche Demokratische Republik.

Vereinigt werden sollen die beiden, seit zwanzig Jahren voneinander getrennten deutschen Gemeinwesen mit diametral entgegengesetzten politischen Systemen und Gesellschaftsordnungen. Beide Systeme sind zumindest nach gegenwärtigen Vorstellungen miteinander unvereinbar. Ihre Koexistenz in einem Staat ist ebenso wenig möglich, wie sich gegenwärtig eine Verbindung ihrer wesentlichen Elemente zu einer neuen Ordnung vorstellen läßt. Wie immer der politische Status des vereinigten Staatswesens sein mag, die

Einigung läßt sich nur vollziehen, wenn ein Ordnungssystem dem anderen weicht.

Die Bundesrepublik verlangt ‚Wiedervereinigung in Freiheit.' Sie soll mittels freiheitlich demokratischen Verfahren vollzogen werden, die eine freiheitlich demokratische Ordnung für den gesamtdeutschen Staat errichten. Mit der nationalen Einigung soll die Befreiung der Deutschen in der Zone von der kommunistischen Diktatur verbunden sein. Man kann auch von Wiedervereinigung im ‚traditionellen Sinn' sprechen.

Die Wiedervereinigung Deutschlands, die zu einer Änderung des seit 1945 bestehenden politischen Status quo führt, bedarf nach unumstrittenem Vertragsrecht der Zustimmung der vier Weltkriegsalliierten: Amerika, England, Frankreich und Sowjetrußland. Die Westmächte haben sich gegenüber der Bundesrepublik verpflichtet, die Zustimmung unter bestimmten Voraussetzungen zu erteilen. Sollte Sowjetrußland die Erlaubnis zu einer Wiedervereinigung in Freiheit geben, so können die Westmächte sie nicht versagen.

Theodor Eschenburg

Aufsätze und Aufsatzübungen

1. Erzählen Sie die Erlebnisse einer Familie, die durch den Bau der Berliner Mauer getrennt wurde.
2. Wie wäre, Ihrer Meinung nach, ‚die deutsche Frage' zu lösen?

AUS
DEUTSCHER
SICHT

Über Weltgeschehen und Persönlichkeiten wird in der seriösen deutschen Presse ausführlich berichtet und diskutiert.

41. Wahlen in der Nachbarschaft: London, Wien und Brüssel

Aus Wahlresultaten in europäischen Nachbarländern lassen sich keine unmittelbaren Prognosen[1] für die Bundestagswahl ableiten. Dennoch haben die Bonner Parteien in den letzten Wochen die Gemeindewahlen in England, die Präsidentenwahl in Österreich und die Parlamentswahl in Belgien aufmerksam verfolgt.

Die CDU sah es nicht ungern, daß die Labour-Partei Harold Wilsons in der Publikumsgunst erheblich abgesunken ist. Eine Woche nach der Labour-Niederlage in den Kommunalwahlen ergab eine Meinungsumfrage, daß die Konservativen—würden jetzt Parlamentswahlen angesetzt—wieder als Regierungspartei ins Unterhaus einziehen würden. Die Prozentzahlen wären: Labour 41 (Oktober 44), Konservative 49 (44), Liberale 10 (10). Am größten war die Enttäuschung über Labour bei den mittelständischen Wählern und bei den Frauen.

Die SPD registrierte währenddessen mit Genugtuung die Wahl ihres politischen Freundes Jonas zum neuen österreichischen Bundespräsidenten. Der sozialistische Bürgermeister von Wien siegte mit 50,69 Prozent knapp über den Kandidaten der Österreichischen Volkspartei, Altbundeskanzler Alfons Gorbach. Noch nie hatte ein ÖVP-Kandidat nach 1945 soviel Stimmen auf sich vereinigen können. Die Mehrheit der Österreicher entschied sich jedoch dafür, daß wie bisher die Sozialisten das Staatsoberhaupt und die Bürgerlichen den Regierungschef der Großen Koalition stellen.

Die FDP schließlich wurde durch den Wahlerfolg der belgischen Liberalen ermutigt und hofft, daß der Mißerfolg der Großen Koalition in Brüssel Nachahmer in den großen Bonner Parteien warnen wird. Christlich-Soziale und Sozialisten, die seit vier Jahren das Land gemeinsam regierten, verloren zusammen 39 Mandate und büßten ihre Zwei-Drittel-Mehrheit ein. Die bisher schwache liberale Oppositionspartei gewann fast zehn Prozent an Stimmen. Auch die Extremen (die rechtsstehende flämische Volksunie und die Kommunisten) wurden stärker.

42. Ein Cowboy als Präsident? Washington, nicht Texas hat Johnson geprägt

Vor kurzem zeigte die amerikanische Fernsehgesellschaft NBC einen Film mit Lyndon Johnson auf seiner heimatlichen Ranch in Texas. Man sah den Präsidenten in der weiten und zugleich intimen Atmosphäre der kargen Landschaft, man sah ihn unter Farmern und Kirchgängern. Es wurde zurückgeblendet in die Jugend, als Johnson sich sein Studium als Straßenbauarbeiter verdiente oder aufsässigen Schulkindern mit mexikanischem Einschlag das Alphabet und die Geschichte Amerikas einbleute.

Dann erzählte der Präsident, wie er großgeworden war und sich aus einer mit materiellen Gütern nicht gesegneten Familie hochgerackert hatte. Er sprach mit der an ihm gewohnten Mundart, dem breiten und leicht singenden südlichen Akzent; er brauchte sich nicht zu genieren, um ganz so zu wirken, wie er am liebsten vor dem amerikanischen Volk erscheint: Ein Mann einfacher Herkunft, der die Sorgen aller versteht und dem die elementaren Dinge des Lebens, eine anständige Behausung, gute Schulbildung, satt zu essen und eine gleiche Chance des Fortkommens für jedermann mehr als alles andere am Herzen liegen.

Es war ein Film ohne Phrasen. Hier offenbarte sich der willensstarke, aber schlichte Mann, der nicht von des Gedankens Blässe angekränkelt werden möchte, der die Dinge um sich und das eigene Leben einfach und vereinfacht sehen und gestalten will, der mehr auf die Erfahrung als auf eine gedankliche Konzeption setzt.

Aber Lyndon Johnson, der sich so gern als Texaner zeigt, hat zwar alle Eigenarten des Menschenschlages dieser Landschaft—und doch ist er kein ranker, unbekümmerter Cowboy in der Verkleidung des Präsidenten der Vereinigten Staaten. Vielmehr ist er ein waschechter Washingtoner, der ohne das Getriebe der Hauptstadt und die ungezählten Verantwortlichkeiten seines Amtes, ohne das verzehrende Spiel der Selbstbestätigung und ohne die niemals schwindenden Sorgen um den Bestand Amerikas in der Welt gar nicht auskommen kann. Der Texaner Lyndon—das ist die Flucht in eine Wirklichkeit, in der sich der Washingtoner Johnson nicht lange wohl fühlen könnte.

Bei dem Image vom Texaner wird zumeist übersehen,

daß Lyndon Johnson—wie kaum ein zweiter amerikanischer Politiker und wie fast kein anderer Präsident vor ihm—mit Washington verbunden ist. Von den knapp 58 Jahren seines Lebens hat er fast 35 Jahre in der Hauptstadt verbracht. Hier und nicht an den Ufern des Pedernales vollzog sich seine wirkliche Entwicklung. In dieser Stadt, nicht im Staate Texas, gewann er seinen Schliff als Politiker. Nach dem Mord an Kennedy übernahm er das Präsidentenamt wie eine erwartete Berufung, die er mit der Wiederwahl höchst eindrucksvoll bestätigte.

Johnson fühlt sich nicht als irgendein Präsident der USA, sondern als einer ihrer bedeutendsten. Er handhabt seine Geschäfte mit einem Selbstvertrauen, das in diesen drei Jahren noch durch keinen wirklichen Rückschlag erschüttert worden ist. Seinen Auftrag will Johnson ganz erfüllen, und er legt alles darauf an, Widerstände zu umgehen—wo sie sich nicht mit Gewalt beiseite schieben lassen.

Von diesem Johnson ist vorauszusetzen, daß er Amerika als Mittelpunkt der Welt und sich als Zentrum Amerikas betrachtet, daß er Macht bis zur Brutalität gebraucht, wenn er keinen anderen Weg sieht, daß er ein Präsident bleibt, der leicht zu verletzen, aber schwer zu gewinnen ist—und an dem das Texanische allenfalls Oberfläche ist.

Joachim Schwelien

43. Gewissensforschung in Washington: Die große Debatte über den Vietnam-Krieg

Kaum waren die öffentlichen *hearings* des außenpolitischen Senatsausschusses in Washington beendet, da machte Senator Robert Kennedy mit dem Vorschlag Furore, der Vietcong müsse in Vietnam an der Macht beteiligt werden, wenn der Krieg beendet werden solle. Diese Erklärung trug ihm zwar den Beifall der demokratischen Linken ein, aber auch Mißfallenskundgebungen von der Regierung. Vizepräsident Humphrey meinte, dies heiße, einen Brandstifter zum Feuerwehrmann zu ernennen.

Tatsächlich läuft der Gedanke Robert Kennedys auf den Versuch hinaus, eine kommunistische Bewegung wie den Vietcong mit einer Scheibe am Kuchen der Macht zu beteiligen, in der Hoffnung, sie werde davon absehen, ihn ganz zu verzehren. Dafür hat es jedoch in Ländern, die an starke, kommunistisch regierte Nationen grenzen, freilich noch kein Beispiel gegeben. Kein Wunder, daß sich in der amerikanischen Regierung niemand auf ein Experiment dieser Art in Vietnam einlassen möchte.

Dennoch hat der Vorschlag des jungen Senators insofern einen Sinn, als er auf das Dilemma und auf die auch nach der großartigen öffentlichen ,Vernehmung' im außenpolitischen Senatsausschuß noch unbeantwortete Frage verwies, wie der Konflikt denn eigentlich abgeschlossen werden soll, wenn die USA nicht davon ausgehen, in Südvietnam einen totalen militärischen Sieg zu erringen. Denn worauf das amerikanische Engagement in Vietnam hinausläuft, diese Frage ist immer noch nicht geklärt.

Joachim Schwelien

44. Im Westen nichts Neues

Die Pressekonferenz von General de Gaulle hat nichts wesentlich Neues gebracht, aber einige Aspekte seiner Politik klarer hervortreten lassen. Das gilt für die Begriffe ,Unabhängigkeit und Souveränität', und es gilt auch für seine Ansicht über das Verhältnis von Amerika und Europa und über die NATO.

Die Organisation des atlantischen Bündnisses enthält in de Gaulles Augen ein Element der Unterordnung, das ihm nicht mehr zeitgemäß erscheint. Mit der Rolle Frankreichs hält er es für unvereinbar: „Unser Land ist durch seine eigene Kraft eine Atommacht geworden und nimmt die politische und strategische Verantwortung auf sich, die damit verbunden ist—eine Verantwortung, die ihrer Natur und ihrer Ausdehnung nach unveräußerlich ist. Außerdem ist Frankreich entschlossen, seine eigenen Entscheidungen zu treffen, was unerläßlich ist, damit es an seine Aufgabe glaubt und damit es den anderen nützlich sein kann."

Seinen Entschluß, die gegenwärtige Bündnisorganisation aufzulösen und sich nur an die Präambel zu halten, mit der 1949 die westliche Verteidigungsgemeinschaft ins Leben gerufen wurde, wird außerdem mit den veränderten weltpolitischen Bedingungen erklärt. Ein Krieg um Europa sei heute weniger wahrscheinlich, als die Ausweitung eines anderwärtigen Konflikts, in den Amerika verwickelt ist, zum Weltkrieg. De Gaulle will von Frankreich die Gefahr abwenden, in eine solche Entwicklung einfach hineingezogen zu werden. Daher fordert er ein Ende „des Einbaus seines

Territoriums, seiner Verbindungswege, einiger seiner Streit-
kräfte, mehrerer seiner Luftbasen, dieser oder jener Häfen
in das amerikanische Befehlssystem".

Weil zu erwarten steht, daß die NATO an Komplika-
tionen eingeht, die ihr Paris jetzt bereitet, hat de Gaulle
gleichzeitig mit großer Geste die Tür für die europäische
Zusammenarbeit zu öffnen versucht. Er fordert die sechs
EWG-Länder zu Gesprächen auf „über ihre Sicherheit
unter Berücksichtigung ihrer engen Nachbarschaft und ihrer
geographischen Bindungen und damit zu strategischen
Gesprächen . . ." Es ist wohl nicht schwer, den Gedanken zu
Ende zu führen.

Ernst Weisenfeld

45. Erziehung zum Schlaukopf

Erfahrungen eines wohlerzogenen jungen Mannes in Paris

Die Franzosen, die im Lauf der letzten fünfzig Jahre viele
Illusionen über sich selbst verloren haben, sind nichtsdestoweniger überzeugt, das kultivierteste Volk der Erde zu sein.

Die Erziehung hierzulande ruht auf mehreren mächtigen
Grundsteinen, die hübsch der Ordnung nach aufgezählt
werden sollen. Zu allererst der Snobismus.

Oft hört man sagen: „Mein Kind wird nicht im selben
Beruf wie sein Vater arbeiten. Ich habe es auf eine pikfeine
Schule geschickt, wo es mit gebildeten Leuten zusammen-
kommt." Namen, die, wie man so sagt, alle Türen öffnen,
gut im Ohr liegen und nach etwas klingen, werden sehr gern
geführt. Fachleute haben berechnet, daß von 80 000 Familien
mit Adelsnamen höchstens 1 000 ihn authentisch tragen.

Mit der Leibrente einer aristokratischen Abstammung
versehen, legt man sich alsdann gute Manieren zu. In allen
Bussen werden die Sitzplätze stets von Matronen belegt, die
vor Gesundheit strotzen, während sich in den Gängen
Wesen männlichen Geschlechts und erschöpften Ausdrucks
drängen. Der Handkuß ist nicht etwa ausgestorben, im
Gegenteil. Wohlerzogene Menschen verneigen sich tief,
erreichen endlich die anvisierte Hand und küssen sie dann
. . . beileibe nicht.

Die Ernährung bildet einen weiteren fesselnden Bestand-
teil der französischen Erziehung. Alle Welt redet nur von der
Nahrung: was man gestern gegessen hat, was man heute ißt,
was man morgen essen wird. Das fängt schon im Kindergarten an. Die Kinder sitzen rings um den Tisch, sehen

51

wohlgenährt aus, strahlen vor Gesundheit. Die Kindergärtnerin wiederholt in sanftem Ton: „Brot, Wein, Käse, Pudding, Apfel, Birne, Wurst." Ringsum Bilder mit Lebensmitteln. „Und nun, liebe Kinder, wollen wir's uns gut schmecken lassen." Die Kinder sind entzückt. Man serviert ihnen Kakao und Butterbrote.

Ganz Frankreich ißt von früh bis spät, und ein gesellschaftlich gewandter Herr würde nicht als normal angesehen, wenn er sich nicht mit riesigem Enthusiasmus zu Tisch begäbe.

Ferner lernt der junge Franzose einige Redensarten, mit Hilfe derer er dann immer das treffende Wort findet: „Der Spatz in der Hand ist besser als die Taube auf dem Dach." „Was man nicht im Kopf hat, muß man in den Beinen haben." „Man soll den Tag nicht vor dem Abend loben." „Unrecht Gut gedeiht nicht." Sprüchlein wie diese deuten an, daß das Leben im Grunde von Weisheit regiert wird, —dem Anschein nach wenigstens. Denn in Frankreich zählt allein der Anschein.

Bernard da Costa

46. Der Besuch der Königin

Elisabeth II. und der Herzog von Edinburgh sind in der Bundesrepublik mit großer Freude empfangen worden. Dieser Staatsbesuch ist nur vergleichbar mit zwei vorangegangenen: mit dem Besuch de Gaulles (*„Sie sind ein großes, ja ein großes Volk!"*) und dem Kennedys (*„Ich bin ein Berliner"*). Aus dem Munde der englischen Königin sind solche schlagkräftigen Komplimente, in denen gleichwohl politische Absichten staken, nicht zu erwarten. Und doch übt ihre Erscheinung bei aller Kühle, Korrektheit und bei einer Liebenswürdigkeit, die immer ein wenig nach Routine und Pflicht aussieht, einen bezwingenden Zauber aus.

Englands Königin hat nicht das Recht, politisch zu handeln; sie hat die Pflicht, politischer Haltung Ausdruck zu geben. Mag es rührend oder erheiternd wirken, daß allein ihr Anblick schon genügt, viele Menschen in romantische Stimmung zu versetzen—wichtiger als die Ereignisse ihrer Reise ist die Tatsache ihres Besuches.

Sieben Jahre sind es her, daß der erste deutsche Bundespräsident, Professor Heuss, in England war: freundlich bei Hofe, kühl vom Volk empfangen. Dies ist nun der Gegenbesuch, und es liegt nahe, den Satz aus Schillers *Wallenstein* zu zitieren: „Spät kommt Ihr, doch Ihr kommt. Der weite Weg entschuldigt Euer Säumen." In der Tat ist in den verflossenen sieben Jahren ein weiter Weg zurückgelegt worden, denn kaum irgendwo in der westlichen Welt hatte sich das Mißtrauen gegen uns Deutsche so lange wach erhalten als in England.

Die englische Regierung und Diplomatie haben sich geringere Mühe gegeben, als die deutschen Verantwortlichen im Bund und in den Ländern es taten, um einem historisch bedeutsamen Geschehnis Form zu geben, dessen Inhalt heißt: *Wiederversöhnung.* Gleichgültig, ob dieses Wort im Strom der offiziellen Reden anklingt und im Schwall der sentimentalen Kommentare verschlissen wird—die britische Regierung weiß, was sie will: sie hat die Königin gebeten, auf dem Wege europäischer Politik voranzugehen.

J.M.-M.

47. Treibhaus der Traditionen

Verpaßt Großbritannien den Anschluß an die moderne Welt?

Deutsche, die England bewundern, vergleichen nicht selten mit wehmütigem Neid die Atmosphäre eines Landes, in dem sich historische Kontinuität so vielfältig äußert, mit der traditionslosen Realität der Bundesrepublik.

Aber ist der Fluch britischer Traditionen nicht tatsächlich viel augenfälliger als ihr Segen? Es geht nicht bloß darum, daß so viele Traditionen im Grunde längst anachronistisch geworden sind. Gefährlicher ist die Pflege eines Geistes, der dem Alten den Vorzug vor dem Neuen gibt, und allzu oft sich dem Schein zuwendet, nicht dem Sein. Schein, historisches Theater beherrschen geradezu das politische Leben. Das schlagendste Beispiel ist ‚die gnädige Rede vom Thron‘, mit der alljährlich im Herbst die neue Parlamentssaison eröffnet wird. Die Königin verliest die Rede vom Thron im Oberhaus. Das Unterhaus muß warten, bis der Herold, der ‚schwarze Stab‘, erscheint, um die ‚Commoners‘ aufzufordern, an der Schranke des Oberhauses zu erscheinen.

Dann traben sie hinüber, geführt vom Premierminister und dem Führer der ‚treuen Opposition ihrer Majestät‘, und stehen—sie, welche die wahre und einzige Macht in dieser repräsentativen Demokratie verkörpern—hinten zusammengedrängt, während die edlen Lords, die so gut wie keine Macht mehr haben, auf den Bänken sitzen. Und die Königin verkündet Regierungspläne in Worten, die alle vom Premierminister stammen, und die sie aussprechen muß, ob sie will oder nicht; denn wenn sie nicht wollte, müßte nicht der hinten stehende Premierminister abdanken, sondern sie, die auf dem Thron sitzt. Wenn die Tradition solchen historischen Theaters zur allgemeinen Vorstellung beiträgt, daß sich im Grunde seit den glorreichen alten Zeiten nicht gar so viel geändert habe, so schadet sie einem Volk, das vor allem begreifen muß, wie viel sich geändert hat.

Der Gelderwerb, zum Beispiel, ist zwar nicht mehr verächtlich, nur gar so ernst darf man's nicht nehmen; ,hartes Verkaufen' ist noch immer nicht wirklich fein. Ein Pressemogul sagte vor kurzem, es sei „grausam klar, daß unsere Methoden auf vielen Gebieten, besonders in der Industrie, im Vergleich zu denen anderer Länder verschwenderisch und unrationell sind . . . Als Sündenbock werden gewöhnlich die Gewerkschaften genannt, aber die Hauptschuld trägt ein Management, das weich und untüchtig ist und vor positiven Aktionen zurückscheut . . ." Die Managerklasse lebt eben noch immer möglichst nach dem Vorbild der ,landed gentry'. Wenn der Tag nicht erst mit dem Drink in einem Klubsessel beginnt, so beginnt doch das Leben erst auf einem grünen, ländlichen Rasen und womöglich hoch zu Roß.

Wenn nun das Management nicht sehr abenteuerlustig ist, so sind die Gewerkschaften durch und durch konservativ. Unter führenden Industrieländern wird allein in England industrielle Ausbildung nach veralteten Lehrlings- und Gesellenmethoden betrieben, die fünf Jahre erfordern —anstatt drei, wie auf dem Kontinent—und deren Ergebnisse wahrscheinlich schlechter sind. Der jüngere Arbeiter wird einem älteren zugeteilt, dem er auf Schritt und Tritt zu folgen hat; von ihm soll er sein Fach durch Nachahmung lernen, als wäre es ein Mysterium (wie man im Mittelalter ein Handwerk nannte). Behördlich überwachte Prüfungen gibt es nicht; die Handwerksromantik muß gewahrt bleiben—„die sicherste Formel", schrieb Andrew Shonfield „um mit dem größten Zeitaufwand die Technologie der vorigen Generation zu lernen."

Nicht darum geht es, warum die Engländer im 19. Jahrhundert so traditionsbesessen wurden—ganz Europa

wurde es damals—sondern nur darum, warum sie es
geblieben sind—im Gegensatz zu den Völkern des Kon-
tinents.

Edmund Wolf

48. Schwarzer Sand im Zucker der Weissen

Die Einwanderung der Farbigen ist in England zum Problem geworden

Wenn morgen alle in London lebenden Schotten oder
Iren die Stadt verließen, so gäbe es eine große Zahl freier
Stellen, vom Bauarbeiter bis zum Bankdirektor. Gingen
jedoch alle farbigen Einwanderer, so bräche das Chaos aus.
Die U-Bahn stünde still, die Busse führen nicht, die
Briefe blieben auf dem Postamt liegen, in den Kantinen
stapelte sich das ungespülte Geschirr, in den Straßen der
Müll.

Die schwarzen und braunen Commonwealthbürger sind
nicht länger eine Randerscheinung, sie sind ein notwendiger
Faktor. Nur, daß das zu ihrer Beliebtheit nicht gerade
beigetragen hat.

In England leben gegenwärtig etwa 800 000 Farbige—
1,5 Prozent der Bevölkerung (gegen 12 Prozent in den
USA). Aber was die Einwanderung zum Problem macht,
ist nicht der Prozentsatz, sondern die rapide Zunahme
innerhalb des letzten Jahrzehnts und die gleichzeitige
Konzentration der Einwanderer in etwa 30 Städten.

Es begann in der Zeit des Arbeitskräftemangels nach
1945, als die Einwanderungsbestimmungen demonstrativ
gelockert wurden. In den überseeischen Gebieten warben
die Briten privat und offiziell für die Reise nach England.
Angezogen von vielversprechenden Filmen und angetan
von der Lebensart und der praktischen Toleranz, die sie
bei den englischen Ingenieuren und Lehrern sahen, machten
sich die arbeitslosen Männer pakistanischer Kleinstädte
und jamaikanischer Slums auf den Weg nach Liverpool—
die selbst bestellte Invasion eines Landes, das gegen
nichts so allergisch ist wie gegen Invasionen.

Trotz dieser Ballung in den letzten Jahren hätte es ein
Farbigenproblem in England nie gegeben, wenn sich die
Ankömmlinge nicht auf einige Städte konzentriert, inner-
halb dieser Städte auf engem Gebiet dicht beieinander

angesiedelt und auf das Wohnen und Arbeiten in England nur ungenügend vorbereitet hätten.

Zu den Widrigkeiten, die sie vorfanden—Wohnungsnot, wechselnde Wirtschaftslage und rassische Vorurteile— kamen hinzu mangelnde Kenntnisse der englischen Sprache und unzureichende Vorstellungen von dem nötigen Start- kapital in einer vergleichsweise wohlsituierten Gesellschaft.

Die Einwanderer zogen dorthin, wo Arbeit wartete. Sie verdingten sich als Schaffner, Briefträger, Fließbandarbeiter, Straßenreiniger, Küchenpersonal, Krankenpfleger, Kinder- schwestern, Club-Diener und Ärzte. „Unsere Kranken- häuser sind nur deshalb noch geöffnet, weil es 4000 Mediziner aus Indien, Pakistan und Afrika im Lande gibt", sagte der Generalsekretär einer der Ärztegewerkschaften.

Die Westinder kamen meist, um zu bleiben, daher holten sie nach und nach ganze Sippen von Angehörigen nach. Die Inder und Pakistani dagegen wollten in erster Linie Geld verdienen, um irgendwann zurückzukehren; unter ihnen überwiegen die Junggesellen. Die Westinder können Englisch. Bei den Asiaten hapert es damit, sofern nicht eine bessere Schulbildung hinzukam.

Sie alle fanden entgegenkommende Unternehmer und abwartende Kollegen vor. Aufstiegschancen boten sich kaum; wer es dennoch schaffte, spürte sofort die eisige Reserve der einheimischen Untergebenen. Farbiger Vormänner wegen ist schon gestreikt worden. Die Einwanderer rächen sich dafür durch betonte Unlust am Beitritt zu den Gewerk- schaften, deren offizielle Politik zwar alle Rassen-Diskri- mination verpönt, deren untere Chargen aber mit den Wölfen heulen, wenn es ums Nachbeten von Vorurteilen geht.

Denn aus dem Vorurteil resultieren alle Übel.

Die Hauswirtin in Nummer 9, die den zimmersuchenden Pakistani abweist, wundert sich, wenn er dem Vorbild seiner Landsleute folgt, für teures Hypothekengeld ein Haus kauft— vielleicht zufällig Nummer 11 nebenan—und dann fünf von sechs Räumen untervermietet an etwa zehn Personen, darunter sechs lärmende kaffeebraune Kinder, die durch ihren bloßen Anblick jeden künftigen Käufer des Hauses Nummer 9 abschrecken, dessen Wert daraufhin um 50, 60 oder 70 Prozent sinkt. Dennoch wird die Hauswirtin die Schuld nie bei sich selbst suchen. Sie wird einem ‚Bürger- verein' beitreten und für einen örtlichen Rechtsextremisten stimmen.

Dagegen hilft kein Gesetz, und das würde auch eine Einwandererquote nicht ändern, die nur noch Atomforscher und Cricketspieler ins Land ließe.

Karl Heinz Wocker

Aufsätze und Aufsatzübungen

1. Beschreiben Sie eine Persönlichkeit des öffentlichen Lebens.
2. Zeichnen Sie das Bild eines typischen jungen
(a) Deutschen   (b) Engländers   (c) Amerikaners.
3. Deutschlands Gastarbeiter.
4. Herr Wolf sieht Englands schwächste Seite in seiner Traditionsgebundenheit; schreiben Sie nach diesem Muster einen Artikel, in dem Sie Deutschlands größte Schwäche angreifen.

E

Glossary of Educational Terms

In the *Bundesrepublik*, there is no Federal Ministry of Education: schooling is the business of the *Länder*, of which each has its own *Kultusministerium* (although a consultative *Ständige Konferenz der Kultusminister* has its offices in Bonn).

Nevertheless, there are certain main features which are broadly common to school types in the public sector. Children begin their schooling at the age of six in the *Grundschule*; from the age of 10 they may continue to the age of 15 (or later) in the *Volksschule*, after which, on starting work, they will continue part-time education in a *Berufsschule*; or else by means of internal assessment and/or examination they may pass into the *Realschule* (with a technical and practical bias) or into one of several types of *Höhere Schule*: the *Gymnasium* in which there may be a choice between 'arts'—*geisteswissenschaftlicher*—and science—*naturwissenschaftlicher Zweig*—while the emphasis in the *humanistisches Gymnasium* lies on the study of the ancient languages; the *Realgymnasium* (modern languages and science bias) or the *Oberrealschule* (scientific bias). The *Höhere Schulen* lead to the *Abitur*, the senior leaving examination, in a minimum of 9 years, and open the way to university or other advanced study. More recent experimental types of schooling include *Abendgymnasien* and *Aufbaukurse*, which offer later chances to pass from the *Volksschule* to more advanced educational opportunities.

Broadly speaking, primary schools are coeducational but separated according to denomination, *Konfession*, i.e. either Catholic or Protestant —which determines also the religious basis of teacher training colleges, *Pädagogische Akademien*. Secondary schools are rarely coeducational, and are not usually separated according to *Konfession*.

JUGEND STEHT ZUR DISKUSSION

7

Wie überall in der Welt stehen auch in Deutschland Probleme der
Erziehung und Bildung, der Reform von Schulen und Universitäten
und der Verständigung zwischen den Generationen im Mittelpunkt der
Diskussion.

49. Staatsstudenten und Privatschüler

Der Schultyp der Zukunft, der alle Altersstufen umfaßt und von sozialdemokratischen Bildungspolitikern wie von nicht parteigebundenen Schulreformern propagiert wird, hieß einmal ,Einheitsschule'. Jetzt verzichtet man auf dieses Wort. Es war werbepsychologisch falsch. Zu sehr erinnerte es an Eintopf, Einerlei, Einheitsbrei. Dort, wo es diese Schule bereits gibt, nennt man sie ,Gesamtschule'.

Wie immer sie jedoch genannt werden mag, sie dürfte bei ,bürgerlichen' Wählern noch lange auf Mißtrauen stoßen. Waren sie denn gar nichts, sind sie denn gar nichts: die Realschule, das Realgymnasium, das humanistische Gymnasium?

Ist denn die gleiche Schule, ob Einheits- oder Gesamt-, für alle Kinder das Richtige? Und die Hochbegabten? Und die Katholiken? Und die Gegner der Koedukation? Und die Kinder, deren Eltern bei den Schularbeiten nicht helfen können? Und die Eltern, die ein paar tausend Mark lieber in die Ausbildung ihrer Kinder als in ein neues Auto investieren möchten? Und . . . und . . . und . . .

Nun ist es nicht nur möglich, sondern wahrscheinlich, daß die ideale Gesamtschule viel mehr Sonderwünsche erfüllen, auch mehr Sonderbegabungen gerecht werden kann als die existierenden Schulen. Gerade in einer sehr großen Schule—und Gesamtschulen sollten große Schulen sein— lassen sich gewiß mehr Differenzierungen ermöglichen, als manche Schulweisheit sich träumen läßt.

Doch diese hochdifferenzierte, diese ,,ideale'' Gesamtschule ist auch ein Traum, vorerst jedenfalls noch. Vertretbare Elternwünsche jedoch sollten keine Träume, sollten erfüllbar sein—um so leichter, je eher die Eltern bereit sind, sich die Erfüllung etwas kosten zu lassen.

Ein Musterfall sind die Konfessionsschulen. Ich kann es nicht bestätigt finden, daß Religionsfriede hergestellt wird, wenn *von Staats wegen* oft im gleichen Gebäude katholische Fahrradständer von evangelischen Fahrradständern geschieden werden (das ist kein Witz). Es scheint mir absurd, *von Staats wegen* Kinder zwischen sechs und zehn Jahren nach Konfessionen, Kinder zwischen zehn und neunzehn Jahren nach Geschlechtern zu scheiden und danach bei den ,höheren' Lehrern (Universität) die Konfession zu ignorieren, bei den ,niederen' (Pädagogische Akademie) die Konfession zur Existenzfrage[1] zu machen.

Andererseits wünschen offenbar viele deutsche Wähler, daß Kinder nach Konfessionen oder nach Geschlechtern getrennt erzogen werden. Und keine deutsche Regierung hätte das Recht, solche auf tiefe Überzeugungen gegründete Bildungsforderungen zu verweigern.

Privatschulen bieten hier Auswege, die bei uns zu wenig genutzt werden.

Rudolf Walter Leonhardt

50. Ein englisches Modell für die Schule der Zukunft

Die *Comprehensive School* wurde nach dem Krieg von den Sozialisten in England eingeführt und hat noch heute mit dem leidenschaftlichen Widerstand des traditionellen Schulwesens und seiner um dessen Existenz bangenden Vertreter zu kämpfen. Immer wieder kommt es zu turbulenten Demonstrationen, wenn irgendwo in Großbritannien eine der alten, traditionsreichen *Grammar Schools* durch eine *Comprehensive School* ersetzt werden soll, die eine Art simultaner Volks-, Mittel- und Oberschule darstellt und, wenn sie sich auf die Dauer durchsetzt, alle anderen Schultypen überflüssig machen wird.

Der Aufbau einer solchen Schule ist zugleich kompliziert und genial einfach. Eine Reihe von traditionellen englischen Schulcharakteristiken, wie etwa das pädagogisch bewährte Housemaster- und Tutoren-System, wird beibehalten.

Jedem Kind, das mit zehn oder elf Jahren die fünfklassige Grundschule verläßt, soll durch diese Schule die Möglichkeit geboten werden, eine seinen Anlagen und seinem Interesse entsprechende Ausbildung zu erhalten, ohne sich schon im Kindesalter entscheiden zu müssen, ob es den geistes- oder naturwissenschaftlichen Zweig oder überhaupt eine höhere Schule besuchen will.

Um den verschiedenen Begabungsrichtungen und Begabungsstufen möglichst gerecht zu werden, ist jeder Schülerjahrgang in sieben Ströme, *streams,* eingeteilt, zwischen denen die Schüler, je nach ihren Leistungen, hin- und herpendeln können. Das hat den unschätzbaren Vorteil, daß kein Kind am falschen Fleck sitzt; daß sich also niemand mühsam und freudlos zum Abitur schleppen muß, wenn sein geistiges Wachstum später einsetzt, als das in der Regel der Fall ist.

Abgesehen von einem festen Kern an Fächern (Sprache,

Rechnen, Sport), werden den Schülern in diesen sieben Strömen eines jeden Jahrgangs die mannigfaltigsten Ausbildungschancen eingeräumt. Es gibt in jeder *Comprehensive School* Laboratorien, Werkräume, handwerklichtechnische Abteilungen und Kurse, in denen jedes Kind seine spezifische Begabung entdecken und weiterentwickeln kann. Für die intellektuell Begabten existieren Klassen, die leistungsmäßig den traditionellen *Grammar Schools* entsprechen oder sie sogar durch moderne und intensivere Lehrmethodik übertreffen sollen.

Nach dem Willen ihrer Schöpfer soll diese Schule alle Begabungsreserven ausschöpfen und verhindern, daß ein Kind durch die Wunschvorstellungen der Eltern oder durch soziale Hemmungen in eine Stellung gedrängt wird, die seinen individuellen Anlagen nicht entspricht. Hier wird also versucht, einen neuen Schultypus für die Anforderungen einer neuen Zeit zu finden, einer Zeit, die keine Klassenunterschiede und Bildungsprivilegien mehr duldet, sondern gleiche Entwicklungsmöglichkeiten für alle fordert und in der Eskalation ihrer Wissenschaft und Technik auf die Entfaltung aller Begabungsreserven drängt. Die Gesamtschulen in England sollen der jungen Generation in stärkerem Maße als bisher die Möglichkeit bieten, eine individuelle und ihre Anlagen berücksichtigende Ausbildung zu erhalten, wobei auf die gemeinsame Erziehung von zukünftigen Akademikern, Technikern, Kaufleuten, Handwerkern und Arbeitern besonderer Wert gelegt wird, um sozialen Spannungen von Anfang an entgegenzuwirken.

Da alle Lehrer in allen Alters- und Begabungsstufen eingesetzt werden, bleibt der Unterricht frei von Routine, und die Lehrer sind gezwungen, pädagogische Vielfalt, Einfallsreichtum und psychologisches Verständnis zu entwickeln.

Das Faszinierende an dieser Schule ist der ungeheure Bildungsoptimismus, die Kühnheit und Experimentierfreudigkeit des vorwiegend jungen Lehrerkollegiums und der mitreißende Impetus, der von einer im Werden begriffenen großen Sache ausgeht.

Heidewig Fankhänel

51. Assistentin an einer englischen Schule

Im Rahmen des britisch-deutschen Assistentenaustauschens unterrichtete ich im Schuljahr 1964/65 an einer Londoner

Schule, wo ich Gelegenheit hatte, mich als Deutschlehrerin in die dortige Schulpraxis einzuleben.

Was mich an der Schule besonders beeindruckte, ist das kollegiale Verhältnis zwischen Schülern und Lehrern (im wohltuenden Gegensatz zum deutschen Schulwesen, das noch immer recht patriarchalisch, um nicht zu sagen autoritär ist).

Da alle Prüfungen nicht von den Lehrern, sondern der lokalen Erziehungsbehörde abgenommen werden, sind Schüler und Lehrer Bundesgenossen im Kampf gegen ,die von oben'. Da der Lehrer keine offiziellen Zensuren oder Abschlußzeugnisse (höchstens Übungsnoten) verteilt, fällt das recht fragwürdige disziplinarische Moment der Furcht vor dem allgewaltigen Zeugnisgott völlig weg, und auch das noch viel fragwürdigere Kriechen vor ihm, wie man es zuweilen an deutschen Schulen findet.

Einer der Grundsätze an jener Schule lautete: ,,Wenn Schüler ungezogen und unaufmerksam sind, ist immer der Lehrer schuld." Eine sehr gesunde Einstellung, die es dem Lehrer verbietet, auf einsamer Höhe zu dozieren.

Als Deutschlehrerin konnte ich selbst von dem sehr tiefgehenden Spezialwissen der älteren Schüler profitieren. Die Abiturklasse verfügte über ein germanistisches Wissen, das es erlaubt, literarische Werke oder Zeitungsartikel aus Deutschland auf deutsch zu erörtern.

Das pädagogisch interessanteste Feld sind jedoch die unteren Begabungsströme, deren Schüler, obwohl sie zum Teil kaum richtig Englisch sprechen und schreiben können, durch audio-visuelle Unterrichtsmethodik zumindest eine Fremdsprache lernen, so wie das Kind durch Nachsprechen und Wiederholen die eigene Muttersprache lernt.

Heidewig Fankhänel

52. Deutsche Abiturienten[1] sind zu alt

In all unseren Oberprimen[2] sitzen 21jährige, in vielen 22-jährige,—Altersklassen, die man nicht mehr auf der Schulbank festhalten sollte. Die Überalterung der Abiturienten, die es nirgendwo sonst in der Welt gibt und die es früher auch in Deutschland niemals gegeben hat, ist ein menschlich und sachlich unerträgliches Ärgernis.

Das hat noch niemand zu bestreiten gewagt. Aber niemand ist bereit, diese Erkenntnis in Aktion zu verwandeln. Während sich die Hochschulen lebhaft um die Verkürzung der Studienzeiten bemühen und erfreuliche Ergebnisse erwarten dürfen, herrscht hinsichtlich der Verjüngung der Abiturienten völliger Immobilismus. Man wagt es nicht, die Verkürzung der Schulzeit auch nur anzufassen, und setzt die Arbeitskraft der Experten immer wieder auf andere Aufgaben an, zum Beispiel die Entwicklung immer neuer Schulformen, die ebensoviel Schulzeit vorsehen wie die bisherigen. Gleichmütig sieht man zu, wie durch die Umstellung auf den Herbstbeginn[3] die Schulzeit noch einmal einige Monate länger wird.

Offenbar ist diese erneute Belastung unserer Gymnasiasten kein Tatbestand, der die Konferenz der Kultusminister aufregen könnte.

Hans Dichgans

53. Studienrätliches[1]
(Leserbrief)

In Ihrem Artikel über Generalmajor Werner Haag schrieben Sie: „Dabei liegt ihm alles Studienrätliche fern." Es ist mir unverständlich, warum der Beruf des Studienrates in der Öffentlichkeit immer wieder abgewertet wird, und zwar von den gleichen Journalisten, die bei jeder Gelegenheit vorgeben, sich für die Verbesserung der Ausbildung unserer Jugend einsetzen zu müssen. Glauben Sie, durch Ihre spitzen Bemerkungen dazu beizutragen, daß tüchtige und aufgeschlossene junge Menschen sich für diesen Beruf, der Taktgefühl und Begabung voraussetzt, interessieren werden? Möchten Sie selbst einem Berufsstand angehören, der in der Öffentlichkeit bei jeder Gelegenheit karikiert wird?

W. Bondorf, Idstein

54. Die Wandlung einer Universität

Die Universität Tübingen ist jetzt 488 Jahre alt. In ihren ersten Jahrhunderten wurde sie, wie alle Universitäten der Zeit, von den ‚oberen Fakultäten‘ der Theologie, Jurisprudenz und Medizin beherrscht. In ihr hatten die Studenten vor allem zu lernen, wie dies noch heute in den Hörsälen geschieht.

Dann kam das 19. Jahrhundert und mit ihm die von Berlin sich ausbreitende neue Idee der Universität als einer Stätte, an der Magister und Scholaren in ‚Einsamkeit und Freiheit‘ dem reinen Gedanken huldigen. In dieser Zeit gewann das philosophische Gespräch seine Bedeutung, das kleine Seminar, in dem die Schüler sich um ihren Lehrer scharen. Aber dasselbe 19. Jahrhundert hat auch schon eine neue Form der Wissenschaft, damit eine neue Form der Ausbildung hervorgebracht, nämlich die der modernen Naturwissenschaften. Hier wird der Student nicht einfach belehrt, hier sitzt er auch nicht pfeiferauchend im Gespräch mit dem Professor, hier steht er vielmehr an der Laborbank, an modernen Apparaten und nimmt teil an der Forschung.

Rolf Dahrendorf

55. Reform oder Revolution?
Diskussion um die deutschen Hochschulen

I

Die deutschen Hochschulen sind ins Gespräch gekommen. Wir leben heute in einer ‚verwissenschaftlichten Welt‘, wie ein unschöne, aber richtige Formel es will. Was morgen in unseren Fabriken und Krankenhäusern, Ministerien und Schulen geschieht, hängt auf vielfältige, auf komplizierte Weise von der Wissenschaft ab.

Diejenigen, die es wissen müssen, sind heute übereinstimmend der Meinung, daß etwas geschehen muß, um die deutsche Hochschule auf die Ansprüche von morgen einzustellen. Entschließen wir uns nicht bald zur Reform, dann wird die Revolution, der innere Zusammenbruch der Hochschule uns das Heft aus der Hand nehmen. Denn es ist heute nicht mehr zu leugnen: Die deutschen Hochschulen laufen nicht nur Gefahr, im internationalen Vergleich zur Zweitrangigkeit abzusinken; sie sind auch dabei—in der Lehre wie in der Forschung—regelrecht zu versagen. Statt unsere Zukunft für uns zu bestimmen, sind die deutschen Hochschulen dabei, eben diese Zukunft zu verraten. Das sind harte Worte, die der Begründung bedürfen.

Universitäten sind Stätten der Bildung durch Wissenschaft. Das bedeutet aber zunächst einmal, daß in ihnen Studenten für die Schlüsselberufe der Gesellschaft von morgen ausgebildet werden: Lehrer und Ärzte, Richter und Pfarrer, Chemiker und Ökonomen, nicht zuletzt auch Wissenschaftler aller Disziplinen.

Doch hier schon wird das Versagen der deutschen Hochschule der Gegenwart erkennbar. Die Bilanz läßt sich in vier Sätzen ziehen, und sie ist erschreckend:

Die deutsche Universität nimmt zuwenig Studenten auf. Von denen, die sie aufnimmt, brechen zu viele ihr Studium vorzeitig ab.

Diejenigen, die zum Schluß kommen, studieren zu lange. Was sie lernen, ist zudem weder quantitativ noch qualitativ genug.

II

Wenn wir hören, daß es in der Bundesrepublik heute 280000 Studenten gibt, dann klingt das eindrucksvoll, und Sie mögen zweifeln, ob man wirklich von „zu wenigen" sprechen kann. Das gilt umso mehr, wenn wir die 280000 etwa mit den 140000 Großbritanniens vergleichen. Aber Statistiken trügen bekanntlich oft. Von den deutschen Studenten kommen nur 170000 zum Abschluß, von den englischen 120000. Nimmt man hinzu, daß deutsche Studenten im Durchschnitt fast doppelt so lange studieren wie ihre englischen Kommilitonen, um zu entsprechenden Abschlüssen zu kommen, dann werden aus den 280000 kaum mehr als 80000, die in der gleichen Zeit Akademiker werden wie in England 120000. Das Bild sieht jetzt recht anders aus.

Es gibt noch eine andere Rechnung, und sie ist nicht minder relevant. Unter den Studenten deutscher Hochschulen sind nach wie vor manche gesellschaftlichen Gruppen weit überproportional, andere dagegen nur sehr dürftig vertreten. Jeder zwanzigste berufstätige Deutsche ist Beamter, aber die Kinder dieser fünf Prozent machen nicht weniger als ein Drittel aller Studierenden an wissenschaftlichen Hochschulen aus.

Umgekehrt ist jeder zweite Erwerbstätige Arbeiter, und doch kommen aus ihren Familien gerade sechs Prozent aller Studenten. Noch immer machen es die deutsche höhere Schule und die Universität den Arbeiterkindern schwer.

Allerdings sind es nicht nur die Schulen, die den Kindern von Arbeitern und Bauern, den Katholiken und den Mädchen den Weg zur Universität erschweren—sondern auch die Eltern, die oft meinen, die Hochschule sei nur für bevorzugte Gruppen da.

III

Daß es im übrigen auch den Erfolgreichen auf der Universität nicht gerade gut ergeht, kann niemanden trösten. Vier von zehn Studienanfängern kommen nicht zu einem Abschluß; viele von ihnen brechen überdies nicht etwa nach einer kurzen Stippvisite auf der Universität, sondern nach Jahren des Studiums ab. Daß der Studienabbruch bei Mädchen noch weit häufiger ist—mehr als die Hälfte aller Studentinnen verlassen die Universität vor dem Abschluß —kommt zwar weit verbreiteten Vorurteilen entgegen; doch sind hier wie sonst Vorurteile keine Erklärung.

Eine Untersuchung hat ergeben, daß die Heirat der Studentin als Grund des vorzeitigen Abganges von der Universität nicht die Hauptrolle spielt; daß die Hilflosigkeit in dieser anonymen Institution ein noch viel wichtigerer Grund für den vorzeitigen Abgang ist.

Die in Festreden gern gepriesene akademische Freiheit, die Freiheit des Studenten, sich seinen Studienplan selber zu machen, erweist sich oft als höchst zweideutiges Geschenk der *alma mater* an ihre Kinder.

In nahezu allen Fächern ist in den letzten Jahren die für Abschlußprüfungen verlangte Studienzeit angestiegen. Noch mehr aber hat sich das tatsächliche Studium ausgedehnt. Deutsche Studenten studieren im Durchschnitt um 50 Prozent länger, als es die Prüfungsordnungen von ihnen verlangen.

Man muß sich einmal vergegenwärtigen, was das bedeutet. Das Durchschnittsalter der Abiturienten liegt in Deutschland bei $20\frac{1}{2}$ Jahren. Es folgt der Wehrdienst, das lange Studium, das erste Examen, meist noch eine ‚Vorbereitungszeit‘ auf ein zweites Examen—so daß junge Akademiker im günstigsten Fall mit 30, häufiger mit 32, 34, 36 Jahren aufhören, Lernende, also Menschen mit halber Verantwortung, zu sein zu einer Zeit, wo andere eine Spezialausbildung hinter sich gebracht, in ihrem Beruf mancherlei geleistet und gesehen, eine Familie gegründet, für ein eigenes Haus gespart haben und längst voll verantwortliche Staatsbürger sind.

Denkt man an den Massenbetrieb in einigen Fächern, an die überfüllten Hörsäle, die gemeinsamen Klausuren[1] von tausend und mehr Studenten, dann meldet sich doch der Zweifel an der Qualität eines deutschen Hochschulstudiums —ein Zweifel, der noch wächst, wenn man, wie ich, Gelegenheit hatte, Studenten und Examenskandidaten in verschiedenen Ländern kennenzulernen.

Zu wenige Studenten, zu viele Abbrecher, zu langes Studium, mangelnde Qualität—das bleibt unsere Bilanz.

Rolf Dahrendorf
(Auszug aus einem Fernsehskript)

56. Jung gefreit[1], besser studiert

Die Frühehe hat sich im nichtstudentischen Bereich längst durchgesetzt. Ein Maurer, ein Bankangestellter, der mit 24 Jahren ein neunzehnjähriges Mädchen heiratet, wird kaum noch schief angesehen. Wehe aber dem Studenten, der es in diesem Alter wagt! Seine ,Frühehe' verfällt noch mit 26 dem Verdikt der Familie. Warum? Weil seine Frühehe nichts mit dem Alter zu tun hat, sondern mit seinem Stand: Ein Student hat eben nicht zu heiraten. Er ist noch nicht fertig, weil er noch kein Examen hat, noch nichts verdient; er ist deshalb natürlich auch noch nicht fertig als Mensch.

Einem 24jährigen Autoschlosser wird, weil er schon vor sechs Jahren ,ausgelernt' hat, mehr Reife zuerkannt als einem 28jährigen Studenten der Chemie, weil er noch nicht ,ausgelernt' hat. Wann eigentlich hat man ausgelernt? (Daß sich Eltern weigern, auch noch die Ehe ihrer Söhne zu finanzieren—das allerdings ist schließlich ihr Recht.)

Wo liegt da der logische Bruch? Er leitet sich her von der gängigen Meinung, ein Akademiker sei heute wie vor zwanzig, dreißig Jahren schon mit sechs bis acht Semestern examensreif. Dann wäre er in der Tat wie einst mit 25 Lebensjahren schon Assessor[2] oder Doktor. Aber in derselben Zeit, in der die nichtstudentische Frühehe sich durchgesetzt hat, verlängerte sich das Universitätsstudium erheblich.

Nach wie vor aber wird dem Studenten abverlangt, nicht zu heiraten und ein halbes Jahrzehnt länger auf die Ehe zu warten als seine Altersgenossen. Er darf sich Jugendtorheiten, sogar sexuelle Eskapaden leisten; denn er ist so etwas wie ein ,verlängerter Schüler'. Nur binden darf er sich nicht. Denn zur Klischeevorstellung gehört, daß ein als Lernender die Wissenschaft Betreibender zölibatär zu leben habe. Das uralte Wissenschaftlerideal, das noch aus dem Mönchtum stammt: Armut, Keuschheit, Gehorsam, hat sich umgesetzt in die moderne Theorie, eheliche Bindung sei geistiger Arbeit abträglich. Seltsam nur, daß dies in dem Augenblick nicht mehr gilt, wo einer Dozent, Professor ist oder einen anderen geistigen Beruf ausübt. Hier wird unbewußt mit zweierlei Maß gemessen.

Zwei andere Einwände gegen die Studentenehe sind ebenso widerlegbar. Der eine heißt, sie verlängere das Studium. Darüber gibt es keine statistischen Unterlagen. Eine Untersuchung an der University of California (über

100 000 Studenten an verschiedenen Orten) jedoch ergab, daß verheiratete Examinanden im Durchschnitt besser bestehen als unverheiratete.

Der andere Einwand wiegt schwerer: der eine Partner, meist die Frau, gibt das Studium auf, um zu verdienen. Wenn man bedenkt, daß es sechsmal mehr verheiratete männliche als weibliche Studierende gibt, ist dieser Verdacht wohl begründet, obgleich für das Ausscheiden aus dem Studium weder exakte Zahlen noch Begründungen bekannt sind. Demgegenüber ist nun aber zu fragen, ob es nicht gerade im Interesse der Mobilisierung aller Bildungsreserven stünde, wenn die Öffentlichkeit der Studentin, die heiratet, den Studienabschluß ermöglichte, wenn sie den Willen dazu hat. Wie bei vielen Junglehrerinnen, die heiraten, besteht doch heute die begründete Hoffnung, daß sie in späteren Jahren wieder in ihren Beruf zurückkehren möchte und könnte.

Trotz aller Hindernisse, Vorurteile und Schwierigkeiten wird unter Studenten geheiratet. Das zeugt von großem *élan vital*. Das spricht aber auch dafür, daß offenbar viele Studenten die Chancen für ihre Ehe höher einschätzen als die Gefahren.

Über die Möglichkeit anderer junger Ehen hinaus, sich einen Stil zu schaffen, sich geschmacklich aneinander zu gewöhnen, birgt die Studentenehe die Chance, das große geistige Experiment des Studiums gemeinsam zu unternehmen.

René Leudesdorff

57. Der Knabe Arzt, das Mädchen Krankenschwester

Sollen Söhne lernen, Töchter nur heiraten?

„*Meine Tochter braucht die Reifeprüfung*[1] *nicht zu machen,*" hielt mir ein Vater entgegen, als in einer Sendung von Radio Bremen die Frage erörtert wurde, ob wir mehr Abiturienten[2] brauchen. „*Freilich ist sie begabt genug*", so fügte er hinzu, „*aber sie ist auch wohl anzusehen und wird sicherlich früh heiraten. Geht sie jetzt ab—sie hat nach dem zehnten Schuljahr die mittlere Reife*[3] *erlangt—kann sie in den Jahren, die sie sonst noch in der Schule verbringen müßte, annähernd* 4500

Mark für eine ordentliche Aussteuer verdienen und sparen."
Auf die Frage, ob er zu dem gleichen Entschluß gelangt
wäre, wenn es sich um einen Jungen gehandelt hätte, meinte
er ein wenig zögernd: *„Bei einem Sohn wäre das wohl etwas
anderes . . ."*

Allem Anschein nach ist diese Ansicht so selten nicht.
Bei einer Erhebung, die durchaus als repräsentativ gelten
kann, bezeugen einige Oberschülerinnen, daß sie bei ihren
Eltern und Bekannten auf die gleiche Einstellung stoßen:

*„Meine Verwandten sagen mir fast bei jeder Gelegenheit,
daß es unnütz für ein Mädchen sei, das Gymnasium zu
besuchen, ich würde doch bald heiraten. Dabei habe ich mir
mein Ziel gesteckt und möchte es gern erreichen. Auch bin ich
keine schlechte Schülerin. Sollte man mir nur den Mut nehmen
wollen?"*

*„Ich habe den Eindruck, daß die Erwachsenen kein Ver-
ständnis dafür haben, daß wir etwas Richtiges werden wollen.
Wenn ich erzähle, ich möchte das Abitur machen, dann kann
ich sicher sein, daß der größte Teil sagt: ‚Ach, noch so lange.'
Dann folgen Ratschläge, was ich sonst noch werden könnte . . .
und so weiter. Weiterhin schlagen sie Berufe vor, die viel Geld
einbringen, und wenn man dann solche wählt (eventuell auch
gezwungen), achten sie uns. Aber ob wir Freude daran haben,
das kümmert sie nicht . . ."*

*„Meine Mutti sagt auch: Du heiratest ja doch bald, und
dann bist du froh, wenn du schon Geld hast. Aber an das
Heiraten denke ich noch gar nicht; und ich finde, daß man an
seinem Beruf Freude haben muß. Viele Frauen sind auch in
der Ehe noch berufstätig."*

Es ist doch wohl einiges geschehen, das die Eltern unserer
Tage hätte lehren können, das künftige Geschick ihrer
Töchter sorgsamer, nämlich verantwortlicher zu bedenken.
Oder genügt die Erfahrung nicht, daß der Krieg, die
Flucht aus der Heimat, der Verlust aller Habe, die Entnazifizierung,[4] der Beginn nach dem Zusammenbruch,
viele Frauen genötigt haben, Hand anzulegen und sozusagen
ihren Mann zu stehen? Oder genügt die Beobachtung nicht,
daß die Mehrheit aller berufstätigen Frauen sich mit unteren und allenfalls mittleren Stellungen bescheiden muß,
so daß mit einigem Grund gefragt werden kann, ob sie
an ihrem Beruf „Freude haben"? Und die Industriegesell-
schaft ist in zunehmendem Maße auf die Leistungsfähigkeit
der Frauen angewiesen. Schon jetzt machen die Frauen ein
gutes Drittel aller Erwerbstätigen in der Bundesrepublik

aus, und mehr als fünf Millionen sind davon verheiratet. Dennoch bleibt es in der Erziehung anscheinend so, wie es immer war. In einer Studie, die schon 1929 veröffentlicht wurde, schreibt die Verfasserin Susanne Engelmann:

„Wir erleben es heute leider noch vielfach, daß aus den gleichen Elternhäusern der Knabe Arzt wird und das Mädchen Krankenschwester ... die Bevorzugung der Knaben nicht von ihrer überragenden Begabung abhängig gemacht wird, sondern ihnen mit Selbstverständlichkeit zusteht."

Horst Wetterling

58. Warum sind Halbstarke[1] halbstark?

Warum randalieren junge Leute? Eine Antwort auf diese Frage fand der 31 Jahre alte Niederländer Wim Buikhuisen, Doktor der Sozialwissenschaft an der Universität Utrecht. Seine Erfahrungen sind wichtig, auch wenn es so scheint, daß ‚die Halbstarken' hier kein ‚Problem' mehr seien und die Aufmerksamkeit gelegentlich nur noch von den englischen ‚Mods' und ‚Rockers' und ihren Verwüstungen in Brighton und Margate angeregt wird. „Mein Interesse für die Provos", wie Buikhuisen die zum Provozieren neigenden Jugendlichen kurz nennt, „ist nicht vom üppigen Haarwuchs oder der ungewöhnlichen Kleidung angeregt worden, sondern von eigentümlichen gesellschaftlichen Gepflogenheiten." Und er verlangt: „Es muß etwas gegen die periodisch auftretende Unruhe dieser Jugendlichen getan werden, damit Krawalle sich nicht zu einer Tradition festigen."

Der Provo ist weniger gefährlich und bösartig als man denkt, trotz seines recht oft schrecklichen Benehmens bei Schlägereien auf der Straße, in Kneipen und Kinos oder auf den Tanzböden, mit oder ohne Polizisten als Gegner Seine Neigung zur Kriminalität ist auch weit geringer, als man auf den ersten Blick annehmen könnte. Er ist seelisch verkorkst. Die Ursache dafür ist Langeweile, intensive, quälende Langeweile. Er weiß nichts anzufangen mit seiner Freizeit und befriedigt seine Sehnsucht nach Sensation und Aufregung mit Krach, sturem Benehmen: Er schneidet auf und prahlt.

Dies ist Dr. Wim Buikhuisens Urteil. Er fand es auf folgende Weise: Buikhuisen spielte Provo mit den Provos, er begab sich zwischen seine lärmenden Studienobjekte. Er ließ sich die Haare bis auf die Schulter wachsen, zog sich schlampig an und schloß sich jugendlichen Gruppen an.

So entstand Buikhuisens Skizze über die Provos. Das Ergebnis: Die Intelligenz dieser jungen Leute bleibt unter dem Durchschnitt; viele von ihnen stammen aus dem Arbeitermilieu, sie kommen aus verhältnismäßig kinderreichen Familien, die Väter sind mehr als üblich von zu Hause weg.

Bisher galt die Behauptung, das gesellschaftsfeindliche Benehmen der Halbstarken sei eine Reaktion auf die Verhältnisse im Elternhaus. Es sei eine Meuterei gegen die Eltern, hieß es beispielsweise in einem Bericht der UNESCO. Buikhuisen indessen bestreitet dies. Für Provos, so hat er beobachtet, gäben ungünstige Familienverhältnisse nicht den Antrieb zu den typischen Reaktionen Halbstarker. Bei diesen jungen Menschen handele es sich also nicht um eine Rebellion gegen die elterlichen oder sonstigen Gewalten, obgleich den Provo ein ungewöhnlich starker Freiheitsdrang beherrscht. Er will nicht bevormundet sein und haßt die üblichen Erziehungsversuche.

Er scheut prinzipiell Einsamkeit. Er ist meist ungeduldig und kurz angebunden und reagiert leicht hochfahrend. Allerdings: Er sehnt sich nicht nach Macht, Sicherheit und Selbstvertrauen, aber er liebt das Abenteuerliche, vor allem wenn es begleitet wird von irgendeiner Art von Unordnung wie Krawallen, Raufereien und ähnlichem Unfug. Auf feine Manieren und Anstand pfeift er. Für Klubs, Sport und Liebhabereien ist er nicht zu haben. „Aber es wäre falsch zu meinen, daß der Provo sich unglücklich fühlt", meint Dr. Buikhuisen. Provos leiden keineswegs unter unbefriedigten und enttäuschten Wünschen. „Und es glaube bitte niemand, seine Handlungen seien ihm eingegeben von irgendeiner Angstpsychose, die mit dem Krieg zu tun habe."

Provos sind freilich leicht zu erregen. Sie lassen sich gern auf die Straße holen, wenn es gilt, gegen die Atombombe und den Atomkrieg zu demonstrieren—mit der gleichen Begeisterung verwandeln sie einen Tanzboden in ein Trümmerfeld. Sie stellen nur eine einzige Bedingung: Krawall muß dabei in Aussicht sein. Auf jeden Fall muß die Möglichkeit dazu vorhanden sein, denn dies ist es, was den ersten und letzten innerlichen Antrieb gibt. Krach ist ihr Ziel—und nicht die Herausforderung der Gewalt.

Herman W. M. van Wordragen

59. Unter Gammlern[1] und Trampern[2] (Leserbrief)

Bis vor eineinhalb Jahren war ich öfters mit Gammlern zusammen. Das Abenteuer, an der Straße zu stehen—irgendwohin zu trampen—barfuß und schmutzig—Lieder singen—Freiheit—und ‚Ich bin Ich‘ sein . . . war eine schöne Zeit.

‚Gammeln‘ heißt ‚verfaulen‘. Und Gammler sind eine europäische Beat-Generation. Es ist sehr existenziell—ohne Idealismus—und auf längere Zeit langweilig, zwischen Gammlergruppen zu leben. ‚Koksen‘[3] und ‚Kiff‘, ‚Aufputschmittel‘, ‚Schnorren‘ sind Hauptgesprächsstoffe. Der Gammel ist in sich selbst spießig, er verträgt keine Toleranz. Die Originalität beschränkt sich auf einige wenige Gedichte und Ausdrücke und wenige Bildmotive, die gekreidet werden . . .

Karin Fries, München

Aufsätze und Aufsatzübungen

1. Skizzieren Sie das Porträt
   (a) eines Lehrers, den Sie gut kennen.
   (b) des idealen Lehrers.
2. Beschreiben Sie das Schulwesen in Ihrem Lande.
3. Schildern Sie
   (a) die Geschichte der Hochschulen in Ihrem Lande
   (b) den gegenwärtigen Stand des Hochschulwesens.
4. Der Sprachunterricht der Vergangenheit, der Gegenwart und der Zukunft.
5. Vielseitigkeit und tiefes Spezialwissen: sind diese Bildungsideale vereinbar?
6. Wieviele Jahre sollten junge Menschen auf der Schule verbringen?
7. Sollten Studenten vom Staat oder von den Eltern unterstützt werden, später zurückzahlbare Anleihen erhalten, sich während ihres Studiums als Werkstudenten den Unterhalt verdienen, oder erst dann die Universität besuchen, wenn sie sich durch eigene Arbeit etwas erspart haben? Begründen Sie Ihre Ansicht.
8. Die Jugend von heute.

F

REISE
UND
SPORT

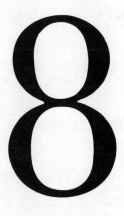

In einem Lande, das im Mittelpunkt des europäischen Verkehrsnetzes liegt, dessen Einwohner sich gerne *auf Achse* begeben, und das seine Erholung fast so ernst nimmt wie die Arbeit, spielt das Reisen eine wichtige Rolle. Auch Fragen der Gesundheit schenkt eine größtenteils städtische Bevölkerung viel Aufmerksamkeit: während die Jugend sich in vielen Sportarten betätigt und sportliche Veranstaltungen große Menschenmengen anziehen, schätzt die ältere Generation die unzähligen Kurorte Deutschlands, von denen manche mit ihren Heilquellen als Zentren ärztlicher Betreuung weit in die Geschichte zurückreichen, während andere, meist neueren Datums, hauptsächlich ,gute, frische Luft' und die Gelegenheit zu angenehmen Spaziergängen in ländlicher Umgebung bieten.

74

61. Zwanzig Millionen Deutsche machen eine Ferienreise

Das Meer und die Sonne üben noch immer die größte Anziehungskraft auf den Urlaubsreisenden aus, aber die von Reise-Unternehmen organisierten Möglichkeiten haben den natürlichen Rhythmus, im Sommer zu schwimmen, Boot zu fahren, Wasserski zu laufen, zu wandern und auf die Berge zu klettern und im Winter Ski zu laufen, Besichtigungs- und Studienreisen aber im Frühjahr und Herbst zu machen, schon längst zerstört. Die heutigen Transportmittel erlauben das Seebad im Winter, den Skilauf im Sommer und das ganze Jahr über Sightseeing, Jagd- und andere ‚Hobby-Reisen'.

Aber die große Auswahl der Möglichkeiten und der fernen Ziele ist eben doch eine Sache der Mittel. Die meisten Urlaubsreisenden sparen ein Jahr lang, um sich dann die Verwirklichung eines Traumes zu gönnen, sich von der alltäglichen Arbeit für kurze Zeit zu entfernen, die grauen Betonmetropolen zu vergessen. Und zu den Mittelmeerländern, die Sonne und Wasser verheißen, ist der Weg am kürzesten und gesuchtesten.

62. Notizen für Reisende

1. *Leihfahrräder für Sommergäste*
Mit dem Fahrrad können künftig die Feriengäste der ostfriesischen[1] Bäder Borkum, Juist, Langeoog und Norderney die Inseln durchstreifen. Die Kurverwaltungen stellen den Urlaubern in dieser Saison zum erstenmal Leihfahrräder zur Verfügung.

2. *Auf allen Schienen Europas*
Egal wohin man fährt, nach Frankreich, Großbritannien oder Polen, der Preis für den Liegewagen 2. Klasse wird überall derselbe sein: 11,50 Mark. Mit dem neuen Sommerfahrplan, der vom 30. Mai an gilt, wurde der Liegewagenpreis im internationalen Verkehr einheitlich festgesetzt.

3. *Das Urlaubsgeld kommt in Mode*
Im ersten Vierteljahr 1965 ist es den Gewerkschaften gelungen, in zunehmendem Maße mit den Arbeitgebern

ein tarifliches Urlaubsgeld zu vereinbaren. Nach Angaben des Bundesarbeitsministeriums erhalten bereits mehr als vier Millionen Arbeitnehmer ein Urlaubsgeld, das entweder als fester Prozentsatz des Lohnes oder in festen Beträgen (meist 7 bis 10 Mark je Urlaubstag) festgelegt ist. Verhandlungen über Arbeitszeitverkürzungen sind gegenüber diesen Forderungen in den Hintergrund getreten.

4. *Wohin reisen Engländer?*

Wenn die Engländer Ferien machen, fahren sie immer noch am liebsten auf den europäischen Kontinent (93 Prozent). Spanien und Italien gefallen ihnen besonders gut, dorthin reisen die meisten. Dann folgen Frankreich, die Schweiz, Belgien, Luxemburg und Österreich. Die Bundesrepublik ist (noch) nicht dabei. Und was nehmen die Briten in den Urlaub mit? Den Photoapparat an erster Stelle (72 Prozent). dann Schwimmanzüge (64), Landkarten (44), Reiseführer (38 Prozent) und Aspirintabletten: die Hälfte aller auf Urlaub fahrenden Briten vergißt sie auf keinen Fall.

5. *Abenteuer Trampen?*[2] *(Leserbriefe)*[2]

Lassen Sie mich von meiner Art Autostopp[2],tourismus' berichten. Ich bin Student und habe auf dem Gebiet einige Erfahrung. Seien Sie gewiß, daß für mich das Abenteuer im Trampen längst aufgehört hat. Trotzdem mache ich weiter— warum? Von meiner Mutter (sie ist seit 20 Jahren Witwe) bekomme ich monatlich 180 DM Studienunterstützung. Vater Staat gab mir im letzten Semester monatlich 39 DM. Eine Rückfahrkarte vom Studienort Berlin zum Heimatort in Süddeutschland kostet 90 DM. Soll ich deswegen an einer Universität in Süddeutschland studieren, wenn mir das Trampen (und nur das!) erlaubt, in Berlin zu studieren, wo die Universität meinem Studium mehr entgegenkommt?

In Großbritannien erhält jeder Student ein großzügiges Stipendium vom Staat und trotzdem wird getrampt. Keiner nimmt in diesem Land daran Anstoß; man gibt vielmehr den jungen Menschen fairerweise eine Chance.

So wie heute der Großteil der Autofahrer, die Tramper mitnehmen, aus Ex-Autostoppern besteht, wird sich ein Teil der Autofahrer von morgen aus Trampern von heute regenerieren. Ich werde einer von ihnen sein.

Michael Richter, z.Zt. Glasgow

Nach meinen und meiner Freunde Erfahrungen sind nicht

die Franzosen die freundlichsten Mitnehmer (die Deutschen im Ausland schon mal gar nicht, da sie ihre Autos mit Reisegepäck vollgeladen haben), sondern die Holländer und Engländer, ja man kann sagen, daß England unter den Trampern als das ‚gelobte Land' gilt.

Anselm Faust, Bonn

63. Für junge Leute: Urlaub von der Stange[1] und nach Maß

Junge Leute bis zu dreißig Jahren bilden das Gros[2] der bundesdeutschen Urlauber. Kein Wunder also, daß sich nun nach den vielen Jugendreiseorganisationen auch die großen Reiseunternehmen mit eigenen Programmen ausdrücklich an jugendliche Kunden wenden. Man weiß inzwischen ziemlich genau, welche Urlaubswünsche junge Leute haben.

Das Angebot von Reisen von der Stange ist groß: Liegewagen oder Flugzeug in Richtung Süden, nach Mallorca, Teneriffa, an die italienische und französische Riviera, nach Spanien und Jugoslawien. Der Komfort ist bemerkenswert, denn man weiß, daß die jungen Leute heute für ihren Urlaub ‚etwas springen lassen'.

Andererseits macht das Jugendherbergswerk jungen Leuten einen ungewöhnlichen, aber gar nicht unzeitgemäßen Vorschlag: *Ferienwanderungen*. Diese Wanderungen, die im Durchschnitt zehn bis sechzehn Tage dauern und einen Betrag von 60 bis 80 Mark erfordern, führen in die schönsten deutschen Wandergebiete.

Wem es auf Schusters Rappen fürs erste noch zu mühsam ist, der kann es zunächst einmal mit einer *Radwanderung* versuchen.

Wer den *Kontakt mit jungen Ausländern sucht*, wer etwas mehr von andern Ländern sehen will als nur den Badestrand am Tage und das Tanzlokal bei Nacht, der findet auch in diesem Jahr wieder unzählige interessante Möglichkeiten. Im großen Stil werden Treffen zwischen deutschen und französischen Jugendlichen vom Deutsch-Französischen Jugendwerk (Bad Honnef-Rhöndorf) organisiert.

Auch wird es offensichtlich zur Mode, *in den Ostblock* zu reisen. Die Sensation besteht darin, sich ein wenig illegal und beschattet zu fühlen, abgehorcht und bespitzelt. Schuld daran ist der Eiserne Vorhang, dessen Löcher allerdings gerade noch so groß sind, den Devisenstrom ungehindert fließen zu lassen. Aber trotz allem Sensationellen, das einer solchen Reise anhaften mag—ihr Informationswert, gerade für junge Leute, kann nicht hoch genug eingeschätzt werden. Mit der Auslandsstelle des Bundesstudentenringes kann man an die Danziger Bucht fahren, an den ungarischen Plattensee, an die bulgarische Goldküste und in die Pußta. Moskau gehört ebenfalls zum Reiseprogramm, der Kreml inklusiv.

Jugendliche zwischen 18 und 28 Jahren können an dem Programm *Gast bei amerikanischen Familien* teilnehmen. Die jungen Leute fliegen von Deutschland nach New York, dort sind zwei Tage Aufenthalt vorgesehen. Dann geht es mit Omnibussen in den mittleren Westen. Vier Wochen wohnen die Jungen und Mädchen in amerikanischen Familien in den Bundesstaaten Iowa und Nebraska.

,Ferien, die etwas einbringen', nennt die Gesellschaft für praktisches Auslandswissen in Köln ihr Sommerprogramm. Das sind vierzig verschiedene *Ferien-Sprachkurse* in England, Frankreich, der Schweiz und Spanien. Man macht im doppelten Sinne Urlaub: von daheim und von der Muttersprache. Damit das ganze aber auch noch Urlaub ist, werden in der Regel nur drei Stunden Unterricht pro Tag gegeben. Die Teilnehmer wohnen in Familien des jeweiligen Landes. Dauer der Kurse zwischen zwei und zwölf Wochen.

In den *Internationalen Aufbaulagern* geht es nicht um Broterwerb, auch nicht um ,Beschäftigungstherapie'. Der Verdienst wird gegen Kost und Unterkunft aufgerechnet. Vielleicht sind Aufbaulager die billigste Art, eine Auslandsreise zu machen und dabei seinen Mitmenschen ziemlich genau kennenzulernen. Die Arbeitsprojekte sind unterschiedlich: Bohnenernte, Kartoffel- und Obsternte, Weinlese (in Frankreich), archäologische Ausgrabungen. Arbeitsorte: verschiedene Städte in Deutschland, England, Frankreich, Italien und Israel. Aufbaulager-Organisationen in der Bundesrepublik arbeiten vornehmlich an Bauprojekten (Wohnungen, Schulen, Kindergärten, Straßen, Sportplätzen). Anschrift: Internationale Jugendgemeinschaftsdienste, Bonn.

Ferdinand Ranft

64. Ein Oktober wie in Cannes: Ferien an Englands Südküste

England soll für deutsche Touristen Mode werden. Reisefachleute haben die Südküste Großbritanniens entdeckt. Was könnte den deutschen Touristen reizen, statt an das Mittelmeer dorthin zu fliegen?

Zunächst wohl das gemäßigte Klima. Die Isle of Wight beispielsweise, die nun in das Charterprogramm einer deutschen Reisegesellschaft aufgenommen wird, war schon vor 1914 ein beliebtes deutsches Urlaubsziel, das sich vor allem als Seglerparadies einen Namen gemacht hat. Die Liste prominenter Segler ist lang. Der berühmteste deutsche Name auf dieser Liste: Kaiser Wilhelm II.

Wer auf der Isle of Wight nicht segelt oder badet, liegt faul in der Sonne. *„Unser Indien-Sommer während der Herbstmonate hat Mittelmeercharakter."* Allerdings steigen die Wassertemperaturen im Oktober kaum über 15 Grad. Da hört für die meisten die Gemütlichkeit beim Baden auf.

Angeln kann dann immer noch Spaß machen, ebenso wie Reiten, Tennisspielen oder Golf. Für Sportler ist in Bournemouth und Umgebung reichlich gesorgt. Noch reichlicher ist das Hotelangebot. Für jeden Geschmack und Geldbeutel etwas: Vom Fünf-Sterne-Haus internationaler Extra-Klasse bis zum gemütlichen Familienbetrieb reicht die Auswahl. Auch der Tagesrhythmus der Engländer entspricht unseren Gewohnheiten eher, als der lang in die Nacht hineinreichende Trubel im Süden. Nicht zuletzt mag manchen auch ein Ausflug in die englische Geschichte locken, der man überall im Lande sehr dicht auf den Fersen ist.

Die normannischen Kathedralen von Winchester und Salisbury sind keine Autostunde von Bournemouth entfernt. Auch die römischen Badeanlagen in Englands ältestem und berühmtestem Kurort Bath gehören zu den Ausflugszielen interessierter Archäologen. Oder, wenn es ein altes, noch immer bewohntes Schloß sein soll: In Berkeley Castle unweit von Bristol kann man sich über einen echten Holbein freuen. In Longleat, dem 400 Jahre alten Sitz des Markgrafen von Bath, findet man herrliche Gobelins aus dem 16. Jahrhundert. An Zeugnissen einer uralten Geschichte ist kein Mangel. Mangel, großer Mangel sogar, herrscht an Engländern, die eine andere Sprache als ihre eigene sprechen. Das könnte ein Argument gegen die England-Reise sein. Zwar gibt es vereinzelt in den Hotels bereits deutsches Personal, aber das sind Ausnahmen und werden Ausnahmen bleiben. Ganz ohne Sprachkentnisse geht es also nicht.

Auch wer schnell und viel Kontakt sucht in den Ferien, dürfte in England nicht auf seine Kosten kommen. Die Aufgeschlossenheit vieler Südländer mag manchem Besucher aufdringlich erscheinen, hier auf den britischen Inseln wird ihn die Teilnahmslosigkeit, die sich hinter allzu viel Korrektheit verbirgt, irritieren. Man muß englische Hotelgäste an der Bar beobachtet haben oder in der Halle, um zu wissen, wie schnell man frieren kann in dieser Umgebung. Der Fremde wird selten Gelegenheit haben, festzustellen, daß der äußere Eindruck gelegentlich auch täuscht.

Wer Ferien an Englands Südküste macht, wird sich den Abstecher nach London nicht entgehen lassen. London läßt sich nicht in drei Stunden erobern, auch nicht in drei Tagen oder Wochen. Aber wer einmal abends am Picca-dilly-Circus gestanden und in die Lichtreklame und in den Verkehr gestaunt hat, der vergißt die Vergleiche mit Paris, Berlin, Kopenhagen oder Brüssel. London hat keine Vergleiche. Wer sich in London verliebt, tut es vielleicht nicht auf den ersten, aber gewiß auf den zweiten Blick. Und diese Liebe hält. Sie läßt sich auch durch den dicksten Nebel und die schmutzigsten Hafenstraßen nicht verdrießen.

Horst Zetzsche

65. Fußballsport zwischen Idealismus und Materialismus

Die Spieler der Münchner Vereine, die in der Spielzeit 1965/66 sowohl die deutsche Meisterschaft in der Bundes-liga als auch den Pokal errangen, sind fast ausnahmslos ganz junge und recht einfache Burschen. Der Sportruhm trifft sie überwiegend mit 18 bis 25 Jahren, in einem Lebens-alter also, in dem sie zumeist recht anfällig sind—der Sportruhm und—das Geld. Während sie ohne den Fußball als Arbeiter, Handwerker, kleine Angestellte im Monat mit 500 bis 1 000 DM hätten auskommen müssen, verdienen sie jetzt durch den Fußball mit Gehalt, Tor- und Sieges-prämien, Teilnahme an Europapokalspielen, Sonderzuwen-dungen und so weiter das Drei- bis, na sagen wir mal vorsichtig, Sechs- bis Achtfache, in Ausnahmefällen, wie zum Beispiel Petar Radenkovic, ‚bestes Torwart von Welt‘, sogar durch Schallplatten- und Buchhonorare noch mehr. Soeben haben die Borussen[1] aus Dortmund mit der gesamten Mannschaft ihre Siegesgesänge in die Rillen einer Schallplatte einpressen lassen, und es scheint nur eine Frage der Zeit zu sein, wann andere Mannschaften, zum Beispiel die Münchner, folgen.

Während diese jungen Männer, wenn der Fußball nicht vor ihren Füßen rollen würde, allenfalls einen Kleinwagen fahren würden, kutschieren sie in nicht gerade billigen Sportwagen über Münchens Boulevard, die Leopoldstraße. Ihre Frauen und Freundinnen erschienen zur Siegesfeier in Kleidern, die nicht von der Stange gekauft, sondern in erstklassigen Ateliers gearbeitet waren und mit Frisuren, die sie nicht dem Vorstadtfriseur um die Ecke, sondern dem Meisterfigaro im vornehmen Innenstadtsalon verdankten.

Diese jungen Spieler bindet größtenteils nicht viel anderes an der Verein als das Geld, das sie in ihm verdienen. Bietet ein anderer mehr, so verkaufen sie sich an ihn. Nur ein Träumer und Narr wird anderes von ihnen erwarten.

Doch die Gefahren, die dem Sport von heute gerade auch durch den Berufs- und Halbberufsfußball drohen, sind riesengroß. Arnold Kaech schreibt in seinem ausgezeichneten ‚Magglinger Stundenbuch‘: „Je glänzender und verbreiteter der Profisport ist, desto weniger Leute üben sich in den harmlosen Spielen der Amateure. Es wirkt leicht lächerlich, in Dingsda um die Meisterschaft der 5. Spielklasse zu kicken, wenn man mit dem Motorroller in die Stadt fahren und dort Fußballkünstler sehen kann, welche für die Wunder, die ihre Füße verrichten, das dreifache Gehalt eines Hochschullehrers beziehen.“

Rudolf Hagelstange hat es einmal ganz klar ausgesprochen: „Man kann den Sport nur im Zusammenhang mit unserer Zeit sehen. Die Umwelt denkt und handelt heute rein materiell. Wer will es also dem Sport vorwerfen, wenn auch in ihm die materielle Gesinnung den Idealismus mehr und mehr vertreibt?“

Heinz Maegerlein

66. Wer ist der Größte?
Ron Clarke weltbester Sportler

Nur einer unter den Sportlern dieser Tage hat von sich

selbst behauptet: „Ich bin der Größte!" Er krähte es so oft und so laut, daß der simple Satz fast zum geflügelten Wort geworden wäre. Doch Cassius Clay, Boxweltmeister im Schwergewicht oder, in aller Titelwürde herausposaunt, ‚Weltmeister aller Klassen‘, betätigt sich, was weltweite Popularität angeht, in der falschen Branche. Als man jetzt eine Anzahl von Sportredakteuren nach dem ‚weltbesten Sportler‘ fragte, blieb der Boxer unter ‚ferner liefen‘. Ihm lief der Leichtathlet Ron Clarke auf und davon.

Ron Clarke ist 28 Jahre alt und bestätigt die Regel, die wie so viele Regeln ihre Ausnahme hat: daß eben Langstreckenläufer ‚ausgewachsene Männer‘ sein müssen und folglich im forgeschrittenen Twen-Alter[1] zu stehen haben. Er ist 1,83 Meter groß und 75 Kilogramm schwer, verheiratet übrigens. Zwischen drei englischen Meilen (in 12:52,4 Minuten) und 20 Kilometern (in 59:22,8 Minuten) gibt es niemanden, der mit ihm Schritt hält; und die Ausnahme ist hier Kipchonge Keino, ein Polizist aus Kenia, der dem Australier den 5 000-Meter-Weltrekord in der exakt gestoppten Fabelzeit von 13:24,2 Minuten entriß.

Und so ist der Australier also ‚weltbester Sportler des Jahres‘, oder wie immer man's nennen will.

Die ‚wesentliche‘ Sportart, Inbegriff des uralten klassischen wie des modernen Sports, ist die Leichtathletik; und so kamen im Urteil der Sportredaktionen nach Ron Clarke noch zwei Leichtathleten am besten weg, der Franzose Michel Jazy, Weltrekordläufer über eine Meile (3:53,6 Minuten) und der Zwei-Meter-Texasboy Randy Matson, der mit einhundertzehn Kilogramm Lebendgewicht die Kugel 21,57 Meter weit stieß, auch Weltrekord, versteht sich.

Ein Automobilrennfahrer, der Brite Jim Clark, folgt auf dem vierten Platz der weltweiten Urteilsliste vor abermals einem Leichtathletiker, eben dem schwarzen Star Kipchonge Keino, hinter dem wiederum Spaniens Tennis-As Santana placiert wurde. Auf dem siebten Platz erscheint die erste Frau, die Russin Irina Press, beste Fünfkämpferin und vielseitigste Leichtathletin der Welt. Ein Deutscher, der Schwimmer Hans-Joachim Klein, taucht an dreizehnter Stelle auf.

Alexander Rost

67. Jedes Jahr fährt er vierzig Autos: der Motor-Journalist

Die Mehrzahl der Zeitungen hat die Motorseite seit ungefähr sieben Jahren. Das Interesse der Leser ist groß: F. Gert Pohles ‚Welt des Motors‘ bekommt nach den drei klassischen Ressorts (Politik, Wirtschaft, Kultur) die meisten Leserbriefe. „Manchmal komme ich mir wie ein halber Pastor vor", spöttelte Pohle, „mit der Aufgabe, menschliche Seelen zu retten und vor sich selbst zu schützen".

Er hatte mich frühmorgens zu einer Spazierfahrt in einem neuen Testwagen abgeholt: einem roten VW–Varianten mit der Maschine des VW 1600. Wir fuhren durch Hamburg, über die Elbbrücken, auf die Autobahn Hamburg-Hannover. Die Sicht im Wagen war schlecht, nicht nur weil es draußen regnete, sondern weil die Scheiben beschlagen waren. „So etwas ist eine Katastrophe", stellte Pohle sachlich und ruhig fest, während er nach einem Tuch angelte, um die Windschutzscheibe abzuwischen: „Schlechte Sicht macht nervös und unruhig. Der Fahrer wird unsicher und ermüdet schneller."

Ein Sportwagen hatte uns auf der Autobahn elegant überholt, obwohl nur sechzig Stundenkilometer gestattet waren; an der Bahn wurde gebaut. Pohle: „Vom sogenannten sportlichen Fahren halte ich überhaupt nichts. Auf Kosten anderer rasant zu fahren, ist rücksichtslos. Und wenn es darauf ankommt, wenn es gefährlich wird, dann fingern die an ihrem Armaturenbrett herum, das ausgestattet ist wie beim Sportflugzeug, und drücken auf den Knopf für die Scheinwerfer statt die Scheibenwischer anzustellen. Das habe ich gern . . .‘‘

Auf der Gegenfahrbahn war der Verkehr von der rechten Fahrbahn auf die neu erbaute Standspur umgeleitet worden. Pohle machte mich darauf aufmerksam: „Hier kann irgend etwas nicht stimmen. So oft ich in der Dunkelheit die Strecke befahre, liegt irgendein Lastwagen im Graben und streckt alle viere nach oben. Wenn das so oft passiert, dann überlege ich mir doch: Entweder ist es für LKW-Fahrer zu schwer, auf dieser Bahn die Spur zu halten, oder es liegt an einer falschen Straßenführung."

Vor uns war ein Wagen mit einer englischen Nummer aufgetaucht. „Achtung", sagte Pohle, „wenn der Autofahrer so einen Wagen sieht, muß er aufpassen und Abstand halten. Die Leute sind fremd hier, und Autobahnfahren können Engländer sowieso nicht. Wahrscheinlich werden sie jetzt gleich einen entscheidenden Fehler machen . . ."

Der Engländer schien zu zögern, ob er beim Autobahnabzweig nach Bremen abbiegen sollte. Er verlangsamte das Tempo, dann zeigte endlich der Blinker nach rechts. Pohle: „Naja, sie haben es geschafft."

Der Pädagoge am Steuer—er saß gelöst und ruhig da und schaute vergnügt über das verregnete Niedersachsenland: Autofahren macht ihm Spaß. „Das ist wie beim Schachspielen", sagte er, „wichtig ist, vom anderen im voraus zu wissen, was er tun muß, was er ganz bestimmt machen wird. Der Autofahrer soll nach vorne, nach hinten und nach der Seite denken."

Er wird nicht müde, seinen Lesern immer wieder zu sagen, solange, bis sie es im Schlaf können: „Das Überholen vor einer Bergkuppe und in einer Kurve ist eine lebensgefährliche Dummheit. Parken in der Kurve bringt andere in Gefahr."

Als notwendige Routine-Artikel tauchen immer wieder auf seiner Seite auf: ‚Kaltstart im Winter', ‚Wie fahre ich an einem Berg an', ‚Urlaubsreise mit dem Auto', ‚Nebelfahrten auf der Autobahn'. Zu seinen Lieblingsthemen gehören die Fußgänger, die Zebrastreifen und die ‚gute Sicht'. Dabei ist immer die Sicherheit sein Generalthema und auch der wichtigste Gesichtspunkt, unter dem er seine Testberichte schreibt, die er lieber ‚Fahrberichte eines normalen, vernünftigen Mannes' nennt.

Nina Grunenberg

68. Was ist ein Sportwagen?

Sind Sie schon einmal aus dem Stand in 18 Sekunden 400 Meter weit gekommen, in 18 Sekunden auf rund 120 Kilometerstunden? Dieses Gefühl müssen Sie selber erleben —in einem ‚Porsche 912' zum Beispiel. Und dafür brauchen Sie nicht einmal eine Betonpiste.

Das ist kein Fahren. Das ist ein Gleiten. Man gleitet über gute und schlechte Straßen, über Betonpisten und Katzenköpfe. Man gleitet durch jede Kurve—auch wenn man kein durchtrainierter Rallye-Fahrer ist.

Das Auto namens ‚Porsche' ist ein Sofa. Aber: Soll ein Sportwagen ein Sofa sein? Mit Wehmut, aber auch mit

Schrecken denke ich an den ‚Triumph' zurück, den ich vor Jahren fuhr. Ein Sportwagen! Da übertrugen die Blattfedern getreulich und mit Akribie jede auch noch so kleine Erschütterung auf den Körper. Auf schlechten Straßen brauchte man in jeder Kurve zwei kräftige Arme. Mein Rücken schmerzt jetzt noch, wenn ich an den alten störrischen Esel denke, der bei üblem Pflaster gar nicht mehr zu bändigen war. Und dennoch denke ich gern an den Wagen zurück, der eben ein Sportwagen war: einfach, robust, schnell und preiswert. Er war für runde 12 000 Mark zu haben.

Das ist das Problem! Ich teile es mit den jungen Leuten: 12 000 Mark sind eventuell möglich. Fast 18 000 Mark—wie beim billigsten ‚Porsche'—sind nur möglich, wenn man für das Auto arbeitet (und das auch nicht immer). Sportwagen sind doch Fahrzeuge für junge Leute oder für solche, die jung geblieben sind!

Heinz D. Stuckmann

Aufsätze und Aufsatzübungen

1. Ist es wahr, daß das Reisen bildet?
2. Wie unnahbar ist der Engländer?
3. Wie sieht der ideale Ferienort aus?
4. Schreiben Sie einen Kommentar zu Heinz Maegerleins Artikel über den Fußballsport.
5. Der Verkehr im Jahre 2000.
6. Sollte der Fahrunterricht auf den Schulen eingeführt werden? In welchem Alter macht man am besten den Führerschein?

FEUILLETON

9

Unter diesem Titel erscheinen die ‚Kulturseiten‘, in denen Literatur und Kunst zu Worte kommen.

69. Unser Seller-Teller[1]

Die Wörter — Sartre
Rowohlt (Reinbek) — 14,- DM

Die schöne Wilhelmine — Salomon
Rowohlt (Reinbek) — 20,- DM

**Paris — Ein Fest fürs Leben —
Hemingway** Rowohlt (Reinbek) — 16,80 DM

**Über tierisches und menschliches
Verhalten — Lorenz** Piper (München) - 14,80 DM

Eine andere Welt — Baldwin
Rowohlt (Reinbek) — 24,- DM

70. Ist das Leichte gleich verächtlich?

Die Rolle der sogenannten Unterhaltungsliteratur in Deutschland.

Macht der Erfolg einen Schriftsteller verdächtig? Muß der Romancier, der sich der Gunst des Publikums erfreut, ein schlechtes Gewissen haben? Ist es mit der Würde eines Künstlers unvereinbar, Bücher zu schreiben, die sich auch für die Eisenbahnlektüre eignen? Sollten wir von dem Autor, der dem Unterhaltungsbedürfnis der Leser entgegenkommt, erwarten, daß er sich schämt?

In der angelsächsischen oder romanischen Welt mögen solche Fragen geradezu unsinnig scheinen. In Deutschland sind sie leider, befürchte ich, weder abwegig noch überflüssig. Das hat nichts mit der Qualität der deutschen Literatur zu tun, wohl aber mit der ihr seit altersher zugewiesenen Rolle.

Nichts liegt mir ferner, als über den ehrwürdigen Traum von der ,heil'gen deutschen Kunst' herzuziehen. Da gibt es nichts zu spotten. Ihm verdanken wir unendlich viel. Die Sehnsucht nach dem erhabenen und erlösenden Wort hat jedoch hierzulande eine hochmütige Geringschätzung jener Literatur zur Folge gehabt, die sich damit begnügte, für den täglichen Bedarf des Publikums zu sorgen.

Das vom Bildungsehrgeiz getriebene deutsche Bürgertum des vergangenen Jahrhunderts suchte Nachfolger für den verwaisten Thron von Weimar.[1] Es schmachtete nach Dichterfürsten. Aber es weigerte sich, das schriftstellerische Handwerk zu respektieren. Es träumte vom edlen Sänger, der auf der Menschheit Höhen wohnen sollte. Aber vom Literaten wollte es nichts wissen.

Und während die Engländer und Franzosen ihren großen Unterhaltungsautoren—denn was anderes waren Balzac oder Dickens?—im Poetenhimmel die ehrenvollsten Plätze zuwiesen, wurde in Deutschland der Begriff ,Unterhaltungsliteratur' fast zum Schimpfwort.

Auf die Dauer läßt sich jedoch das Amüsement nicht fortjagen. Gewaltsam vertrieben, kommt es durch die Hintertür wieder hinein. Kein Zweifel, wenn sich die Schriftsteller dem Geschmack der Leser unterwerfen, kann es um die Literatur nicht gut bestellt sein. Wo indes andererseits die künstlerisch anspruchsvolle Literatur glaubt, das Publikum ignorieren zu dürfen, schlägt die große Stunde der Pseudokunst. Es triumphiert der bare Schund.

Statt nach des Tages Arbeit das Land der Griechen mit der Seele zu suchen,[2] wie es das akademische Bildungswesen vom deutschen Leser erwartete, warf er sich an den Busen der Elfriede Marlitt[3] und später der Hedwig Courts-Mahler, entfloh zu Ganghofer oder mit Karl May.

Der Bann, mit dem man die unterhaltende Funktion der Literatur im neunzehnten Jahrhundert belegt hat, lastet auf einem beträchtlichen Teil der deutschen Kritik bis heute, von der Universitätsgermanistik ganz zu schweigen. Das Amüsante gilt als unseriös, das Spannende wird als dubios empfunden und das Witzige als undeutsch denunziert.

Noch werden allerdings in Deutschland Bücher nicht nur geschrieben und gedruckt, sondern mitunter auch gelesen. Indes: sind es dieselben Bücher, über die wir uns in den Literaturblättern und Zeitschriften verbreiten? Auf einige Titel jährlich trifft dies bestimmt zu. Aber eben nur auf einige.

Sonst gehen die Wege von Kritik und Publikum auseinander. Was die Kenner beschäftigt, findet dank intensiver Werbung zwei- bis dreitausend Leser, nein, seien wir vorsichtiger, zwei- bis dreitausend Käufer. Und was Hunderttausende genießen, kümmert die Kenner nicht.

Ich habe nichts gegen eine Dichtung für Gelehrte. Ich liebe vieles, was Literaten für Literaten schreiben.

Soll jedoch eine solche bisweilen interessante, oft unlesbare und esoterische Literatur tatsächlich vorherrschen? Wir können, denke ich, nicht oft genug daran erinnern, daß es das Geschäft der Kunst ist, wie Brecht einmal sagte, ‚die Leute zu unterhalten‘. Auch der modernen Künste.

Marcel

71. Subventionierte Freiheit des Theaters

Glanz und Gefahr des deutschen Theaterbetriebs—beides ist in dem Zauberwort ‚Subvention‘ begründet.

In der Spielzeit 1963/64 haben die bundesdeutschen Theater 300 Millionen Mark aus öffentlichen Mitteln an Zuschüssen erhalten. Diese Zuschüsse sind inzwischen weiter gewachsen. Theaterleute aus den meisten anderen Ländern blicken wegen dieser Subventionen neidvoll nach Deutschland. Die Mittel der öffentlichen Hand fließen nicht nur den Staatstheatern und städtischen Bühnen zu, es gibt auch kaum ein wichtiges Privattheater, das nicht durch einen Zuschuß aus den Steuereinkünften unterstützt würde. Hans Daiber hat in seinem Buch ‚Theater—eine Bilanz' umgerechnet, daß für das derzeit relativ teuerste deutsche Theater, nämlich in Krefeld, jeder Einwohner pro Kopf und Jahr auf dem Steuerumweg 34,70 Mark ausgibt.

Das Theater ist also, kraß ausgedrückt, ein schöner Luxus, den sich die öffentliche Hand für uns—oder die zehn Prozent von uns, die wir die Theater besuchen—leistet. Keine Bühne von wirklicher Bedeutung wäre in Deutschland lebensfähig, wenn Staat und Gemeinden den Geldhahn zudrehten.

Das hat mehrere Folgen. Gute und weniger gute. Eine der ersten ist das getrübte Freiheitsverhältnis zwischen Parkett und Bühne. Denn so sehr der Zuschauer sein Mißfallen auch kundgeben darf, indem er sich die Freiheit nimmt, zu buhen und zu pfeifen: Er bewirkt damit bestenfalls einen kräftigen Skandal, ändert aber nichts an der Tatsache, daß nicht er über die Spieldauer einer Aufführung entscheidet— sondern der Steuerzahler, der automatisch bezahlt, auch wenn er gar nicht daran denkt, ins Theater zu gehen.

Die Folgen eines völlig freien Theatermarktes, bei dem die Publikumsgunst allein über den Spielplan entscheidet, wären freilich leicht abzusehen. Kein Theaterleiter könnte sich dann einer Aufführung des ‚Land des Lächelns'[1] oder der ‚Lustigen Witwe' widersetzen, vielmehr würden lauter Witwen und lauter Länder des Lächelns die zeitgenössische Dramatik rasch in die Abgeschiedenheit von Nachtstudios vertreiben. Mit den Subventionen ist jedenfalls eines unerbittlich garantiert: der edukatorische Zug des deutschen Theaters, der die Leute oft zu ihrem literarischen Glück zwingt, weil er ihnen in der Miete A 3[2] gnadenlos den literarischen Höhenflug zumutet. Denn das Theater ist nicht nur subventioniert. Es ist auch weitgehend ausabonniert. Ärgert sich ein Gast über das ihm Vorgesetzte, so kann er oft frühestens zu Beginn der nächsten Spielzeit die Konsequenzen daraus ziehen.

Gepolstert mit Subventionen, zugedeckt durch ein Abonnementssystem kann also das Theater in aller Freiheit seiner Freiheit nachgehen. Der Intendant kann mit der theatralischen Freiheit walten und schalten, wie es ihm sein Gewissen gebietet. Die finanzielle Sicherheit beflügelt den ‚Mut zum Experiment'. Nicht zufällig sind beispielsweise die letzten Stücke Ionescos zuerst in Deutschland gespielt worden. Das deutsche Theater mit seinem Experimentier-

und Stoffhunger hat sie, wie so vieles Neue, einfach an sich gezogen. Die gut finanzierten Bühnen können sich daher auch junger, unbekannter Talente wirklich annehmen. Kein Autor, der etwas auch nur halbwegs Spielfähiges zu Papier bringt, muß fürchten, nicht gespielt zu werden— zumindest einmal.

Verdirbt diese Freiheit, die dem deutschen Theater vor allem eine stattliche Reihe dramatischer Eintagsfliegen eingebracht hat, aber nicht vielleicht die jungen Autoren, anstatt sie langsam reifen zu lassen? Ist diese Freiheit nicht auch Nachlässigkeit?

Hellmuth Karasek

72. Brecht[1] galore

Eine Brecht-Welle geht zur Zeit durch England: Im *National Theatre* war vergangene Woche die gefeierte Premiere von *Mutter Courage*; der *Puntila* wird im Juli im Aldwych folgen; im August wird, so es die Weltpolitik will, das Berliner Ensemble[2] zu einem dreiwöchigen Gastspiel eintreffen; zwei Bände ausgewählter Dramen erscheinen in dieser Woche, eine Gesamtausgabe der Dramen ist geplant; der eifrige Leser und Theatergänger kann sich dazu in einer Sondernummer der Zweimonatsschrift *Encore* darüber informieren, was Brecht selber alles zur *Courage* geäußert und angemerkt hat.

73. Film: *Mutter Courage*[1]

(DDR, Verleih: Constantin)

Wer die Aufführung des Berliner Ensembles[2] nicht kennt, hier ist sie, ungelenk, aber einigermaßen präzise abgefilmt, es spielen Helene Weigel, Ernst Busch, Ekkehard Schall, Angelika Hurwitz. Es handelt sich um die Inszenierung, die Brecht zusammen mit Erich Engel noch selber eingerichtet hat. Der Film wurde 1961 beendet; ein früherer Versuch, das Stück zu verfilmen, scheiterte am Einspruch des mißtrauischen Brecht. Der vorliegende folgt streng den Anweisungen des Autors für die Bühne: die Songs werden an der Rampe gesungen—Schwarzblenden schieben sich über einen Teil des Cinemaskopebildes, es gibt keine Details, die Illusionen erzeugen können, die stilisierte

Mutter Courage zählt ihre Einnahmen, während der Feldprediger und der Regimentsschreiber ein Brettspiel spielen. Eine Szene aus der Defa-Verfilmung der Aufführung des Berliner Ensembles mit Helene Weigel als Mutter Courage.

Szenerie ist deutlich erkennbar die der Bühne, Stiche, die den Dreißigjährigen Krieg zeigen, leiten den Film ein und zerlegen ihn in Kapitel. Peter Palitzsch und Manfred Wekwerth haben darauf verzichtet, das Stück für den Film neu durchzudenken, sie halten sich an das Vorgefundene, die Inszenierung, und fallen deshalb hinter diese zurück. Sie wissen mit dem Format nicht viel anzufangen, weite Teile des Bildes bleiben einfach leer und nichtssagend, und sie haben mit ihren Kamerafahrten meistens Pech, der Zufall regiert. Die Frage nach Möglichkeiten einer Brecht-verfilmung wird also auch hier nicht beantwortet.

U.N.

74. Deutsche Oper

Berlins musikalisches Mai-Erlebnis war, was es schon vor 145 Jahren war: der Freischütz von Carl Maria von Weber. So rollte auf der Bühne der Deutschen Oper eine der deutschesten aller deutschen Opern ab.

Nun aber hatte dieses teutonische Spektakulum einen kleinen Schönheitsfehler: An unserer nationalen Opern-weste klebten Fäden amerikanischen Kaugummis, was keineswegs der Inszenierung Sellners, geschweige denn der Stabführung Eugen Jochums zuzuschreiben war, sondern dem Mangel erstklassiger Sangeskräfte in deutschen Landen. Und so passierte es also, daß der Inbegriff deutscher Opernseligkeit, eben der ‚Freischütz‘, in den Hauptrollen mit Amerikanern besetzt werden mußte.

Max, blond, stämmig, sicher auch blauäugig, Prototyp des deutschen Förstergehilfen, sagte zu *Agathe*, blond, keusch, rank, kaum weniger blauäugig—anzunehmen—, Prototyp des deutschen Förstertöchterleins, im zweiten Akt:

„Vuerzaiht, wuenn ihr mainetwuegen aufgebluiben said, laider komm' ich nuer auf wuenige Augenbluicke."

Agathe: „Du wuillst doch nuicht wuider forrt?"

Hans-Jürgen Usko

75. Lydia Schierning empfiehlt Schallplatten

Franz Schubert: Klavier-Trio Nr. 1 B-dur, op. 99; The Stern-Rose-Istomin-Trio; CBS 72 344, 25, – DM.

Beim Zuhören begreift man Robert Schumanns Wort:
„Ein Blick auf das Trio B-dur—und das erbärmliche
Menschentreiben flieht zurück, und die Welt glänzt wieder
frisch!" Kraftvoll und überschäumend, durchweht von
dem weiten ‚romantischen' Atem, ist das Spiel des amerikanischen Trios.

*„Grace Bumbry singt Verdi-Arien"; Orchester der Deutschen
Oper Berlin, Leitung: Hans Löwlein; Deutsche Grammophon
Gesellschaft* 138 987, 25, – DM.
Die üppige, reich gefärbte Stimme von Grace Bumbry, der
‚schwarzen Venus' von Bayreuth,[1] beherrscht die Kunst
des italienischen Bel-Canto. Sie klingt süß und voll im
lyrischen Ausdruck und versagt niemals, wenn es bei
leidenschaftlichen Ausbrüchen darum geht, dramatische
Vorgänge darzustellen.

Nicht zu empfehlen:
Johann Sebastian Bach. Brandenburgische Konzerte Nr. 1–6;
*Marlboro Festival Orchester, Rudolf Serkin, Klavier, Leitung:
Pablo Casals; CBS S* 72 396–97, 50, – DM.
Berühmte Namen garantieren nicht immer entsprechende
Leistungen. Hier sind Bachs Brandenburgische Konzerte
durch ein überhitztes Tempo und eine manierierte Phrasie-
rung völlig entstellt worden. Und wenn dann noch durch
einen motorischen Rhythmus etwas ‚Außergewöhnliches'
hervorgezaubert werden soll, was in Wirklichkeit dem Wesen
Bachs und seiner Zeit total widerspricht, kann selbst das
virtuose Spiel der Solisten diese Interpretation nicht mehr
retten. Die Komposition ist zerstört.

76. Gesellschaftskritik mit Musik

Folksong: Ich finde für dieses Wort, so simpel es scheint,
kein deutsches Äquivalent, weil es für die Sache selber kein
Äquivalent gibt, ebenso wenig wie für die Quellen, die
Geschichte und die Atmosphäre, aus denen das alles kommt.

Gewiß, auch hier in Deutschland singt noch mancher
Schüler, halb grollend, halb gröhlend, mit, wenn der Lehrer
auf der Klassenreise den bekannten frischen Gesang
anstimmt; aber mehr als zwei Strophen von drei Liedern
kann glücklicherweise eh keiner.

Flatternde Wimpel[1], grüne Wipfel, kühler Grund und

herzallerliebster Schatz, davon kann man zur Not mal mitbrummen, aber abgestanden ist es doch und unwahr dazu. Was sollen die Gesänge, wo es das Riesengebirge, die kühlen Gründe und die wandernden Gesellen (aus allerlei Gründen) nicht mehr gibt? Und überhaupt: Wer singt bei uns schon gern in der Öffentlichkeit, und sei es auch nur der des Gartens, des Wohnzimmers oder des Brunnens vor den Toren der Universität?

In Amerika jedoch kann man zur Zeit keine Universität betreten, ohne nicht mindestens einer Gitarre zu begegnen (geschultert oder in Aktion); jedes zweite abendliche Beisammensein von Studenten endet, geplant, oder ungeplant, mit allgemeinem Singen; es gibt niemanden, der nicht wenigstens die bekannteren Lieder auswendig kennt.

Ein großer Teil der Lieder, die hier vorgetragen werden, von beruflichen und nebenberuflichen Folk-Sängern, von Professionals und Amateuren, sind Lieder aus dem amerikanischen Süden, Neger- Strafgefangenen- und Sklavenlieder, auch Kirchenlieder, die teils unverändert übernommen, teils mit aktuellen Strophen oder ganz neuen Texten versehen werden. Es sind einprägsame Melodien, voll von gläubiger Klage und sanftem Protest.

Das Lied *We shall overcome* zum Beispiel, das heute jeder Amerikaner mit der *Civil Rights*-Bewegung identifiziert, war ursprünglich ein Kirchenlied, wurde dann von Tabakarbeitern in Tennessee als Gewerkschaftslied übernommen und schließlich, seit den frühen fünfziger Jahren, von Weißen und Farbigen im Kampf gegen die Rassendiskriminierung gesungen. Es ist nicht übertrieben zu sagen, daß dieses Lied, das von nichts als geduldiger Überwindung und Hoffnung auf Frieden handelt, inzwischen eine quasi leitmotivische Bedeutung im *Civil Rights*-Kampf hat. Präsident Johnson wußte, was er tat, als er dessen erste Zeile zum Anfang und Motto seiner großen Rede zur Rassenfrage machte.

Petra Kipphoff

77. Jazz-Gottesdienst in Düsseldorf

Das Himmelfahrtsfrohlocken[1] in der Düsseldorfer Neander-Kirche war ungewöhnlich. Eine zwölfköpfige Combo mit Jazztrompeten, Saxophonen und Schlagzeug spielte Art Blakey's *Moanin*. Einer der bekanntesten Düsseldorfer Jazzmusiker, Hermann Gehlen, intonierte zusammen mit

Kantor Oskar Gottlieb Blarr Psalmenstrophen, Spirituals, traditionelle Kirchenlieder, das Vaterunser und eine Bach-Fuge. In den Bänken der evangelischen Neander-Kirche saßen überwiegend ‚Sachverständige‘, junge Leute zwischen 17 und 25 Jahren. Sie hocken für gewöhnlich in den gleich neben der Kirche gelegenen Jazzkneipen der Düsseldorfer Altstadt. An diesem Feiertag öffnete Düsseldorfs älteste Kirche für eine Stunde ihre Pforten zum jährlichen ‚Gottesdienst für junge Leute‘.

Seit vier Jahren experimentieren die Düsseldorfer an einer zeitgemäßen Form des Gottesdienstes. Sie sind damit nicht allein. Auch an anderen Orten füllen Jazzgottesdienste die Gotteshäuser mit jungen Leuten, die sonst nicht in eine Kirche gehen. Das Treiben der Neutöner indessen ist nach wie vor umstritten. „In der evangelischen Kirche ist kein Platz für liturgische Playboys“, meinte erst kürzlich Kirchenrat[2] Friedrich Hofmann.

Kantor Blarr und viele andere evangelische Kirchen-musiker sind anderer Ansicht: „Wir müssen doch das, was unsere Zeit empfindet, auch in der Kirche zum Ausdruck bringen!“ Blarr kann sich dabei auf den Hilfsprediger Joachim Neander berufen, nach dem die Altstadtkirche benannt wurde. Im siebzehnten Jahrhundert dichtete er zur Melodie eines damals beliebten Studentenliedes den bekannten Choral ‚Lobe den Herrn‘. Der aufgeweckte Kantor folgt ihm: „Lebendigkeit und Dichte brauchen wir auch in unseren Gottesdiensten. Nichts tötet mehr als die lauwarme Routine!“

Auch Pfarrer Dr. Paul Seifer, der zu den Initiatoren der modernen Gottesdienste gehört hatte, trat den Kritikern entgegen: „Wir leiden doch darunter, daß über unserem gottesdienstlichen Leben so oft der dichte Nebel der Gleich-gültigkeit und der Gewohnheit liegt. Dieser Nebel ist im ‚Gottesdienst für junge Leute‘ jedenfalls davongeblasen worden. Die Predigt soll modern sein, das wird allgemein anerkannt. Warum dann nicht der ganze Gottesdienst?“

F.R.

78. Der Hörfunk im Zeitalter des Fernsehens

Als der Rundfunk, 1923, zu senden begann, hatten schon seit mehr als zweihundert Jahren die Komponisten für ihn

komponiert, seit zweitausend Jahren die Geschichtener-
zähler für ihn fabuliert. Zwar hatten sie an bescheidenere
Verbreitungsmittel gedacht, nicht an ein so mächtiges; an
Konzertsäle etwa und Bücher. Die Breitenstrahlung machte
nun, was bisher wenige besaßen, allen zugänglich, ein
Riesenschritt vorwärts ins Zeitalter eines kulturellen Sozialismus.

Dementsprechend wurde der Rundfunk damals auch
gesetzlich als universales Volksbildungsmittel struktuiert.
Man versuchte für ihn zwei Unabhängigkeiten zu erreichen:
die wirtschaftliche, um ihn von der Sklaverei des Massen-
geschmacks, und die politische, um ihn von Staats- und
Parteizugriffen freizuhalten. Diese Grundkonzeption hat
sowohl in Deutschland wie zum Beispiel in England, wo
man eine ähnliche Struktur schuf, aus dem Hörrundfunk ein
hochangesehenes Instrument kultureller Wirksamkeit werden lassen.

Die Bilanz des Fernsehens ist fragwürdiger. Musik und
Erzählvortrag fallen als Programmöglichkeiten fast ganz
aus; das genuine Fernsehspiel ist weder praktisch noch
theoretisch ein gültiger Begriff. Es werden fast nur vor-
handene Bühnentexte gesendet in Bearbeitungen als Thea-
tersurrogat; und die rund fünfzigjährige Filmgeschichte
liefert Spiel- und Dokumentarfilme; aber die Mittel des
Filmes sind reduziert durch die Grobzerlegung des Bildes
mit der festgesetzten Rasterzahl 625. Der Fernsehschirm
erlaubt bei weitem nicht, die Bildtradition der Filmkamera
fortzusetzen.

Nur in zweierlei Hinsicht ist das Fernsehen sehr viel
mächtiger als der Hörfunk. Man kann an den Sendungen mit
Unterhaltungsmusik kaum mehr wie an einer ‚Musik-
wasserleitung‘ vorbeihören. Und in Reportagen und Doku-
mentarsendungen beweist das Instrument seine Macht.
Es hat darüber hinaus die Möglichkeit direkter Ansprache
und Einflußnahme der einzelnen prominenten Persönlichkeit, auch der politischen auf die Allgemeinheit.

Nun werden Hörfunk und Fernsehen jeweils im selben
Haus und an der Spitze unter Verantwortung derselben
Personen produziert. Niemand wird Zweifel haben können,
welches der beiden inkommensurablen Instrumente auf die
Dauer den kürzeren ziehen muß.

Es muß einem alten Rundfunkmann in dem Augenblick,
in dem stimmstarke Mächte mit dem Einsatz aller Kraft für
das Fernsehen plädieren, aber erlaubt sein, zu sagen, daß

es auch noch intellektuelle Gesichtspunkte gibt. Man bedenke, was das Hörspiel—bei so bescheidenem Aufwand —für die Geschichte der deutschen Nachkriegsliteratur seit Borcherts[1] ‚Draußen vor der Tür' und seit Eichs[2] ‚Träumen' bedeutet!

Der Hörfunk ist heute in Gefahr, eine Art Wurmfortsatz des Fernsehens zu werden und als solcher um seiner Lästigkeit willen eines Tages vielleicht gar als operabel zu gelten. Wenn er in den Funkhäusern nicht als eine Reservation des Geistes angesehen wird, statt als Unterhaltungsinstrument für Autobahnreisende und Küchenfeen, wenn nicht die Mächtigen hier eine besondere Verantwortung verspüren, dann wird eines Tages ein neuer Anlaß sein zu sagen, daß die Deutschen lieber der Macht Opfer bringen als dem Geist.

Heinz Schwitzke

79. Fernsehen: Sonnabend, 21 Uhr [2]

Er hat eine kleine, verplüschte Wohnung und eine bieder-besorgte Frau, er raucht Pfeife und trägt zerknautschte Hüte, den Mantelkragen hat er meistens hochgeschlagen; im Büro setzt er sich auf die Schreibtischkante und zupft sein rechtes Ohrläppchen; er angelt gern und ist nett zu seinen Untergebenen; er hat viele Freunde, in der Hauptstadt und in der Provinz, mit denen er früher einmal, es ist schon so lange her, das Gymnasium besucht hat; er ist fleißig und liebt seinen Beruf, der ihn nicht zur Ruhe kommen läßt; er träumt davon, irgendwo an der Loire seine Pension zu verzehren, zweijährige Austern, einen guten Chablis, seine Frau und seine Dunhill einmal in Frieden genießen zu können, Jules Maigret, der rundliche *petit bourgeois*, der gefürchtete Kommissar vom *Quai des Orfèvres*.

Zweiundfünfzigmal, Sonnabend um Sonnabend, eingeschaltet zwischen dem professoralen Wochen-Kommentar und dem leutselig-derb-dreisten Sportstudio wird seine Stunde geschlagen haben, die gemütliche Sonnabend-einundzwanzig-Uhr-Stunde, wenn die deutsche Ausgabe der BBC-Serie *Maigret und . . .* am Ende des Jahres ausgelaufen ist; zweiundfünfzig Mordfälle werden geklärt sein, den ersten wird man vergessen haben, ehe der letzte gelöst ist—nichts steht im Wege, die zweiundfünfzig Filmchen zu wiederholen (wie es in England bereits geschehen ist), von vorn zu beginnen, die Runden noch einmal auszuzählen, das Spiel endlos zu repetieren: *Maigret und der Schatten am Fenster, Frau Maigret als Detektiv, Maigret hilft einem Dienstmädchen, Maigret und die sonderbaren Geschwister, Maigret wird wütend, Maigret hat Angst, Maigret ad infinitum* . . .

Jules Maigret alias Rupert Davies—er ist der Held des Kriminal-Marathons, dieser unermüdliche, joviale Mann, ein Augenzwinkerer und Sorgenfaltenleger, ein Genie emsiger Identifizierungskunst, ein Zauberer an zweiundfünfzig Abenden: Die Papierfigur ist zum Leben erweckt, eine vollkommene Metamorphose hat stattgefunden— Davies ist Maigret, Maigret nur noch Davies, Davies-Maigret ist ein Star, die zahllosen Regisseure, Bearbeiter, Kameraleute und Chargen, die er verschlissen hat, sind namenlos geworden in seinem Schatten, hilfreiche und genügsame Handlanger seines Ruhmes.

Mit einer Untat oder ihrer Vorbereitung beginnt es jedesmal, die Welt ist aus den Fugen für die kurzen Augenblicke des Vorspanns,[1] doch der Titel schon, unterlegt mit einer *valse musette,* stellt die Ordnung wieder her, Maigret reißt das Feuerhölzchen an, der Qualm seiner Pfeife verspricht die alsbaldige Katharsis, es ist Zeit, sich im Sessel zurückzulehnen und in Ruhe zu betrachten, wie die Polizei, dein Freund und Helfer, wie Maigret, der liebgewordene Freund und rastlose Helfer, es übernimmt, das gute Ende herbeizuführen.

Das Kriminalstück ist eine bürgerliche Gattung. Ohne die Übereinkunft, daß es gelte, die bestehende Ordnung zu bewahren, wäre Maigret nicht möglich, ohne das Vergnügen an restaurativen Aktionen die Lust am Kriminalstück nicht —sie setzt die bedenkenlose Bereitschaft des Zuschauers voraus, mit der Polizei gegen den Desperado, mit dem Kollektiv gegen den Einzelgänger, mit der etablierten Moral gegen die individuelle Unmoral zu paktieren: Zu erfahren, warum ein Mord geschah, ist nicht so interessant, interessant ist nur, zu verfolgen, wie der Schuldige erwischt wird, nicht erklärende Worte werden verlangt, sondern Taten, die das Verbrechen ahnden—Mordfälle als Anlässe, sich vom Funktionieren der Ordnungsmacht beruhigende Gewißheit zu verschaffen. Wo Maigrets Besen kehrt, bleibt die gute Stube sauber, und der Scharfrichter im Brot, Maigret, der Büttel der Nation, er tue seine Pflicht.

Sonnabend um Sonnabend verteidigt Maigret—Blessuren und Überstunden nicht achtend—den *status quo* der bürgerlichen Gesellschaft, ihn ficht nichts an. Seine Beharrlichkeit ist pittoresk, diese so virtuose wie monotone Mörderjagd der kleinen Gesten; sein Geblinzel, Naseschnauben und Achselzucken, seine fintenreichen Recherchier- und Verhör-Orgien haben längst nicht nur quantitativ alle anderen Wer-hat-es-getan-Serien aus dem Felde geschlagen.

Uwe Nettelbeck

80. Ausstellung Lovis Corinth

Mit der Ausstellung der Zeichnungen und Aquarelle von Lovis Corinth[1] feiert die Lübecker Overbeck-Gesellschaft das Jubiläum ihrer 400. Ausstellung seit der Gründung im Jahre 1918.

Die über 100 Blätter kommen aus 20 Museen und Sammlungen, auch Ostberlin und Dresden haben sich beteiligt. Sie umfassen das ganze zeichnerische Werk von 1876 bis zu den letzten Selbstbildnissen von 1925. Die enthusiastische Neubewertung, die Corinth in den letzten zehn Jahren erfahren hat, ist von seiner Malerei und seiner Graphik ausgegangen.

Ob aber der Zeichner Corinth dem Maler ebenbürtig ist, wird man trotz der Lübecker Ausstellung, die dafür den Beweis bringen will, nur mit großen Vorbehalten bejahen können. Es handelt sich meistens um Studien vor der Natur, um Vorarbeiten für die Bilder, etwa bei den Skizzen einer Ziege oder eines nackten Jungen, die Corinth für die ‚Kindheit des Zeus‘ benötigte. Viele Aktzeichnungen, Baumstudien und Landschaftsskizzen würde man mißverstehen, wenn man ihnen einen künstlerischen Anspruch und eine Selbständigkeit beilegen würde, die sie nicht haben und die Corinth ihnen nicht gegeben hat.

Am schönsten sind die aquarellierten und gezeichneten Porträts aus den letzten Jahren, vor allem die Selbstbildnisse—keine Denkmäler der eigenen Kraft und Herrlichkeit wie die Bilder, vielmehr eine distanzierte, ironische, rücksichtslose Selbstaussage. Die Ausstellung dauert bis zum 15. August.

G.S.

Aufsätze und Aufsatzübungen

1. Kann ein Bestseller literarische Qualitäten haben—oder ein literarisches Werk zum Bestseller werden?
2. Beschreiben Sie das Theaterwesen Ihres Landes. Ist es dem deutschen vorzuziehen?
3. Schreiben Sie die Rezension
   (a) eines Theaterabends
   (b) eines Filmes
   (c) eines Fernsehspiels.
4. Die moderne Malerei.

ÜBER
DEN UMGANG
MIT
MENSCHEN[1]

10

Auch eine seriöse Zeitschrift hat ihre leichtere Seite.

81. Deutschlandreise mit Dolmetscher

(Aus einem amerikanischen Wegweiser für reisende Geschäftsleute)

Sie sollten möglichst deutsch sprechen können, oder einen Dolmetscher bei sich haben. Glauben Sie nicht, daß Ihr Geschäftspartner englisch spricht. Das muß nicht unbedingt jeder können. Ungefähr jeder vierte deutsche Geschäftsmann spricht eine fremde Sprache, und nur ungefähr 17 Prozent aller erwachsenen Deutschen sprechen englisch.

Erscheinen Sie zu allen Verabredungen pünktlich, seien sie nun geschäftlicher oder gesellschaftlicher Art. Wenn Sie sich mit Ihren deutschen Geschäftspartnern gut verstehen, werden diese Sie sicher zu sich nach Hause einladen. Hat man Sie zu 20 Uhr gebeten, so halten Sie diese Zeit ein. Die lange Cocktail-Stunde vor dem Essen kennt man hier nicht. Wenn Sie zum Essen eingeladen sind, ist es üblich, Blumen mitzubringen—aber niemals mehr als fünf oder sieben und immer eine ungerade Zahl. Schenken Sie möglichst keine roten Rosen, weil das in Deutschland bedeuten könnte, daß Sie heimlich in die Gastgeberin verliebt sind. Hier eine nützliche kleine Anleitung: Entfernen Sie das Papier, bevor Sie die Blumen überreichen. Wahrscheinlich wird während des Essens nicht geraucht, und die Zigaretten werden erst nach dem Kaffee angeboten.

Reden Sie Ihren Geschäftspartner immer mit seinem Titel an, zum Beispiel ‚Herr Doktor' oder ‚Herr Ingenieur'. Seien Sie nicht zu vertraulich. Man nennt sich erst nach langjähriger Verbindung bei seinem Vornamen. Hier werden Sie wahrscheinlich mehr Hände schütteln als in irgendeinem anderen Land. Seien Sie darauf vorbereitet, ... zig Male am Tag Hände zu drücken, oftmals sogar derselben Person. Dabei streckt der Ältere (oder der in der höheren Stellung) zuerst seine Hand aus. Lassen Sie sich von Ihrem Geschäftspartner in den Mantel helfen. Das ist deutsche Höflichkeit und bedeutet nicht, daß man Sie für altersschwach hält. Helfen auch Sie ihm bei der erstbesten Gelegenheit, das beweist, daß Sie mit deutschen Gepflogenheiten vertraut sind.

Norddeutsche Geschäftsleute sind reserviert und stolz auf ihre Tüchtigkeit. In München sind sie umgänglicher und ein bißchen fröhlicher.

Sie wären schlecht beraten, vom Zweiten Weltkrieg zu reden, wenn nicht Ihr Gastgeber selber dieses Thema anschneidet. Jedermann wird es gefallen, wenn Sie die Mauer[1] beklagen, was auch wirklich nicht schwerfällt. Zwischen Ost- und Westdeutschland besteht eine tiefe gefühlsmäßige Verbindung. Fast jeder hat drüben Verwandte.

Es könnte auch die Rede auf die amerikanische Aktivität in der Deutschlandfrage kommen. Präsident Kennedy war in Westdeutschland sehr beliebt, und viele Leute werden Ihnen von seiner berühmten Berliner Rede erzählen, in der er unter anderm sagte: *,Ich bin ein Berliner'*.

82. Schlafsack für deutsche Studenten

Die Eskimos haben einen Gebrauchsgegenstand, der ihren Lebensverhältnissen gut angepaßt ist: eine Schlaftasche aus Tierpelzen, in der die ganze Sippe (durchschnittlich zehn Leute) für die Nacht Platz hat. Dort drin liegen Schwiegergroßmutter, Vetter, Base und Enkelkind, wenn der Polarsturm ums Iglu heult.

Solche ungezwungenen Gebrauchsgegenstände gibt's bei uns bis jetzt nicht; dafür wurde jetzt hierzulande eingeführt: das Doppelzimmer im Studentenwohnheim (natürlich, bitte schön, mit der herkömmlichen Geschlechtertrennung). In den vier neuen Wohnheimen in Heidelberg haust etwa die Hälfte der achthundert Studenten und Studentinnen in Doppelzimmern.

Dafür gibt's gute Gründe. Es ist Geld und Platz gespart, und man gibt den Studenten Gelegenheit, ihre Erziehung in Sachen Rücksichtnahme und Anpassungsfähigkeit zu vertiefen.

Außerdem können auf diese Weise die ausländischen Kommilitonen[1] Deutschland und seine Bewohner besser kennenlernen: Wie lange wälzt sich der Deutsche durchschnittlich, bis er einschläft? Wie schnarcht der Deutsche? Wann hört er am liebsten Radio, und wie hat er's mit dem Zähneputzen?

In der alten Idee der ,Studentenbude'[1] waren einige kräftige Widerwärtigkeiten enthalten, die es zu ertragen galt: eine Wirtin, die um 23 Uhr die Sicherung 'rausschraubt, Waschwasser, das im Winter auf der Waschkommode gefriert, und ein Ofen, der Kohlen frißt, ohne ausreichend zu wärmen.

Diese ‚klassischen' Kümmernisse gibt's in den neuen Studentenwohnheimen nicht; die Erbauer haben jedoch mit ihrem Doppelzimmer-Trick ohne große Umstände neue geschaffen. Der Qualmempfindliche bekommt einen starken Raucher, der Nachtarbeiter einen entschlossenen Frühaufsteher, der konzentriert und still arbeitende Streber eine Stimmungskanone mit großem Freundeskreis und der geruchsempfindliche Säuberling ein herzliches, fröhliches Stinktier als Sozius auf die Bude.

Manfred Schwengler

83. Männer für Anfänger

Das echte Abenteuer besteht aus drei Teilen: überraschendem Anfang, stürmischem Ablauf und dramatischem Schluß. Fehlt nur eines dieser drei Elemente, so kann man nicht von einem wirklichen Abenteuer reden. Wenn, zum Beispiel, der bis dahin so gemütliche Briefträger plötzlich zudringlich wird, dann gibt es einen überraschenden Anfang und einen dramatischen Schluß. (Es fehlt der stürmische Ablauf.) Wird der Bürochef zudringlich, dann gibt es bestenfalls einen stürmischen Ablauf und einen dramatischen Schluß. (Doch wo bleibt der überraschende Anfang?)

Der Flugkapitän einer gigantischen Düsenmaschine verläßt über dem Atlantischen Ozean seinen Platz, setzt sich neben die Anfängerin und erklärt ihr seine Liebe. (Das war der überraschende Anfang.) Die Anfängerin erwidert die Gefühle des trefflichen Piloten aus vollem Herzen, will aber—schon weger der Flugsicherheit—nicht augenblicklich nachgeben. Der verschmähte Verehrer entfernt sich und vollführt in der nächsten halben Stunde mit der Riesenmaschine die tollsten Flugkünste, um durch diesen Beweis seines todesverachtenden Mutes das Herz der Anfängerin zu erweichen. Erleichtert schließt sie ihn nach der Landung in die Arme. (Das war der stürmische Ablauf.) Allein, der Flugkapitän wird von seiner Ehefrau erwartet. Die Anfängerin wirft dem Verführer seine Gewissenlosigkeit vor, und straft ihn, obwohl er von Scheidung spricht, mit eisiger Verachtung. Einsam fährt sie vom Flugplatz in die Stadt. Der Flugkapitän verfolgt das Taxi mit einem Helikopter, doch verfehlt er bei der Landung das Dach des Hotels und stürzt in die Tiefe. Die Anfängerin

aber tritt ihre Stellung als Stubenmädchen an. (Das war der dramatische Schluß.)

Wie aus dem Beispiel ersichlich, muß das Abenteuer auch gefährlich sein.

Für den geborenen Abenteurer ist das Abenteuer dasselbe wie für die geborene Hausfrau das Großreinemachen. Alles steht zwar auf dem Kopf, ist aber dennoch in Ordnung. Deshalb soll die Anfängerin, wenn sie's auf ein Abenteuer abgesehn hat, dem geborenen Abenteurer aus dem Wege gehen. Tut sie es nicht, so läuft sie Gefahr, den routinierten Fachkräften ihres Partners zu unterliegen. Diese Gefahr ist bedeutend, denn im echten Abenteuer geht es zuweilen um Leben oder Tod. In diesem Fall sind darum auch alle Männer zu meiden, die eine Schießwaffe, einen Schlagring oder ein Küchenmesser besitzen. Die Anfängerin hingegen muß über ein kleines Waffenarsenal verfügen, auch soll sie für ein Abenteuer folgende Gegenstände stets griffbereit halten: parfümiertes Briefpapier, lilafarbenes Seidentuch (um damit Zeichen zu geben), Strickleiter, Reisekostüm samt Hut mit dichtem Schleier, Giftfläschchen, Diamantkollier (um es versetzen zu können), Siegellack, Wundpflaster, warme Unterwäsche (bei nächtlicher Flucht unerläßlich), Reisekoffer mit Geheimfach, garantiert stumpfe Rasierklingen (zwecks Vortäuschung eines Selbstmordes), direkte Telephonleitung zu Scotland Yard, Schaukelstuhl (um über das Erlebte hinterher nachzusinnen). Mit dieser Ausrüstung wird das Abenteuer für jede Anfängerin ein Vergnügen sein.

Lena Dur

84. Über den Umgang mit der Queen

Die Bundesrepublik hat ein Problem weniger: In den Ostertagen erfuhren die Deutschen, wie sie der *Queen* zu begegnen haben, wenn sie am 18. Mai zum Staatsbesuch kommt. Der ‚Fachausschuß für Umgangsformen‘,[1] hat, mit Ratschlägen von Publizisten und Diplomaten unterstützt, eine Liste von ‚Selbstverständlichkeiten‘ zusammengestellt, die aus den Bundesrepublikanern ein Volk von Ladies und Gentlemen werden lassen.

Hans-Georg Schnitzer, wortgewandter Presseparlamentär[2] des Verbandes, konnte berichten, daß in den letzten Wochen ungezählte Briefe beim Fachausschuß eingegangen seien, in denen man um Auskunft darüber gebeten habe, wie man sich verhalten solle, wenn einem die Queen die Gunst ihres Anblicks schenke.

Nun, bei einem Staatsbesuch gibt es—sieht man von Frankreichs General einmal ab—kaum Zufälligkeiten. Das Protokoll regelt jede Bewegung. Deshalb war auch die Anfrage einer Lehrerin, was sie tun solle, wenn die Königin plötzlich in ihr Klassenzimmer käme, überflüssig. Die queenstreue Magisterin braucht ihr Gewissen nicht damit zu belasten, ob es angebracht sei, das Wort an Elisabeth zu richten. Überhaupt: Wir Deutschen haben angesichts des hohen Gastes überhaupt nichts zu sagen, wenn uns die Gunst der Stunde eine Begegnung mit der Monarchin einräumen sollte. Wir haben zu schweigen und zu warten, bis Majestät oder prinzlicher Gemahl uns die Ehre persönlicher Ansprache geben sollten.

Und daß sich ja niemand unterstehe, der Königin die Hand küssen zu wollen! So etwas tut man nicht. Allerdings braucht eine junge Dame, die der Königin vorgestellt wird, auch nicht unbedingt zu knicksen. Diese Geste zu vollführen ist heutzutage ihr überlassen.

Die Zaungäste des Staatsbesuches wollen jubeln, wenn Ihre Majestät huldvoll von Balkonen oder aus Kaleschen winkt. Aber wie jubelt man einer englischen Königin zu? Diese, für das nationale Prestige so ungeheuer wichtige Frage hat Deutschlands Takt-Experten unendlich lange beschäftigt. Schließlich gaben sie diese Empfehlung:

„Die Königin wird sich freuen, wenn sie in Deutschland herzlich begrüßt wird. Diese Herzlichkeit kann man durch Händeklatschen oder Winken zum Ausdruck bringen. Von Staatsbesuchen in anderen Ländern ist bekannt, daß dort die Königin auch gern mit dem Ruf ‚Queen Elisabeth!‘ empfangen wird. Infolgedessen wird ihr in Deutschland wohl der Ruf ‚Königin Elisabeth‘ Freude bereiten. Der Fachausschuß für Umgangsformen teilt selbstverständlich die Auffassung, das Wort ‚Heil‘ als Ausdruck des Jubels auszuschließen . . ."

Horst Hachmann

85. Tschüs, Tschau, Servus

Fasse dich kurz—der fürs Telephon geprägte Imperativ macht Schule, und ganz unmerklich erweist es sich, daß unsere Konventionen im Umgang mit den (Mit-)Menschen dehnbar sind und mancherlei Verzerrungen vertragen. Wer

‚Tschüs' sagt statt ‚Auf Wiedersehen, Frau Sowieso',
verstößt keineswegs mehr gegen die guten Sitten. Immerhin
ist der sich verbreitende Brauch salopper Grußformeln für
wert befunden worden, die Leute danach zu fragen. Die
Demoskopen,[1] die ihre Forschungen nach der Volksmeinung
gelegentlich auch solchen Nichtigkeiten widmen, teilen mit:
67 Prozent sagen, wenn sie ‚guten Bekannten' begegnen,
immer noch ‚Guten Tag', 21 Prozent ‚Grüß Gott', je fünf
Prozent ‚Servus' oder ‚Wie geht's?' und drei Prozent rufen
‚Hallo'. Der Rest grüßt offenbar nicht, denn er wußte keine
Antwort.

Beim Abschied sagt nur noch die Hälfte ‚Auf Wiedersehen', aber schon 22 Prozent rufen ‚Tschüs' oder ‚Tschau'.
Zehn Prozent wünschen ‚Mach's gut', je fünf Prozent sagen
‚Ade' und ‚Adieu' oder ‚B'hüt Gott' und ‚Grüß Gott'.
‚Servus' hört man bei vier Prozent, und je einer von hundert
sagt ‚Guten Tag', ‚Lebe wohl', die übrigen irgend etwas
anderes. Was, ist nicht angegeben.

Daß ‚Tschüs' vor allem in Norddeutschland, ‚Grüß
Gott', ‚Adieu' und ‚Servus' im Süden im Schwange sind,
das ist nicht neu, auch, daß junge Leute besonders gern
‚Hello' rufen und Tschau (vom italienischen Ciao). Aber
unbekannt war wohl, daß neben Landwirten besonders die
Beamten ‚Mach's gut' für schicklich halten.

M.S.

Aufsatz

Schreiben Sie einen humoristischen Essay.

Notes and Exercises

Notes have been provided for proper names of a more than ephemeral interest and some terms and expressions not easily found in average-size dictionaries: it is, however, suggested that students at this stage should start familiarizing themselves with works of reference other than bilingual dictionaries: a small-sized encyclopedia such as *Knaurs A–Z* or *Duden* and a mono-lingual dictionary such as *Brockhaus Sprachwörterbuch*, a German dictionary of synonyms such as Wehrle-Eggers' *Deutscher Wortschatz*, *Stilduden*, and a copy of Roget's *Thesaurus of English Words and Phrases* will be found to be indispensable aids in the search for information, linguistic usage and the right word.

1. Land ohne Hauptstadt

1 **Deutschland von oben zu vereinen** Attempts, following abortive revolutionary risings in 1848, to unite Germany were a failure: Frederick William IV of Prussia refused the Emperor's crown, offered by an all-German parliament—'von unten'. In 1871, however, the King of Prussia was proclaimed German Emperor by Bismarck—a unification imposed 'from above'. The phrase 'Revolution von oben und von unten' was originally coined by Friedrich von Schlegel (1772–1829).

aus verschiedenen Gründen Translate.
Translate into German: 'For this reason, for a reason unknown to me' (two ways: 'for a to me unknown reason', or use relative clause).

in der Regel Translate.
Find German synonyms for this phrase.

will man ein Land kennenlernen Translate.
Translate into German: 'If one wishes to get to know a person *(Mensch)*'.
Find a substitute for *dann* in the main clause following.

die Bundesrepublik There are eight words, phrases or abbreviations which may be used for 'Germany', past or present. Can you enumerate them?

die Beobachtung: *ansehen, zusehen, beobachten, betrachten* Use the appropriate verb in the following contexts: watching children at play, watching a TV show, studying a painting, studying animals at play.

in des Wortes eigentlicher Bedeutung Note pre-position of genitive and form of dative phrase. This construction gives the writing a literary flavour and should not be imitated except in the case of a standard phrase or where it is appropriate to the style of the passage, its *Stilebene*. Note other examples as they occur.

bestenfalls Translate.
Form by analogy: if the worst comes to the worst (use *schlimm*).

genausowenig The antonym of this is *genausosehr*.

aufhören: *stoppen, anhalten, halten, aufhören, fertig werden, zu Ende -en, stehenbleiben.* Use the appropriate verbs in the following contexts: the work is not finished, I must just finish this letter, the car stopped, the train stopped for 10 minutes at O., the rain stopped, you really must stop now, he stopped at the edge of the pavement, the policeman stopped the traffic.

2. Zwei Völker

zu einer Feststellung kommen Translate. Synonyms for this phrase: *feststellen, zu dem Schluß kommen.*

Es gibt zwei deutsche Völker Translate.
What is the significance of the phrase 'two nations' when applied to England?

den Krieg mitgemacht . . . erlebt Translate.
Mitmachen, erleben, erfahren : Which verb would you use in the following contexts: to have had many sad experiences *(viel Schlimmes)*, an interesting experience, to have lived through many good and bad experiences?

schon physisch . . . schon optisch Note the use of *schon.* Translate.
What is the equivalent of *optisch*, here?

zu tun haben mit Translate.
Translate into German: You will have me to deal with (use *bekommen* to render the future sense instead of *haben*).

vor wichtige Fragen gestellt werden Translate into English.

Prosperität Note all the *Fremdwörter*, i.e. words of obviously foreign origin, in this and the previous passage. Are the shades of meaning identical with their English versions?

Es bleibt zu hoffen Translate.
Translate into German: It is to be hoped; nothing was to be seen; it was to be expected.

3. Deutschland ist doch anders

1 **Baden-Württemberg** *Bundesland* in the S.W. (capital Stuttgart).
2 **IG-Metall** *Industrie-Gewerkschaft Metall,* the metal-workers' trade-union.

damals, als . . . Find a German synonym for *damals* in this sentence.
Make up two sentences to illustrate the difference between *damals* and *dann.*

IG-Metall Other names of German trade unions are: *IG Bergbau G. der Eisenbahner Deutschlands, IG Bau, Stein, Erden, G. Erziehung und Wissenschaft, Deutsche Postgewerkschaft.*
Find German equivalents for Amalgamated Engineering Union, National Union of Seamen, Electrical Trades Union.

dieses höfliche . . . Fischgrätenmuster Use these words as a pattern to describe your own country, or another you have visited, by altering adjectives and other attributes: *Dieses . . . aber . . . Land mit seinen . . . und . . . Menschen, . . . und alle in . . . mit . . . .*

den Tag herbeisehnen, an dem . . . Find three completions for a sentence beginning: *Ich sehne den Tag herbei, an dem . . .*

Eine mächtige . . . kontrolliert Note that in this lengthy word-cluster, there are three participial phrases, which in a pedantic *Papierdeutsch* would have to precede their head-word, *Organisation*. Re-write in this way, being careful to position the participles correctly, and compare the stylistic effect with that of the article.

4. Die öffentliche Meinung

1 **die politischen Wochenzeitungen** Apart from *Die Zeit*, one might mention *Rheinischer Merkur* (Koblenz), *Vorwärts* (Bad Godesberg), *Christ und Welt* (Stuttgart) and the *Time*-style *Der Spiegel* (Hamburg).

2 **die Tagespresse** The Federal Republic has more than 200 daily papers published in all major and many quite small centres. Many of these attempt a high standard of serious comment, especially on world affairs, and devote much space to cultural affairs as well as to sport and local matters. Lighter articles and fiction, especially in the week-end editions which appear on Saturdays, are often syndicated. Very often a town or district will be found to have two papers, broadly allied to the two major political parties.

3 **in den großen Tageszeitungen . . . Tageszeitungen mit der höchsten Auflage . . . ‚die Illustrierten'** Among the first are the *Frankfurter Allgemeine (FAZ)*, *Süddeutsche Zeitung* (Munich), *Stuttgarter Nachrichten*, *Die Welt* (Hamburg); the best-known among the second is *Bild-Zeitung* (Hamburg); among the third group *Stern* (Hamburg), *Kristall* (Hamburg) and *Neue Revue* (Cologne).

Ich möchte . . . eingehen Translate this clause into English.
Translate into German: I do not want to go into further details (supply 'about it'); he did not expand this any further (use perfect tense).

Presse, Funk, Fernsehen Translate into German: in the Press, on radio, on television (note that the preposition is *in* in every case, and the definite article is used).

ich habe den Eindruck gewonnen Find two other possible ways of introducing the following clause (one occurred in Passage 2).

wenn es darum geht Translate.
Find a synonymous clause.

wurden . . . geschildert Translate.
Rewrite: *Die Methoden wurden im Fernsehen geschildert*, replacing the verb by *beschreiben* and *berichten* (take care!)

An zweiter Stelle Translate into German: in the first place, lastly, here.

vielfältig, reichhaltig, achtenswert Translate. Find antonyms for these adjectives.

Translate: *einfältig, sorgfältig, eisenhaltig, liebenswert, beachtenswert.*

redigiert Translate.

Note and translate the expressions: *die Redaktion, der Chef-Redakteur, Briefe an die Redaktion.*

Note verbs in *-ieren* used in this passage. This suffix is very productive in verb-formation, as it permits the adoption of useful, often technical expressions from foreign roots. What is the meaning of *Sind Sie motorisiert?*

6. Hitler und seine Zeit

[1] **Das Dritte Reich** Term adopted by the National Socialists for Germany under their regime. The expression goes back to the Middle Ages and originally described an Utopian 'Golden Age' to come, which would last a thousand years; the Nazis reckoned the Holy Roman Empire which perished in 1806 as a consequence of Napoleon's triumphant victories, as the first *Reich*, and as the second, the national state founded after the conclusion of the Franco-German war in 1871, which lasted until the end of the First World War in 1918.

2 **bundesdeutsch** 'Federal German', adjective relating to the *Bundesrepublik.*

3 **Revolution von 1848** see Note p. 111.

4 **Weimar** The 'Weimar Republic' is the name by which the German republic of 1918 was known, as it was established by the *Nationalversammlung* which met in the little town hallowed by its associations with Goethe and his circle. It lasted until Hitler's rise to power in 1933.

5 **Hitler-Putsch** In 1923, Adolf Hitler and some of his associates, planning to overthrow the Bavarian government, staged an unsuccessful coup in Munich.

6 **Röhm, SA** Ernst Röhm, one of Hitler's earliest followers, became Chief of Staff of the *SA (Sturm-Abteilung)*, the armed brown-shirted storm-troopers, originally the Nazi leaders' private para-military guard. Röhm and other prominent Nazis were shot on Hitler's orders in a 'cleaning-up operation' in June 1934, a year after Hitler came to power.

7 **Präsident der gestorbenen Republik** Field-Marshal of the Imperial Army General Paul von Benckendorff und von Hindenburg was the last elected President of the Weimar Republic. As such he formally invested Hitler with the seals of office after the 1933 elections.

8 **Mädchen schwingen ... Arbeitskolonnen** references to compulsory sports in the Nazi *Bund deutscher Mädchen* and to the compulsory term of *Arbeitsdienst* during which young people had to work on road-building and on the land.

9 **Richter ... Hitler-Gruß** The independence of the judiciary was abolished by the Nazis.

10 **im gleichen Schritt und Tritt** A quotation from Uhland's *Ich hatt' einen Kameraden*, but a reference, too, to the Nazi term *Gleichschaltung*, i.e. Nazification.

11 **Österreich ... Sudetenland ... Prag** Austria and the Sudeten

province of Czechoslovakia were annexed to Germany in 1938, the rest of Czechoslovakia invaded in 1939.

12 **Ribbentrop and Molotow unterschreiben** In 1938, Germany's Foreign Minister Joachim von Ribbentrop signed a surprise pact of non-aggression and consultation with Russia, represented by its then Foreign Secretary.

13 **Rotterdam, Warschauer Getto** The bombing to destruction of the city of Rotterdam and the heroic stand of the doomed Jews in the Warsaw ghetto were two memorable events in the Second World War.

14 **Himmler** Heinrich Himmler, an important figure in the Nazi movement, became *Reichsführer* of the *SS (Schutzstaffel)*, the black-uniformed elite of Hitler's para-military organisations, head of the dreaded *Gestapo (Geheime Staats-Polizei)*, the secret police, Minister of the Interior, and Hitler's foremost aide in his policy of cruelty and extermination. He committed suicide in 1945.

7. Auch die Gerechtigkeit braucht ihre Zeit

1 **Frankfurter Auschwitz-Prozeß** Auschwitz was the site of one of the Nazis' extermination camps. Eighteen years after the fall of the Nazi regime, the Federal Republic was ready with its evidence to prosecute twenty of those responsible. The case lasted altogether 20 months.

2 **SS-Männer, Gestapo-Männer** see Note on Himmler, above.

3 **in Nürnberg** At the Nuremberg trials, 1945/6, at which 22 of the surviving Nazi leaders were tried for war crimes.

8. Suche nach den unbesungenen Helden

1 **den gelben Stern tragen** Among the restrictions imposed on Jews in Germany after 1933 was the order to make themselves immediately recognisable by wearing a large yellow star on their clothing, as they had had to do in certain places during the Middle Ages.

9. Fünfundvierzig Milliarden Wiedergutmachung

1 **Wiedergutmachung** Term used to describe Germany's payments of compensation to those who had suffered in health, prospects or property through the Nazi persecutions.

10. Von Zeit zu Zeit 1

1 **Freier Demokrat, Christ-Demokrat** *Abgeordneter,* or *Mitglied des Bundestags (MdB),* respectively, of the *FDP* and the *CDU,* then the governing parties.

2 **Konrad Adenauer** (1876–1967) Postwar Germany's first *Bundes-*

kanzler (1949–1963), a greatly respected figure in world politics, the 'architect of the Federal Republic'.

3 **die nächste Bundestagssitzung in Westberlin** As a sign of solidarity with the divided city, the *Bundestag* met there, instead of in Bonn, the usual venue.

4 **DGB** *Deutscher Gewerkschafts-Bund,* The (West) German Federation of Trade Unions.

5 **Siegerland** District on the river Sieg, a tributary of the middle Rhine, rich in mineral ores which were formerly mined extensively.

6 **AG** *Aktiengesellschaft,* (public) limited company, corporation. *Aktie* = share.

7 **Exmatrikulation** Leaving the university, here: expulsion. A student on joining the university is said to *sich immatrikulieren.*

8 **Ernst Jünger** (born 1895), author of *Auf den Marmorklippen* and other novels.

Mit einer Mahn-Rede . . . Parteitag Re-write this sentence in terms of political figures and parties of your own country.

Parteitag Translate.
What is the connection between the words *Parteitag, Bundestag, Landtag, der Tag,* 'diet' and 'The Diet of Worms'?

Trotz . . . Außenpolitik Re-write this sentence, replacing *außen–* by the designation of other ministerial spheres.

Nach dem Rücktritt . . . Mit einer Mahnrede . . . Trotz einer fiebrigen Erkältung Analyse the form of these sentences and consider their stylistic effect. Where does the emphasis lie? Find other sentences in this extract, and the final extract in this section, which have a similar pattern. This is also a common pattern for news-flashes on the radio.

Die indische Regierung . . . US-Hubschraubern . . . Die von Ranger . . . Translate these three sentences into English. What difficulty have they in common? What is the stylistic effect of this characteristic?

Neuwahlen, Nachwahl Collect political terms to be found in this extract, and compare them with their English equivalents.

11. Blitzkrieg im Nahen Osten

Blitzkrieg List terms relating to warfare from this passage.

Ägypten behauptet Re-write the rest of this paragraph in direct speech.

12. Zwanzig Jahre UN

20 Jahre UN Write a news item of not more than two sentences for a radio or television announcer (*Ansager*), summarizing this article. Bear in mind the stylistic considerations mentioned above. Use reported speech where necessary.

noch leidlich über die Runden gekommen, immer noch lieber,

weniger denn je Translate.
Use each phrase in a new context.
die Abrüstung Antonym: *die Aufrüstung*.

13. Die Einfuhren stiegen schneller
14. Wandel im Außenhandel
15. Bonn in der Finanzklemme

1 **Bundesfinanzminister Strauß** Franz Josef Strauß (born 1915), *CSU*, an important political figure in postwar Germany, after a stormy career as Minister of Defence (1956–62) and a period in the wilderness became Minister of Finance in the *Große Koalition* of 1966.

Die Einfuhren . . . Wandel . . . Bonn in der Finanzklemme Collect terms relating to economics *(die Wirtschaft)* and finance from the two news items and the diagram.

Ausfuhr-Einfuhr Write a news item on the *Außenhandel* of your own country during the last financial period.

Sozialhaushalt From *Bonn in der Finanzklemme,* collect terms relating to spheres of ministerial responsibility.

mittelfristig Translate.
Note expressions: *kurzfristig, langfristig.*

16. Tod für Taximörder?

1 **Taximörder** Germany was swept by a wave of disquiet at the recurrent cases in which taxi-drivers were held up by late-night fares for their takings.

2 **Adenauer** See Note p. 115f.

3 **Brentano** Heinrich von B., Minister for Foreign Affairs 1955–61.

4 **Bundeskanzler Erhard** Professor L. Erhard (born 1897), *CDU*, as Minister for Economic Affairs was largely responsible for postwar Germany's currency reform and the 'economic miracle' which followed. He briefly succeeded Dr. Adenauer to become West Germany's second postwar Chancellor.

5 **Carlo Schmid** Professor C.S. (born 1896), *SPD*, became *Bundesminister* in charge of *Länder* affairs in the *Große Koalition.*

6 **Innenminister Schröder** Gerhard S. (born 1910), in 1966 became Minister of Defence.

Abgeordnete Collect terms relating to politics from this news item.

der bürgerlichen Parteien Which political parties does this term refer to? What would be the equivalent in terms of the politics of your own country? Can you find an English equivalent for the expression?

die Todesstrafe Collect terms relating to this topic from the passage.

Carlo Schmid Try to paraphrase Professor Carlo Schmid's two quoted utterances in simpler language.

17. Von Zeit zu Zeit 2

1 **An der Schwelle des Wahlkampfes** The general election which took place on 19th September 1965.

2 **Ludwig Erhard** See Note p. 117.

3 **Kanzlerkandidat Willy Brandt** The then *Regierende Bürgermeister* of Berlin (born 1913) was the leader of the *SPD* opposition. He became Foreign Secretary in the *Große Koalition*.

4 **Berlins Regierender Bürgermeister** See preceding Note.

5 **die Berliner Mauer** The wall dividing Berlin was erected by the *DDR* in 1961, following an unprecedented wave of emigrants leaving East Germany through Berlin. See Section *Geteiltes Deutschland*.

6 **Passierscheinregelung** After several years during which West Berliners were forbidden to visit East Berlin for any reason whatsoever, the DDR government relented to the extent of issuing *Passierscheine* on the occasions of the high church festivals, to allow families and friends to be temporarily reunited.

7 **uk** *unabkömmlich* (military service).

8 **zu den Gebirgsjägern einrücken** to join the mountain troops.

Wahlkampflosung Invent German *Wahlkampflosungen* for the political parties in your country.

Kanzlerkandidat Willy Brandt English language newspapers usually preface German names by *Herr*. Collect examples of German usage from the news items and articles in this section. Then find German expressions to preface the names of: the Prime Minister, the Leader of the Opposition, the President of the US, the Secretary of the UN, the Leader of the Conservative Party, the Deputy Premier, the Chancellor of the Exchequer.

Berlins Regierender Bürgermeister Which other cities have a 'governing' mayor? What is the significance of the term?

wurde . . . empfangen News items frequently appear in the passive voice. Collect other examples from this passage, and this section. Write four news flashes on the day's news, using the passive voice.

18. Sind die Deutschen noch zu erkennen?

1 **Lodenmantel** The dark green weather-coat, made of hard-wearing water-resistant *Loden* cloth, a mixture of wool and linen, is still quite common, especially in Bavaria and Austria.

die Jugend Translate.
Find synonyms for this expression. What is its antonym? Note also: *ein Herr in den besten Jahren, ein älterer Herr, ein jüngerer Herr* all of which may mean 'middle-aged'.

wogegen Translate.
Find a synonym for this conjunction.

keineswegs Make a list of words and phrases of negation, to be used as synonyms for simple *nicht*.

Es ist schwierig . . . Summarize the argument of this passage in your own words, in one sentence.

19. Ein Student unter Berliner Arbeitern

1 **die Bild-Zeitung** See Note on p. 113.

2 **‚Kies'** (slang) money.

Ruhe gönnen Translate this phrase, and: *Er gönnt sich keine Ruhe; Na ja, der kann sich so was gönnen; Es war ihm nicht vergönnt, es noch zu erleben; Glauben Sie mir, ich gönne es Ihnen!* Make up German contexts for each phrase.

Die Wohnung enthielt List words and phrases relating to furnishing contained in this passage. Write a similar paragraph about a simply furnished home in your own country.

das höfliche Bemühen der Leute Collect noun-and-adjective combinations from this passage which relate to people's character, attitudes or behaviour.

Describe the attitude the writer evinces towards his host family. Choose quotations from the text to support your view.

ein ‚anständiger Kerl', Ganzheits-methode Define these terms in German.

20. Der Index der Lebenshaltungskosten

1 **Arbeitnehmerhaushalt** *Arbeitnehmer* (employee), *Arbeitgeber* (employer), terms used in law and economics.

Monatliche Verbrauchsausgaben Translate all the terms used in this diagram.

Write two German sentences summarizing the picture conveyed by it.

From statistical tables relating to your own country, make up a similar diagram, with the descriptions in German.

21. Was stimmt?

1 **Professor Hallsteins Brüsseler Kommission** The German ex-civil servant Professor Hallstein was the first President of the Commission of the *EWG* with its seat in Brussels.

2 **die Spannen** the profit margins.

nützen, der Verbraucher, frohlocken, Hausfrau, Familienvater, verteuern Find antonyms for these words.

Was stimmt? erfreulicherweise, nicht unrecht haben, die Konsumenten, realisieren Find synonyms for these words and phrases.

Konsumenten See Note on *Prosperität*, p. 112.

einmal . . . zum anderen Is this expression synonymous with *einerseits . . . ander(er)seits*? Write two examples, to illustrate the usage of both.

läßt sich feststellen Translate.
This phrase is equivalent to: *ist festzustellen*. Translate into German (using both patterns): it may be recognized, it cannot be denied (use *leugnen*), it is indescribable. With *lassen* only: it may be imagined *(denken)*; with *zu*+ infinitive only: it is not surprising *(verwundern)*.

Es ist hinzuzufügen The construction here has the force of 'must', 'ought'. Translate the clause beginning with *wenn* . . .

Es ist zu konstatieren See Note on redigiert, p. 114. Translate. Re-write, using form with *lassen*.

22. Marktplatz für Mütter und Kinder

1 **Tivoli** Here, Copenhagen's amusement park.
2 **Pommery** A marque of champagne.

Man nehme This expression does, in fact, usually introduce the ingredients of a cookery recipe, *Kochrezept*. The construction is continued where English uses imperatives: 'weigh', 'mix' etc. Write the German equivalent of a simple English cookery recipe, bearing in mind the need to use German terms for weights and measures.

Einzelgeschäfte Collect from this passage all the expressions relating to shops and shopping; translate them into English.

Parkplätze Collect all the expressions relating to traffic and communications.

Elbe-Einkaufszentrum Summarize briefly, in your own (German) words, advantages and drawbacks of this shopping-centre.

23. Fünfundsiebzig Jahre deutsche Gewerkschaften
24. Die Deutschen sind friedlich

Gewerkschaften List terms relating to trade unionism and labour relations from the two passages. See also *Sprachübung* on *IG Metall*, p. 112.

25. Handwerk auf goldenem Boden

Handwerk Write a sentence for each of the trades listed, describing the tradesman's occupation. Try to use a different verb in each case. For *machen*, use synonyms such as *verfertigen, erzeugen*.

auf goldenem Boden Define in German the meaning of the sayings: *Das Handwerk hat einen goldenen Boden; Morgenstund' hat Gold im Mund.*

26. Kastenmerkmale

Re-write this passage in terms of your own country: consider carefully where a foreigner might make the casual acquaintance of one of your countrymen, and whether the make of motor-car would equally serve as a distinguishing label.

die einen VW fahren Translate (not, here, drive!).

die sich einen Mercedes leisten können Translate into German: I'm sorry, not my class (use *sowas*, coll., for 'a thing like that'); in those days we could not afford holidays abroad.

27. Autofahrer-Partei in Hamburg

1 **am Stammtisch** The traditional institution of the 'club' table frequented daily by the *Stammgäste*, the 'regulars' of inn or beer-garden, where the ways of the world are discussed over one's favourite beverage.

2 **Ratsweinkeller** The *Ratskeller*, a hoary institution in many towns, is the important hostelry snugly ensconced in the cellars of the town hall, and naturally much frequented by the most influential citizens, the *Honoratioren*.

3 **ins Vereinsregister eintragen,** which made it into a legally *eingetragener Verein, e.V.,*—a frequently encountered abbreviation.

4 **PS** *Pferdestärken*: HP.

5 **die Fünf-Prozent-Kurve** According to the German system of limited proportional representation, no party obtaining less than 5% of second votes may be represented in the *Bundestag*.

jüngste Partei Translate.
Find two synonyms for the adverb *jüngst*, which has slightly bookish overtones.

Stammtisch Give a German definition for each of the following: *Stammtisch, Stammcafé, Stammbaum;* and an example of the use of *stammen.*

tagen Translate. See Note on *Parteitag*, p. 116.

rund, ebenfalls, es dauert sie, das Los, die Annonce, der Experte Find a synonym for each of these expressions.

Mit sieben Getreuen zog der Zahnarzt zum Amtsgericht *Getreue, ziehen* convey a flavour of medieval chivalry. The comic effect of this passage is mostly produced by the contrast between the solemn language and the down-to-earth plans described. Note, e.g. *auf Bundesebene operieren,* a typical phrase of *Beamtendeutsch.* Find other words and expressions which add to this effect.

Weltanschauung Try to find a good English equivalent.

hält nicht viel von Translate.
Make up another example using this expression.

werden noch auf sich warten lassen Translate. What is the force of *werden* in this sentence?

I

Wir müssen zusehen, daß. . . Find a good English equivalent for this phrase.
Translate: Mind you don't forget anything!

wie es sich . . . vorstellt Translate into German: Just how do you imagine (we/you can do) that? (use *eigentlich* for 'just': it follows *das*; omit phrase in brackets); I cannot imagine what it is all about.

28. Perpetuum Automobile

1 **Abschreibemöglichkeiten** tax-deductible expenses, *Spesen*, may be *abgeschrieben*, deducted, from taxable income. In Germany this includes travel expenses to and from work.

2 **TEE** *Trans-Europa-Express*, one of the fast intercontinental through trains, carrying only first-class coaches.

3 **Wolfsburg** near Lüneburg, where the German *Volkswagen*, *VW*, is manufactured.

4 **Parkhaus** multi-story garage.

Finanzamt, Pendler, Baustellen, Menschen am Steuer, mit Abschreibemöglichkeiten Find good English equivalents for these words and phrases.

Produkte deutscher Wertarbeit Here again (see Note on *Mit sieben Getreuen,* p. 121) the comic effect is created by the discrepancy between language and matter. Find two expressions of *Beamtendeutsch*, two taken from warfare, and two from journalese, in this passage.

29. Der Mann am Mast

1 **Struwwelpeter** Once enormously popular book of rhymed 'moral tales' for children. One of its characters is *Konrad*, whom his *Frau Mama* admonished with raised index finger for sucking his thumbs.

Unfall List terms relating to traffic and motoring contained in this passage and in Nr. 67.
Make a further list of German terms for common causes of traffic accidents (e.g. *Glatteis, linksabbiegen, falsch überholen* . . .).
Write a short news item describing a car crash at a city cross-roads.

30. Farbe bekennen

Farbe bekennen Synonym: *die Wahrheit gestehen*. A punning title.

Es lebe der Fortschritt! Translate.
Note that the phrase *es lebe* is invariable, no matter what gender follows. Translate into German: God save the Queen! Let us toast the future!

das Farbfernsehen Make a list of broadcasting and television terms used in this article. See also Nrs. 78 and 79.

31. Bücherliste aus dem Computer

1 **GmbH** *Gesellschaft mit beschränkter Haftung:* Limited Company (Ltd.)

Make a list of terms relating to computer technology contained in this article.

32. Weltraumrausch

1 **flachsig** (coll.) flat, commonplace.

Weltraumrausch Make a list of terms relating to space travel and technology contained in this news item.

am Fernsehschirm miterleben, Wettlauf zum Mond, hinter sich lassen, diese Scharte auswetzen, der Ehrgeiz packte sie, das Unterfangen glückte nur halbwegs, man geizt nicht mit Anerkennung, kostspielige Rivalität Translate these phrases.

33. Nur einen falschen Knopf gedrückt . . .

Schlagzeilen liefern Translate this phrase, and the following: **Zum Tagesgespräch werden, der Alltag, ausfallen, Panne, zusammenbrechen, Stromnetz, erschöpft, ihnen ging die Puste aus, nicht zu fassen.**
Use each of these expressions in a new context.

Invent a news item on a similarly disastrous happening.

34. Barbara bittet

1 This is a regular feature on the 'letters to the editor' page.

Describe Herr H.K.'s conversation with the helpers in the Berlin office of *Die Zeit*. Use dialogue as well as description and narration.

35. Das Tor ging auf

1 **Passierscheinstellen** See note 6 on p. 118.
2 **Fluchthelfer** One actively engaged in assisting East Germans to flee to the West.

36. S-Bahnhof Friedrichstrasse

1 **Wenn . . . erfinden** Allusion to Voltaire's saying about God.
2 **die S-Bahn** *Stadtbahn:* metropolitan railway.

List the expressions which contribute to the feeling of helplessness and hopelessness which this extract conveys.

37. Meine Tante Else

1 **Brandenburg** Part of the *DDR* surrounding Berlin, formerly a province, not now a political unit.

2 **Ulbricht** Walter U. (born 1893), First Secretary of the Central Committee of the *SED* (*DDR*).

3 **Stanniol** Aluminium foil, silver paper.

4 **die Wehrmacht** The German fighting forces, 1935–45.

5 **Gesamtdeutsches Ministerium** of the *BRD*, concerned with questions of inter-German relations.

6 **Greifswald** Ancient university town near the Baltic.

7 **Leipziger Messe** The important annual industrial fair.

8 **in Teufels Küche kommen** (slang) to get into trouble.

Hörerpost List terms relating to radio and television contained in this article.

gesamtdeutsche Untertöne Make a list of terms relating to the two Germanies and the political tension between them. Translate them.

38. Freiburger Studenten in der DDR

1 **TU** *Technische Universität.*

2 **FDJ** *Freie Deutsche Jugend:* communist youth organisation *(DDR).*

3 **Havemann** Professor Robert H., a convinced communist, was deprived of his university chair at the (East) Berlin Humboldt-University, presumably because of his outspoken criticisms.

Make a list of terms describing activities carried out by a visiting delegation.

39. Hochzeit in einer LPG

1 **LPG** *Landwirtschaftliche Produktions-Genossenschaft:* collective farm *(DDR).*

Hochzeit in einer LPG Make lists of expressions relating to
(a) agriculture   (b) wedding customs   (c) Communist institutions.

zu (Ur)großmutters Zeiten a standard phrase. Translate.

Es wurde gut gegessen Translate.
Note this use of the passive of intransitive verbs, to describe a general activity.

Translate into German: There was dancing after supper (Begin with this phrase); people laughed and made jokes *(scherzen).*

Wer Licht anzündete What is the force of *wer* in this clause? Translate: People who do not go to bed early find it hard to get up; Anyone who has experienced this *(erleben,* supply *einmal),* will never forget it.

der Hof Find German synonyms or near-synonyms for this word.

40. Die deutsche Frage

List terms relating (a) to politics in general (b) to German politics, contained in this passage.

41. Wahlen in der Nachbarschaft

1 **Prognosen für die Bundestagswahl** This article appeared in May 1965, four months before the German elections and ten months before the British general election which resulted in an increased Labour majority.

Wahlen List terms relating to politics contained in this passage.

Prognosen ableiten, aufmerksam verfolgen, nicht ungern sehen, eine Umfrage ergab, mit Genugtuung registrieren, knapp siegen, Altbundeskanzler, den Regierungschef stellen, die Mehrheit einbüßen Translate these expressions.

42. Ein Cowboy als Präsident?

ein Mann einfacher Herkunft Find other expressions in this article which underline this point.

von des Gedankens Blässe angekränkelt From which Shakespearean quotation does this derive?

ein waschechter Washingtoner Adj. often used with nouns of nationality. Translate.

43. Gewissensforschung in Washington

Die große Debatte List terms relating to political affairs from this passage.

Furore machen, Beifall eintragen, einen Brandstifter zum Feuerwehrmann ernennen, auf den Versuch hinauslaufen, davon absehen, sich auf ein Experiment einlassen, sie gehen davon aus, die Frage ist nicht geklärt Translate.

44. Im Westen nichts Neues

Politik List terms relating to (a) politics in general (b) European politics, contained in this article.

nichts wesentlich Neues, klar hervortreten lassen, das gilt auch für, zeitgemäß, unvereinbar, die Verantwortung auf sich nehmen, Entscheidungen treffen, unerläßlich, sich halten an, die Gefahr abwenden. Translate.

45. Erziehung zum Schlaukopf

nichtsdestoweniger Find a synonym.

die Erziehung hierzulande List terms relating to (a) education (b) manners (c) social life (d) food and eating.

hierzulande Translate. Find a synonym. Translate into German: nowadays.

hübsch der Ordnung nach Translate. Note this use of *hübsch*. Translate: *hübsch kalt*.

zu allererst Translate. Find a synonym. Form by analogy: lastly. Note the synonymous phrase: *zu guterletzt*.

gebildete Lente, nach etwas klingen, gut im Ohr liegen, mit etwas versehen, sich etwas zulegen, vor Gesundheit strotzen Translate.

Der Spatz in der Hand ... Find English equivalents for the proverbial sayings in this paragraph.

46. Der Besuch der Königin

sind ... empfangen worden List all the perfect tenses used in this article. Re-write the sentences concerned in the preterite: compare the two lists. What is the effect conveyed (a) by the use of the perfect, as here? (b) by the use of the preterite?

bei aller Kühle What is the force of *bei* in this and the subsequent phrases? Note a similar use in expressions such as: ... *dabei ist er noch nicht mal achtzehn!*

mag es ... This is a convenient way to render English 'however ... (it may be)', e.g.: *Mag er auch noch so wohlhabend sein, ...* Note that the following main clause may either begin with *so, (... so finde ich ihn doch ...)* or begin with the subject *(... ich finde ihn doch ...)*, or indeed any other part of the clause. Where is the subject in the main clause following *Mag es rührend ...* in the example? What is the force of this position? (See *Nach dem Rücktritt*, p. 116.)

47. Treibhaus der Traditionen

die gnädige Rede vom Thron List words and expressions relating to English politics and institutions. Compare with terms relating to German politics (s. especially Section 3).

im besten Alter, nicht selten, es geht darum, längst Translate. Find a synonym for each phrase. Use each of the original phrases in a different example.

im Grunde, den Vorzug geben, das schlagendste Beispiel, verkörpern, so gut wie keine, ob sie will oder nicht Find good English equivalents for these words and phrases.

Treibhaus der Traditionen Summarize the argument of this article in one (German) sentence, the examples quoted in two more.

48. Schwarzer Sand im Zucker der Weißen

Wenn alle . . . verließen, so gäbe es . . . This paragraph is wholly written in the subjunctive of condition. Compose a paragraph of equal length and pattern, describing what would happen, if married women with children—or indeed all women—were to cease to work outside the home. (Note the different ways in which condition is expressed.)

Randerscheinung, notwendiger Faktor, nicht gerade, zu ihrer Beliebtheit beigetragen, gegenwärtig, nicht auf den letzten Mann genau, Registrierungszwang, es kommt nicht so genau darauf an Translate into English, taking care to find good idiomatic renderings.

Einwanderer-Problem Note words and phrases specifically relating to this topic from this article.

Was die Einwanderung zum Problem macht . . . Note the preponderance of nouns, particularly abstract nouns, in this sentence. Find other examples of this stylistic feature in this article. Translate the sentences you have found into English, taking care to find idiomatic renderings.

hätte es ein Farbigenproblem in England nie gegeben Summarize the factors which, in the writer's opinion, have brought about and aggravated this problem.

Schaffner, Briefträger . . . Note this list of occupations,—not all of them menial, of course. Make separate lists, in German, of names for manual occupations, skilled and unskilled, clerical and similar occupations, professional workers; and of occupations in industry, distributive trades, and services.

Sie verdingten sich Find a synonym for this expression, and for: **es ·hapert damit, wer es schafft, Arbeitsausstände, Rechtsextremist.**

49. Staatsstudenten und Privatschüler

1 **zur Existenzfrage machen** To make sth. a condition of employment.

Note terms relating to education contained in this article. Supplement them by further expressions from your study of subsequent articles in this section.

Einheitsschule—Gesamtschule What is the English term for this type of school? the American?

Einheitsschule, Eintopf, Einerlei, Einheitsbrei Try to find English terms for these expressions which convey the shades of meaning the phrase *psychologisch falsch* implies.

Realschule, Realgymnasium, humanistisches Gymnasium Explain, in German, the difference between these German school types.

Jetzt verzichtet man auf dieses Wort Find synonymous expressions for this phrase, and: **werbepsychologisch falsch, als manche Schulweisheit sich träumen läßt, vertretbare Elternwünsche, sich etwas kosten lassen, ich kann es nicht bestätigt finden.**

auf Mißtrauen stoßen, Auswege nutzen Certain German nouns seem to demand a characteristic verb: Which verbs are almost invariably coupled with *Verbrechen, Urteil, Bedingung, Beruf, Sport?* can you think of other examples?

50. Ein englisches Modell für die Schule der Zukunft.

Grammar Schools Give the approximate German equivalents for the English terms: primary school, secondary school, grammar school, secondary modern school, comprehensive school, technical school, Public School; and for the American terms public school, junior and senior high school, college. Describe each of these briefly in German, and point out differences from their approximate German equivalents.

um die Existenz bangen Translate this phrase and the following: **es kommt zu Demonstrationen, sich auf die Dauer durchsetzen, beibehalten, eine seinen Anlagen entsprechende Ausbildung, im Kindesalter, gerecht werden, Leistungen, am falschen Fleck sitzen, alle Begabungsreserven ausschöpfen, besonderen Wert legen, der ungeheure Bildungsoptimismus, die Experimentierfreudigkeit.**
Use six of these in new contexts.

51. Assistentin an einer englischen Schule

The author points, sometimes obliquely, to several features which in her opinion make the English school at which she taught superior to German educational institutions: make two lists of terms she uses to convey her approbation of the one, and unfavourable references to the other.

52. Deutsche Abiturienten sind zu alt

1 **Abiturienten** Students about to sit for their senior school-leaving examination, *das Abitur.*

2 **Oberprimen** pl. of *Oberprima,* highest form in a *höhere Schule,* attended by *Oberprimaner.*

3 **Herbstbeginn** Schools in Austria and in Bavaria always followed the common pattern of starting the school year in the autumn, while those in the former Prussian territories started and ended the school year at Easter. A uniform September start has, however, been agreed on and is gradually being introduced everywhere.

Während sich . . . Man wagt es nicht . . . Expand each of these sentences into a paragraph, restating their arguments simply in your own (German) words.

53. Studienrätliches

1 **Studienrat** The title conferred on teachers with permanent appointments to a *Höhere Schule.*

alles Studienrätliche Make a list of adjectives and descriptive expressions which might conjure up the image of *studienrätlich*.
Write a short description of a 'typical' *Studienrat*.

54. Die Wandlung einer Universität
55. Reform oder Revolution?

1 **Klausur(arbeit)** University examination of several hours' duration during which students are not permitted to leave the examination room.

die deutschen Hochschulen Note terms and phrases relating to universities and higher education from this article.

Hochschule, die Ansprüche von morgen, der innere Zusammenbruch, das Heft aus der Hand nehmen, dem reinen Gedanken huldigen, in der Lehre wie in der Forschung, Schlüsselberufe, Kommilitonen, Akademiker, Klausur, Abbrecher Define or explain these terms in German in your own words.

Summarize the arguments of the three sections of this extract.

56. Jung gefreit, besser studiert

1 **Jung gefreit,** *bald gereut,* concludes the old proverb, to which Pastor Leudesdorff here writes a new commentary.
2 **Assessor, Doktor** academic degrees.

Die Frühehe, im nichtstudentischen Bereich, schief ansehen, ausgelernt, examensreif, sich Torheiten leisten dürfen, Klischeevorstellung, mit zweierlei Maß messen, die Mobilisierung aller Bildungsreserven, sich einen Stil schaffen Define or explain these expressions in your own words in German.

57. Der Knabe Arzt, das Mädchen Krankenschwester

1 **Reifeprüfung** = *Abitur.* See Note p. 128.
2 **Abiturienten** See Note p. 128.
3 **mittlere Reife** Certificate obtainable after 10 years' schooling on leaving the *Mittelschule*—in distinction to the *Reifeprüfung* to be taken at the end of 9 years in the *Höhere Schule*.

4 **Entnazifizierung** de-Nazification, policy of screening carried out by the Allied Control Commission in Germany from 1946.
Make a list of (usually) feminine occupations; compare it with a list of masculine occupations, and with those that have traditionally been filled by members of both sexes.

Meine Tochter braucht die Reifeprüfung nicht zu machen Summarize the arguments for and against quoted in this article, employing the expressions here used.

Hand anlegen Look up *Hand* in *Stilduden* or one of the bigger dictionaries: copy out metaphorical expressions using this word; and write short paragraphs employing each phase in context.

58. Warum sind Halbstarke halbstark?
59. Unter Gammlern und Trampern

1 **Halbstarke** Term used for the German manifestations of the anarchic, non-conformist youth which made its various appearances in post-war Europe and America. Other terms used are *Provos*, chiefly in the Netherlands, where the movement is associated with non-participation and peaceful resistance, *Gammler* and *Beatnik*.

2 **trampen** to hitch-hike.

3 **koksen** to take *Koks* (cocaine), **Kiff** hashish, **Aufputschmittel** stimulants, **Schnorren** begging one's way.

Halbstarke Note words and expressions used in the article and the letter to describe youthful non-conformists and their activities.

eigentümliche gesellschaftliche Gepflogenheiten, seelisch verkorkst, stures Benehmen, er spielte Provo, schlampig, er will nicht bevormundet sein, scheut prinzipiell, kurz angebunden, er pfeift darauf, sie lassen sich gern auf die Straße holen, Krach ist ihr Ziel, trampen Define or explain in your own (German) words these expressions.

60. Kur und Ferienparadies

Note words and expressions used in these advertisements describing the special attractions offered. Summarize the various types of holidays on offer. Compare demands made by Germans, judging by these advertisements, with those of your compatriots.

61. Zwanzig Millionen Deutsche machen eine Ferienreise

üben die größte Anziehungskraft aus Translate this expression and: **Reise-Unternehmen, Besichtigungs- und Studien-Reisen, Hobby-Reisen, eine Sache der Mittel, die grauen Betonmetropolen.**

20 Millionen Summarize the argument of this article in two sentences.

62. Notizen für Reisende

1 **ostfriesisch** *die o. Inseln* are a chain of North Sea islands, off the Lower Saxony coast.

2 **trampen, Autostopp** hitch-hiking.

Leihfahrräder, Liegewagen, einheitlich festgesetzt, Arbeitgeber, Arbeitnehmer, Urlaubsgeld, Groschenblatt, Studienunterstützung, Anstoß nehmen Define or explain these terms in your own (German) words.

Describe the *Urlaubsuniform* of your own compatriots and those of other countries' tourists.

63. Urlaub von der Stange und nach Maß

1 **von der Stange . . . nach Maß** expressions taken from outfitting: 'ready-made' and 'made-to-measure'.

2 **das Gros** (pronounced as in French) the majority.

etwas springen lassen, nicht unzeitgemäß, Schusters Rappen, im großen Stil, bespitzelt, Devisenstrom, etwas einbringen, Broterwerb, Beschäftigungstherapie Translate.

64. Ein Oktober wie in Cannes

Summarize, in not more than half-a-dozen German sentences, the argument of this article.

das gemäßigte Klima Note words and expressions descriptive of England.

deutsche Touristen Note words and expressions relating to travel and holidays, used in this article.

Auch wer . . . Kontakt sucht Re-write this paragraph, giving the tourist's view of *Germans* at home.

65. Fußballsport zwischen Idealismus und Materialismus

1 **die Borussen** members of the *Borussia* team.

Summarise, in not more than four (German) sentences, the argument of this article.

Define in German the attitude the writer seems to take towards the *Fußballspieler* he describes. Quote from the article to support your view.

66. Wer ist der Größte?

1 **Twen-Alter** Germans speak of *der Twen* (there is even a magazine called *Twen*) by analogy with 'Teen'(ager) to describe a person in his twenties.

weltbester Sportler Note words and expressions relating to sport from this article.

krähen, zum geflügelten Wort werden, herausposaunen, ferner liefen, im Twen-Alter, Fabelzeit, am besten wegkommen, versteht sich, Tennis-As Define or explain these terms in your own (German) words.

67. Jedes Jahr fährt er vierzig Autos

Der Motor-Journalist Note words and expressions relating to motoring and traffic used in this and the following article. See also Nrs. 28 and 29.

Nur 60 Stundenkilometer waren gestattet Describe (in German) German and international traffic signs and their significance.

englische Nummer Write a paragraph describing the impression made on other road-users by a *German* driver.

68. Was ist ein Sportwagen?

Summarize the argument of this article in one sentence.

rund 120, Betonpiste, Katzenköpfe, mit Akribie, robust, preiswert, wenn man für das Auto arbeitet Define or explain in your own (German) words the meaning of these terms.

69. Seller-Teller

1 **Seller-Teller** phrase coined by *Die Zeit* for the week's list of best-selling books. Note that this particular list contains three translations.

Make a list of five recent English or American books you consider worth translating: translate their titles into German and summarize their contents.

70. Ist das Leichte gleich verächtlich?

1 **der verwaiste Thron von Weimar** Where Goethe, Germany's 'poet-prince', had 'ruled' until his death in 1832.

2 **Das Land der Griechen mit der Seele suchend** was the title Anselm Feuerbach (1829–80) gave to his immensely popular painting of Iphigenia in exile, prints of which at one time graced every German home aspiring to 'culture': it is a quotation from Goethe's drama.

3 **Elfriede Marlitt, Hedwig Courts-Mahler, (Ludwig) Ganghofer, Karl May** All best-selling writers of the late 19th and early 20th centuries: the two ladies wrote sugary sentimental love-stories, Ludwig Ganghofer village tales, Karl May (who had an astonishing revival recently) a vast quantity of adventure stores about hunters and Red Indians.

Unterhaltungsliteratur List terms relating to writing and authorship contained in this article.

Schriftsteller, *Dichter, Romancier, Literat, Autor, Verfasser, Poet, Erzähler, Romanschriftsteller, Dramatiker, Lyriker* Use each of these in context to show shades of meaning.

einem Bedürfnis entgegenkommen, geradezu unsinnig, abwegig, seit altersher, nichts liegt mir ferner, herziehen über, für den täglichen Bedarf sorgen, auf die Dauer, von . . . ganz zu schweigen Find good English equivalents for these expressions.

71. Subventionierte Freiheit des Theaters

1 **Land des Lächelns, Die lustige Witwe** Two popular and tuneful operettas by the Austrian composer Franz Lehar (1870–1948).

2 **Miete A 3** Example of an *Abonnement* (subscription), as offered by all German publicly run theatres and taken out by a great many regular theatre-goers.

Theater Collect words and expressions relating to stage and theatregoing from this article, and the following two notes on Brecht and *Mutter Courage*.

Subventionen, aus öffentlichen Mitteln, die Mittel der öffentlichen Hand, auf dem Steuerumweg, kraß ausgedrückt, lebensfähig, den Geldhahn zudrehen, das getrübte Freiheitsverhältnis, er dankt gar nicht daran, leicht abzusehen, gnadenlos, die Konsequenzen ziehen: Find appropriate English equivalents for these expressions.

Subventionierte Freiheit Summarize the argument of this article in one sentence.

72. Brecht galore

1 **Brecht** Bertolt Brecht (1898–1956), eminent German playwright and lyrical poet, author of *Mutter Courage, Der gute Mensch von Sezuan* and other plays, went into exile in 1933 and after his return in 1948 settled in East Berlin.

2 **Berliner Ensemble** The company created and originally directed by Brecht in (East) Berlin; after the dramatist's death it was directed by his widow, the actress Helene Weigel.

73. Film

1 **Mutter Courage** the central figure of this play is a camp-follower of the Thirty Years' War (1618–48). This magnificent role was created by Helene Weigel.

2 **Berliner Ensemble** see Note above.

es spielen Note this common turn of phrase, used also in radio announcements: *„Sie hörten soeben Mozarts Ouvertüre zu „Die Hochzeit des Figaro". Es spielte das Orchester des Nordwestdeutschen Rundfunks unter der Leitung von . . ."*
Compose the radio or TV announcements introducing and signing off a musical programme of your own choice. See also Nrs. 10, 17 and 74–77.

74. Deutsche Oper

Nun aber hatte . . . Translate this paragraph.

Vuerzaiht Choose a brief speech or exchange from Shakespeare or one of the 18th century English playwrights, and write it down 'phonetically', as a German actor might pronounce the English.

75. Lydia Schierning empfiehlt Schallplatten

1 **die ‚schwarze Venus‘ von Bayreuth** The American Negro singer Grace Bumbry sang the part of Venus in Richard Wagner's *Tannhäuser* during the Bayreuth Wagner-Festival.

Klavier-Trio B-Dur Make lists of (a) musical instruments, (b) musical forms, (c) the names of musical notes and scales in German.

76. Gesellschaftskritik mit Musik

1 **Flatternde Wimpel . . . herzallerliebster Schatz** The phrases quoted in this paragraph are snatches from the *Volkslieder* which were kept alive in Germany by the schools and by the popularity of *Wandern* until fairly recently; it was partly the exaggerations of the folk-cult practised by the Nazis, and perhaps the progressive replacement of *Schusters Rappen* by ‚*Autowandern*‘ that dealt the public unself-conscious chorus-singing of *Volkslieder* its death-blow—though there might be surprises in store for those passing the Lorelei rock on a Rhinesteamer!

Folksong; Volkslied Define or explain these two terms in German.

We shall overcome Try to find German equivalents for the English expressions used in the text.

Kühler Grund und herzallerliebster Schatz Try your hand at translating a well-known German *Volkslied* into an English version, singable to the original tune.

77. Jazz-Gottesdienst in Düsseldorf

1 **Himmelfahrtsfrohlocken** the rejoicing on the occasion of the Church festival of *Christi Himmelfahrt* (Ascension Day).

2 **Kirchenrat** honorific title used in the *Evangelische Kirche*.

Gottesdienst List terms relating to church and church services from this article.

Lobe den Herrn Compare the German and English versions of this or other well-known hymns (e.g. *Ein' feste Burg* . . .)

78. Der Hörfunk im Zeitalter des Fernsehens

1 **Borchert** Wolfgang B., (1921–47), who died of the consequences of his war-wounds, created a powerful image of the *Heimkehrer,* the German soldier returning from war and prisoner-of-war camp, in *Draußen vor der Tür.*

2 **Eich** Günter E. (born 1907), has won wide acclaim with his poetic *Hörspiele.*

Summarize briefly, in German, the argument of this article.

der Rundfunk, das Fernsehen List words and expressions relating to radio and television from this and the following article. See also Nrs. 30 and 37.

Der Hörfunk ist heute in Gefahr . . . Translate this paragraph.

Write an outline plan for a parallel essay to this article on *Die Bühne im Zeitalter des Films.*

79. Fernsehen

1 **Vorspann** 'trailer', 'credits'.

Er hat eine kleine, verplüschte Wohnung Following the example of the first paragraph of this review, write a 'portrait' of some other well-known fictional character.

Das Kriminalstück ist eine bürgerliche Gattung Explain the argument of this paragraph in your own (German) words.

80. Ausstellung Lovis Corinth

List terms relating to the graphic arts contained in this review.

1 **Lovis Corinth** German Impressionist painter (1858–1925).

Über den Umgang mit Menschen

1 **Über den Umgang mit Menschen** is the title of a famous and much re-printed book by Adolf Friedrich von Knigge (1752–96), a primer both on etiquette and on 'how to make friends and influence people'.

81. Deutschlandreise mit Dolmetscher

1 **die Mauer** i.e. *die Berliner Mauer.*

82. Schlafsack für deutsche Studenten

1 **Kommilitonen, Studentenbude** fellow students, 'digs' (slang).

84. Über den Umgang mit der Queen

1 **Fachausschuß für Umgangsformen** protocol office.
2 **Presseparlamentär** public relations officer.

85. Tschüs, Tschau, Servus

1 **Demoskopen** conductors of public opinion poll.

Baillière's Study Skills
for Nurses

20 Cavendish Square
London W1M 0AB
Tel: 0171 872 0840

ROYAL
COLLEGE OF
NURSING

Dear Nursing Student

As a nursing student, you need the support of an organisation
that understands the everyday problems and dilemmas of
nursing students. The Royal College of Nursing is run by nurses,
for nurses, so we share the same concerns and anxieties.

We provide exceptional support, advice and representation on
everything from academic problems to personal crises. You can
access our free personal counselling and advisory service,
wherever you are in the UK. From 1998, members will also have
access to a 24 hour advice and information service for the cost
of a local telephone call.

As a member, you enjoy the best professional indemnity
insurance available – up to £3 million worldwide.

You can get excellent discounts of up to 10% on famous high
street brand names like Waterstones books, Next, and Our Price
Records, and on key nursing textbooks from Baillière Tindall.
Everything from motor to personal insurance is available at an
affordable price from RCN Membership Services.

The RCN's wide range of leaflets on the whole range of
professional and work related issues are free to members.
You can even get information on nursing abroad from the RCN.

You can join any of the RCN professional groups for free. These
are networks of members interested in every field of nursing,
midwifery and health visiting, from paediatric nursing to ethics.

You also gain automatic membership of the RCN Association of
Nursing Students, a powerful voice lobbying for your rights.
Through the Association, nursing students have two places on
RCN Council, to raise the concerns of nursing students at the
highest level. You also have a chance of a free place at the
annual nursing student conference and RCN Congress plus
educational awards and your own free magazine, *No Limits*.

RCN membership is an absolute bargain for nursing students:
£10 a year or only 84 pence a month if you pay by direct debit.
Call freephone **0800 590032** any time for an application form.

Yours sincerely

Christine Hancock

General Secretary

Baillière's Study Skills for Nurses

Edited by
Sian Maslin-Prothero

RN RM Dip N (Lond) Cert Ed MSc
Department of Nursing and Midwifery Studies
Medical School
Queen's Medical Centre
Nottingham NG7 2UH
UK

Baillière Tindall
PUBLISHED IN ASSOCIATION WITH THE RCN

London · Philadelphia · Toronto
Sydney · Tokyo

Baillière Tindall

24–28 Oval Road
London NW1 7DX

The Curtis Center
Independence Square West
Philadelphia, PA 19106–3399, USA

Harcourt Brace & Company
55 Horner Avenue
Toronto, Ontario, M8Z 3X6, Canada

Harcourt Brace & Company, Australia
30–52 Smidmore Street
Marrickville
NSW 2204, Australia

Harcourt Brace & Company, Japan
Ichibancho Central Building
22–1 Ichibancho
Chiyoda-ku, Tokyo 102, Japan

A catalogue record for this book is available from the British Library

ISBN 0–7020–1979–8

Typeset by J&L Composition Ltd, Filey, North Yorkshire
Printed and bound in Great Britain by
WBC Book Manufacturers, Bridgend, Mid Glamorgan

Contents

Section III **Appendices**

Acknowledgements

I would like to thank Jacqueline Curthoys who encouraged me to submit the proposal; and for her continuing support and encouragement throughout the development of the book. I am grateful to the contributors who have provided their knowledge and expertise to make this a very special and different study skills text.

My family have played a large part in nurturing this project. Special thanks go to Paul, who helped to compile the appendices, and proof read my contributions. Charlotte and Jack would never forgive me if they didn't get a mention.

Finally this book is dedicated to Peggy and Mansell who fostered my desire to be a lifelong learner.

Contributors

Elizabeth Anne Girot MN Dip RM Dip N Ed RNT RN RM
Lecturer
Advanced Nursing Studies
Faculty of Health and Social Care
University of the West of England

Matthew Godsell BA (Hons) MEd RNMH PGCE RNT
Lecturer
Faculty of Health and Social Care
University of the West of England

Kym Martindale BA (Hons) PG Dip Lib ALA PG Cert
F/H/AE MA
Research Student in English
Cheltenham and Gloucester College of
Higher Education

Sian Maslin-Prothero RN RM Dip N (Lond) Cert Ed MSc
Lecturer
Department of Nursing and Midwifery
Medical School
Queen's Medical Centre
Nottingham

Abigail Masterson MN BSc RGN PGCEA
Lecturer
School for Policy Studies
University of Bristol

Janscí Sketchley-Kaye RGN RNT Cert Ed (FE)
Lecturer
Faculty of Health and Social Care
University of the West of England

Preface: Why Learning Skills are Important

Introduction

This preface is an introduction not only to the book, but also to being a student of nursing. For some of you, it will be read prior to commencing your initial pre-registration nursing course, whilst others will be undertaking a post-registration course. For whatever reason, you have decided that through study you will be able to achieve some positive change in your life. Certain practices can assist you as a student to be a successful learner. Even people who have been successful learners in the past, and are confident, can benefit from updating their learning skills.

Why do you need this book?

There are a number of reasons why I chose to compile this book. These arose from my experiences as a nurse, a learner and as a teacher. The National Health Service (NHS) has evolved and changed since its inception in 1948; and as healthcare professionals we work in an environment of rapid change, where the expectation is that we can respond to these various and changing requirements. This requires strong core skills, and the right 'mind-set' where the individual is able to identify possibilities and solutions, and change and adapt to meet new challenges.

Professional education

There is a recognition of the 'half-life concept' for professional competence, that is the period of time during which half the contents of a course become obsolete. What is learned today is only valid for a few years. The estimated half-life for a nursing course is less than 5 years. Through ongoing personal and professional development we can reduce half-life obsolescence. This need for updating ourselves as nurses has been formalised with the introduction of Post-Registration Education and Practice (PREP).

Updating our knowledge and skills is now obligatory. To maintain professional registration with the United Kingdom Central Council for Nursing, Midwifery and Health Visiting

See
Appendix B

(UKCC), nurses must be able to demonstrate that they are competent to practice. This can be demonstrated by completing at least 5 days of study activity during the previous 3 years, and recording this in a personal professional profile.

Higher education

Both pre- and post-registration nurse education has been moving from schools of nursing into higher education institutions. Nursing courses have developed from certificate level to diploma and degree level (and beyond to master degree and doctoral degree courses). There is an expectation that we have sound knowledge rooted in evidence-based practice. This can be achieved through continued professional development.

Why learning skills are important for nurses

From personal experience I know how important it is to have skills and strategies which can be used when undertaking a course. These will prepare you for the change you experience through study, and identify strategies to help you, not only for this course, but also for the rest of your life: such as why do I want to do this course; how will it affect my life; what do I (and others) need to do in order that I get the most from the course. This includes strategies to enable you to successfully achieve your aim of completing any course.

Lifelong learning skills

There is a need to promote independent activities which foster skills for lifelong learning. As learners, you need to develop the ability to identify a need, access and retrieve information, filter it for quality and use it to answer a specific problem. This book aims to equip you with these necessary information-seeking and problem-solving skills, essential for the independent learner.

The English National Board for Nursing, Midwifery and Health Visiting (ENB, 1995) identify lifelong learners as being:
 – innovative in their practice;
 – responsive to changing demand;
 – resourceful in their methods of learning;
 – able to act as change agents;
 – able to share good practice and knowledge;
 – adaptable to changing healthcare needs;
 – challenging and creative in their practice;
 – self-reliant in their way of working;
 – responsible and accountable for their work.

These are great expectations. We want to create creative, critical thinkers who can respond to the dynamic health policy environment and the requirements of healthcare consumers, and this book will help you achieve this. As Ferguson (1994, p. 643) stated: 'Learning to learn and learning to practice are essential characteristics of good practice.'

REFERENCES

ENGLISH NATIONAL BOARD FOR NURSING, MIDWIFERY AND HEALTH VISITING (1995) Creating Lifelong Learners: Partnerships for Care. Guidelines for the implementation of the UKCC's Standards for Education and Practice Following Registration. London, ENB.

FERGUSON A (1994) An evaluation of the purpose and benefits of continuing education in nursing and the implications for the provision of continuing education for cancer nurses. *Journal of Advanced Nursing*, 19(4), 640–646.

How to use this book

The book has been divided into two main sections: Section I explores the skills required for successful learning, while Section II examines skills for successful writing.

Each chapter consists of a short introduction, as well as a list of key issues to be covered in the chapter. This will allow you to decide quickly whether the chapter contains the information you need. Whichever order you read the chapters is entirely up to you. Cross-references (appearing in the margin) and links to other chapters have been indicated to help you make the most of the book, whatever order you choose.

Finally there are appendices, including reference and citation systems and useful addresses and information.

Above all, the aim of the book is for it to be interactive. The more you attempt the exercises, the more you will get from the book. Keep a notebook near so that you can write down your thoughts. Scribble notes on the book itself!

The structure of the chapters has been devised to be as flexible and supportive as possible.

EACH CHAPTER BEGINS WITH

■ An introduction
■ A list of key issues, letting you know what is covered in the chapter.

WITHIN THE CHAPTER

Case Studies

Some chapters contain case studies. These are designed to help you reflect on your own experiences.

Reflection Points

These will raise issues that allow you a few moments to reflect on what you are learning and how you might learn from your experiences.

Activities

These invite you as the reader to consider issues which require you to move beyond reflection. They may require you to note down some of your ideas or to carry out some more research into a given topic. You may wish to come back to these after you finish reading the chapter.

Tips/Hints

Useful tips have been indicated and highlighted for quick reference. These are often based on the writer's own experiences and we hope they will help you avoid some of the common pitfalls.

At the end of the chapter, you will usually be asked to reflect on what you have read and how you are going to build on it. More useful tips and suggestions for further reading and research are sometimes provided too.

 **SECTION I**

DEVELOPING YOUR STUDY SKILLS

Preparing for your Course

Matthew Godsell

INTRODUCTION

This first chapter will look at how you can approach studying so that you make the best use of your time and any resources that are available. It will consider timetabling and time management as measures for improving the quality of study time and as strategies for completing important tasks like the production of essays and assignments. The final sections will discuss where you study and some of the resources that you may find useful.

The sections in this chapter will look at these issues:

Key Issues

- Time management.
- Setting realistic goals.
- Making a timetable.
- Making plans.
- Defining priorities.
- Thinking strategically.
- Creating a suitable environment.
- Developing networks for support.

PREPARATION

How you learn, where you learn and when you learn will be determined by a number of factors. If you are attending a university you are likely to receive a timetable which will tell you what to do and where to go at specific periods. A timetable will tell you about the times and locations of lectures and seminars. It may also include study time or reading time which is not linked to a subject. On these occasions you are presented with the opportunity to select 'how' and 'where' you are going to study. A lot of courses are designed with the assumption that you will spend time outside of 'office' hours engaged in activities related to the course. These activities may include:

- reading to support lectures and seminars;
- preparation for assignments;
- writing essays;
- collecting materials for projects.

You may find that these activities conflict with other plans that you have made, such as going out for the evening or watching a film on the television. Making a timetable of your own may help you to avoid or resolve some of these conflicts.

TIME MANAGEMENT

The management of your time, and the activities which fill it, are very important aspects of studying. When you are studying outside of the time that has been allocated to you in college you will have to make all the decisions. Issues such as 'when' and 'for how long' can be added to where and how. Working at home means mixing your studies into all of your other activities. Devoting time to your studies means that you may have less time for some of the other things that you already do. Northedge (1990) identifies three areas which generate activities that are likely to compete for your time. These are social commitments, work commitments and leisure activities.

- **Social commitments** including going out to visit friends, time spent with a partner/family, attending parents' evenings or going to church.
- **Work commitments** include housework and child care as well as attending college and placements (they may also include any agency or part-time work you are engaged in).
- **Leisure activities** include attending clubs or societies, concerts, sporting activities and going to the pub.

Think about the activities that you are involved in during a typical
day.
- Which activities would you describe as social commitments?
- Which activities would you describe as work commitments?
- Which activities would you describe as leisure activities?
- Which activities would take up the most space on your time-
table?

If you devote too much time learning at home, or in college,
then your social life and leisure activities will suffer. If you continue to pursue your other commitments without allowing yourself any time for studying it may impede your ability to handle
course work or limit your participation in discussions and seminars.

Timetabling will help you to avoid the two extremes. You
need to devote some time to studying but it is not desirable to
let it take over your life. Keep these two things in mind when you
start to make plans:

- You need to be **realistic** about what you intend to achieve.
- You need to strike a **balance** between studying and your other
  commitments.

If you are going to get the most out of the course you will have to
be happy and healthy while you study. Studying is not a route to
health or happiness or an effective substitute for them. Remember that you can also learn while you are involved in social or
leisure activities with friends, partners or family.

Being realistic will contribute to your sense of well-being. If
you set yourself demanding goals, and then fail to live up to your
own expectations, it is possible that you will form a poor impression of your performance. You may end up feeling frustrated and
low. If you set an achievable goal you are less likely to fail and
more likely to benefit from the pleasant feelings associated with
achievement and accomplishment. On the other hand if you set
goals which are easy to achieve, because they are too low, you run
the risk of feeling frustrated because you are not making the best
of your abilities. You also run the risk of falling behind because
you are not doing enough to keep up with the demands of the
course.

SETTING REALISTIC GOALS

Setting realistic goals is not a skill that you can put into practice straight away if you are not used to studying. Even people who have learned skills through attending other courses will have to adjust their approach so that it matches the structure and requirements of their current course. Setting goals is a skill that is gained through experience. You may have to learn through trial and error so don't be afraid to experiment and try out all sorts of different things.

- How many hours are you going to work each day?
- Do you prefer to do your work early in the morning or in the evening?
- Do you prefer to arrange set times for breaks (for meals, snacks, drinks, television programmes etc.) or do you like to work straight through until you have finished?
- Are you going to try and do most of your work during the week so that your weekends are free, or are you going to work at weekends so that you can carry on with social and leisure activities throughout the week?

You may feel that you cannot answer these questions until you have tried some of the alternatives. Experimentation may be the best way of finding out what suits you!

- Don't get exasperated, upset or angry when you make mistakes.
- You can learn from your mistakes as well as your achievements.
- Recognise and acknowledge your mistakes.

MAKING A TIMETABLE

One way of developing a realistic timetable is to work out how much time is available for studying. Make a record of the time you spend in college attending lectures or seminars, as well as any other work, social commitments and leisure activities that you are engaged in during a typical week. When you know how much of your week is taken up with these activities you will be able to make decisions about the remaining time and how you want (or need) to spend it. Entering the information into a chart like the one shown below will help you to create an accurate record.

	Mon.	Tues.	Wed.	Thur.	Fri.	Sat.	Sun.
08.00 10.00							
10.00 12.00							
12.00 14.00							
14.00 16.00							
16.00 18.00							
18.00 20.00							
20.00 22.00							

- How many hours do you spend on work commitments, social commitments and leisure activities each day?
- How are the hours distributed throughout the day?
- Which are the busiest periods?
- Which are the quietest periods?

When you have entered all of the information that has been collected over a week you will be able to see where the 'free' periods are. The chart will show you where there are chunks of time that are not occupied with leisure, work or social commitments. The chart will also show you if there are clashes between different activities. You will be able to see at a glance if your plan to start something new will involve stopping or moving an existing activity to another time or day.

This layout has some limitations. These limitations are worth exploring because they are indicative of some of the problems that you are likely to experience whenever you construct schedules of work. The information that has been gathered represents a typical week. If you devise a timetable based on the assumption that all of the weeks which follow are going to be just like it you may find that your plans are unworkable. Problems may occur because the week that you have chosen to record is not typical. There may be fewer things going on than usual so that the chart has given you a misleading impression of the amount of free time available. Problems will also occur if there is very little repetition in your pattern of activities. If the amount of time you spend on leisure, work and social activities fluctuates, the amount of free time available to you will also fluctuate from week to week. This can make long-term planning difficult.

These limitations do not mean the information that you have collected is useless. It does mean that you need to think about the ways in which they may influence your planning. These suggestions may be useful:

- Be generous when you estimate the amount of time allocated for each activity.
- When you recorded different activities did you include time for travelling or changing clothes?
- Did you allocate time for any preparation that has to be done in advance or any tidying that follows an activity?
- **Be prepared to adjust your timetable if you do not think it is working**.

It is better to make changes and modify your expectations instead of abandoning timetabling or time management altogether. If the timetable that you have made is too tiring or too rigid you could write in more leisure time and reduce your work commitments. If it is too loose and you do not feel that you are making any progress then you may need to develop more structured activities.

MAKING PLANS

Daily, weekly and monthly calendars are useful when you start to make plans. Each calendar can perform a different function:

- a **monthly calender** helps to plan long-range assignments;

- a **weekly calendar** helps to develop a consistent approach;
- a **daily calendar** helps you set priorities.

From these descriptions you will be able to see that different time scales involve different types of activity.

- How long is your course? Don't just think about the number of years. Think about the changes that occur during each year. Think about where you will be learning. Where will you be spending most of your time? Will it be on placements or in the faculty? Does this change from year to year?
- When are the significant dates for exams, the submission of essays, clinical placements etc.? Are certain events or requirements located at the middle or the end of the course? What needs to be done prior to these dates so that you are prepared for them?
- Which learning skills do you need to help you prepare for each event? Think about the skills that you have already and then the additional skills you will need to learn. Does the programme show you where you will have opportunities to develop these skills? Does the programme show you where you will learn about research, information technology, statistics or drug calculations?
- How frequently do you need to check your progress and preparation? This could become more than a checklist of things that you have or have not done. It is your chance to reflect on how things are going. Did you meet your learning outcomes? Were you told what they were or did you negotiate them? Did you enjoy learning? What did you enjoy? Why did you enjoy it? What didn't you like? Why? What do you need to check or make a note of each month? What do you need to check or make a note of each week? What do you need to check or make a note of each day?

It may help you to think of planning in two stages: long-term and short-term planning. Long-term planning will make you aware of significant dates in the course. These will include assignments, but you will also want to know about holidays, practice placements, study days and reading weeks. All of these things will exert some influence over the ways in which you manage your time. Short-term planning may include weekly or daily activities.

There may be a clear connection between short-term goals and long-term goals or you may choose short-term goals to indicate an activity that is carried out regularly. Some goals will show that you want to develop consistency in your study habits, while others will show that you are organising your study time so that you can achieve specific tasks that have been defined as priorities.

Think about all of the activities related to learning that you are likely to carry out in the next 2 weeks. Locate each activity on a chart like this so that you can see whether it is more or less urgent, important or not so important:

IMPORTANT

URGENT   NOT URGENT

NOT IMPORTANT

If you put activities near to the important and urgent poles it indicates that you need to think in terms of short-term, rather than long-term, goals. Long-term goals are not always less important. They may indicate something which is ongoing and does not need to be changed or reviewed immediately.

Another useful way of thinking about learning is to make a list of aims and objectives.

- An **aim** is a big, broad heading for something you want to achieve. It may involve a piece of work like the completion of a nursing care assignment, or it may be related to an aspiration such as 'I really want to work on my communication skills during my next placement'.
- An **objective** is one of the small steps you have to take in order to achieve your aim. A single aim may incorporate many objectives. Completing an essay will include objectives like carrying out a literature search, writing a plan, writing an introduction etc. Improving communication skills may involve objectives like using more open questions instead of closed ones, paying close attention to body posture and non-verbal techniques, and improving listening skills.

One of the advantages of sitting down and working out a timetable is that you become more aware of all the demands on your time. You will be able to see if there are periods when you will be under a lot of pressure. There may be specific times in the course when you are expected to do two or three things simultaneously. This may involve producing written work for assignment deadlines, changing practice placements or working with mentors and assessors on specific days. In addition you might also have to complete and submit documentation relating to practice assessments.

Being aware of dates and times will not mean that you can get away with less work, but it does encourage you to think about how and when you will get the work done. Your plans may show activities involving family or friends, such as going on holiday, as well as activities related to learning. You will find it useful to look ahead; for example, it is not realistic to set yourself a lot of work during a weekend when you have arranged for a friend to come and stay!

One of the most anxiety-provoking situations you can be confronted with is being issued a list of submission deadlines and significant dates if you do not have a strategy for dealing with them. Without a plan you will find it hard to know if you have done all the things you need to do, or the best thing to do next. When people do not have a very clear idea about what needs to be done they may be inclined to procrastinate. This involves avoiding certain jobs or activities because they do not know how to go about them. Procrastination may not produce any short-term discomfort, but in the long term it may have serious consequences. The closer you get to a deadline the greater the pressure. If you avoid an assignment until a week before the submission date you will have to work on it non-stop to meet the deadline.

■   A task is done more easily if it is not urgent.

James is in the second month of the Common Foundation Programme (CFP). He has been told to do lots of reading and he has a formative essay of 1000 words to write for each of the three sciences represented in the CFP. The essays are not compulsory but he wants to do them because he would like to have some comments on his essay-writing technique. James has not produced any academic work since the end of his course at college 3 years ago and he is worried because he is not sure what the tutors expect from him. He has 6 weeks to write the essays but he also needs to keep up with the reading that has been recommended for the psychology, biology and sociology components of the course.

Put yourself in James' shoes.

- How would you arrange your study time over the next 6 weeks?
- How many hours does James need to study if he is going to get the work done?
- How will that time be divided between producing the essays and keeping up with his reading?
- James has stated that he aims to complete three essays within 6 weeks. What are the objectives that will help him to reach this aim?

A nursing course involves different themes or modules which require separate assessments. It also involves practical work with other nurses and patients or clients. This range of activities means that it is not always possible to drop your other commitments so that you can complete a single task or assignment. If you do drop everything to meet a deadline it may have immediate repercussions on your other commitments. The pressure to meet all of these demands will accumulate and another crisis will develop. If this is the case you are back where you started: under pressure and stressed out!

If you refer to your thoughts about James (above), you will recognise that planning involves paying attention to many different aspects of learning. If you are going to reduce your stress levels and avoid rushing about at the last minute to get everything done you will have to consider all of them at the planning stage. James needs to think about preparing himself for seminars by consolidating notes from lectures and reading, as well as producing the essays. If he is going to achieve this he needs to allocate time each week for his ongoing reading and consolidation as well as time for the essays. Writing the essay will be the final stage of production. Before he can start this he will need to research the subjects and produce an essay plan; both of these activities could form separate learning objectives. James could also divide the time he spends on essays into preparation and writing time. Four out of the 6 weeks available to him could be spent on preparation and the remaining 2 weeks could be used for writing.

Some people feel that they work well when they are put under pressure. They believe that they are most productive when they are up against a tight deadline. There is nothing wrong with this approach if you are sure that you have the skills to carry it off. There are some disadvantages which go along with it which you may like to consider before you make it your preferred option.

Think about:

■ The availability of resources. If you leave everything until the last minute you can only succeed if everything you need is in the right place at the right time. If you need to borrow books from the library or you require access to computers you will be competing with all of the other people who have put themselves (by accident or design) in the same position.

■ The research that you need to complete before you can start writing. The adrenaline that starts to flow if you leave things until the last minute may help you to write faster, but you will not be able to produce good quality work unless you develop a thorough knowledge of the material. Before you commit yourself to paper you will need to get to grips with the theories and concepts you are writing about. You will need to know what other people have written or said before you can establish your own point of view. Make sure that you allow yourself time for preparation as well as writing time.

There is more on this topic in Chapter 4, which looks at gathering information.

There is more on this topic in Chapter 9, which looks at developing an argument.

DEFINING PRIORITIES

Effective management of your time will involve defining priorities. If everything is left until the last minute then everything seems to be a priority. If you are aware of long-term and short-term goals this situation can be avoided. If pieces of work have different submission dates then the earliest becomes a potential priority. If you ignore all of the other work to complete it in time you may miss the other submission dates. To meet all of the dates you need to devote some time to maintaining work which is not an immediate priority. If you devote three-quarters of your study time to completing your first assignment then it would be a good idea to spend the remaining quarter doing some preparatory reading for the assignment which follows. This is evidence of effective long-term planning.

This chapter has described the advantages of making schedules and timetables. It is worth remembering that they are there to help you and not to hinder you. Even they can become a hindrance if they prevent you from thinking about a situation from a new angle. It will not help you if the process becomes oppressive. Try to avoid being ruled and constrained by plans. If an assignment takes much longer than you expected it may make sense to put all of your energy into completing it. Adopting a different approach can be seen as evidence of flexibility and responsiveness. Under some circumstances it may be wise to assess the relevance of long-term goals and introduce some measures to deal with immediate needs and priorities. When you have completed the assignment it may be possible to catch up with your reading through judicious time management (or spending a couple of nights in rather than going out).

Planning and goals are not only important in reaction to assignments and essays. They also help you to structure your approach to different subjects. For example a Diploma in Nursing Studies has 'core' themes which reflect different academic disciplines. You may be tempted to get hooked into one theme and ignore the others. This can happen if you like one subject more than others, or if you find one subject more difficult than others.

Developing a special interest in a particular subject or knowing that a subject is likely to be your Achilles' heel can be beneficial. Having this knowledge shows that you are aware of your strengths and weaknesses. It can become a disadvantage if preferences encourage you to avoid work related to other subjects. Remember that they have the potential to become problems as well. Being aware of how much time you dedicate to each area will help you to avoid getting hooked into a single theme. It may make you more conscious of the need to maintain a consistent approach to your studies. This does not mean that you have to spend equal amounts of time on each. It may involve making thoughtful decisions and keeping records so that you know how you are using your study time.

THINKING STRATEGICALLY

Creating a plan is useful even if you do not stick to it. Departing from your schedule may be beneficial if an unforseen event becomes a priority. If you find that you are constantly having to change your plans or reorganise your priorities, it is still a productive way of working. Planning means that you have to think about what you are going to do and why you are going to do it. Planning is evidence of thinking **strategically**. Developing a strategy for learning is an antidote to drifting aimlessly or bumping along from one crisis to the next. Forward planning and thinking things over before you take decisions gives you some control over future events. It may not enable you to predict everything that is going to happen, but it will make you aware of some of the options at your disposal. This can boost your self-confidence and allow you to take a more positive approach to course work.

Students think about their work in different ways. Some people will visualise plans as a series of tasks arranged in a hierarchical order. The most important task will be at the top of an imaginary list. Strategies may involve devising ways of working down the list until all the tasks are completed. Other people may imagine an hourly timetable with time slots allocated to different subjects and activities. Strategies may involve working out how many hours will be required to complete an essay or how much time is required for background reading prior to a weekly seminar. These sort of questions may run through your mind:

- Where is there a couple of hours free so that I can visit the library?
- When can I find an hour to read about the composition of the blood? I can make notes to clarify some of the things I did not understand during the lecture.
- I need to make a plan before I can start writing this essay. Where will I find the time to make a start?

Whether you approach an activity by thinking of it as a task or a period of time is less important than the fact that you are aware of the need to make space for it. **Defining the task** and **creating a space for it** are the key ingredients in any plan. The ways in which you mix them together are up to you!

A successful plan will be built around a realistic appraisal of your own habits. You may decide to try and work using long periods for learning rather than more frequent, shorter bouts. This can be useful if you want to tackle some big tasks in one go.

This approach will not suit everyone. If you know that your concentration span is between 20 and 30 minutes then periods of between 2 and 3 hours will not be the best option. Even if you set this amount of time aside you may only work for 20 minutes in each hour because you become distracted after a short time. This results in a lot of time being wasted. You may end up feeling angry and frustrated. Instead of big chunks you may need to plan so that you have shorter but more frequent periods of study. You may do less in each session, but you will stand a better chance of maintaining your interest and enthusiasm if you work in a way that suits you.

There is no single method for drawing up plans that is going to meet every student's needs. Everyone works and studies in the way which suits them. In this chapter there are some suggestions you may like to try to see if they suit you. Don't worry if they do not. Experimentation is a way of finding out what is best for you. Try a variety of methods and see which seems to be the most effective.

Because no one else can prescribe a way of managing your time so that all of your needs are met, you will need to evaluate the situation yourself. Making an evaluation of your own progress is one aspect of **reflection**. You may like to glance at Chapter 3 and make some notes on key points, or spend some time reading it when you have completed this section. Ask yourself the following questions so that you think about the effectiveness of your current study habits:

Reflection is discussed in more detail in Chapter 3.

- Are other activities interfering with my study activities?
- Do my goals and priorities suit my current needs?
- Am I allowing myself enough time to study?
- Is my weekly timetable flexible enough to allow for the un-expected?
- Does my weekly schedule show that I am wasting time?
- Have I established a good balance between work and leisure in my schedule?

The answers to these questions may make you change your habits or amend your timetable. It is unlikely that you will get it absolutely right the first time you do it. Adjustments and amendments are ways of adapting your original ideas so that they meet your current requirements.

CREATING A SUITABLE ENVIRONMENT

When you have determined when and what you are going to study, you will need to decide where you are going to do it. Some activities require a specialised environment like a library or access to computers. On these occasions you will need to plan ahead so that you are in the right place at the right time. On other occasions you will be able to exercise more choice and select where you work. Some people prefer to work in the spaces provided by the college, such as work stations in a library or reading room. These places are set aside for studying so they are free from distractions. Other people like to work at home with familiar things around them. If you prefer this option you may like to think about putting some space aside for studying on a regular basis, to encourage 'regular' study habits. This may amount to nothing more than somewhere where you can leave your books and notes out so that they are not disturbed. It may mean making some adjustments so that your existing space or room provides you with a more conducive environment.

- Make sure there is adequate light, heating and ventilation. You will not be able to work effectively if it is stuffy in the summer or freezing in the winter.
- Try and get a table or desk that is large enough to take all of your books, papers, desk lamp etc.
- Find a place to store dictionaries, files with notes and textbooks that is close to hand.
- Try and use a room where you can be on your own so that you can avoid distractions.
- Choose a chair that will enable you to sit and read without causing you any discomfort.

DEVELOPING NETWORKS FOR SUPPORT

The material that you have read earlier in this chapter indicates that studying can become a big thing in your life. It can impinge on your social life, your family and your relationships with partners and friends. If you are moving to another city to start a degree or diploma the changes in your life may be accompanied by all of the trauma that goes along with moving your posses-ions, bank etc. You may also be leaving home, your parents or your partner. You may look forward to the challenge or you may be anxious because you will have to make sense of all of these changes on your own in an unfamiliar place. One way of reducing your anxiety is to talk to the people that you know about the way you feel. They may not be able to make the unpleasant feelings go away, but they can provide reassurance.

- What can be gained from moving to a new place? What does the accommodation, town or city you are moving to have to offer?
- What can you gain from starting a new course? Will you have an opportunity to meet new friends or colleagues? Will you have a chance to talk about things that interest you or things that you are concerned about?

If you are staying at home, studying may be just as traumatic. Spending time at university or immersing yourself in course work means there is less time to do the things you already do. This includes things like the housework and gardening, as well as time spent with children or partners. Creating time and space to study can involve negotiating with the people around you. If you need peace and quiet to get things done you need to let other people know where and when you are going to study. If you are going to invest a lot of time in your studies you need to sort out who is going to do the jobs that you will not have time for. Students with course work, homes and children will have to enter into negotiations with their families so that they can share or delegate domestic work and child care. You may have to discuss your changing responsibilities and how studying will change your role.

When you are allocated to placements you will often be allocated a mentor or supervisor. You may find that you have similar discussions with them regarding your role in the area and your responsibilities as a learner. In both cases negotiation will be necessary to establish what you expect, and what is expected from you, what you intend to do, and what other people think you should do, and how you are going to organise yourself and other people so that it all gets done.

There is further discussion about mentors and supervisors in Chapter 2.

Joan has recently started an ENB post-registration course. Her employers have agreed to give her study time so that she can attend the parts of the course which are taught at the university. She also knows that she will need more time to complete the project work and essays which are specified in the course requirements.

Joan has two children at school and she is worried about the commitments that she already has. These include managing her responsibilities at work, her work at home and child care. Mike, her partner, has encouraged her to take the course and gain more qualifications but he has not said how he is going to support her while she is studying. Mike has done the housework and looked after the children when Joan has made a specific request for help, but he has never used his initiative and done things without a request from her.

Put yourself in Joan's shoes.
- Where should Joan go for help and advice?
- How should she sort things out with Mike?

If you are finding things difficult it may be helpful to talk to other people who are in a similar situation. Remember that some of the people you meet on the first day of the course are going to be in the same position as you. They may have ways of coping that you have not thought of. If they do not have solutions to your problems they may be able to sympathise with you, which can be a source of comfort. If there are other people who share your problems and concerns it may be possible to form a self-help group which will encourage group members to provide support and advice for each other.

Another strategy is to see what the university can offer. Some courses may allocate you a personal tutor who will be able to offer advice on personal problems as well as problems related to course work. Some student unions have health and welfare officers who can advise you on problems related to accommodation or access to resources. You may also have access to a counsellor if you do not want to approach any of the people mentioned above.

- Look for references to any of these people in your university handbook.
- Look for references to them in any material that you receive from the NUS.
- Look for information on notice boards.
- Make a note if they are mentioned in any presentations made by the staff during your introduction to the university.
- Listen to other students; they may recommend someone who has worked with them to overcome a problem.
- See if there are any clubs or societies that you want to join. They are a good way of making friends and meeting people who share common interests.

It is always worthwhile attending orientation sessions and picking up handbooks. You may not need to contact any of these people straight away, but it is useful to know who and where they are in case you require their services in the future.

During this chapter you have considered timetabling and organisation. Remember the following key points when you begin to study:

- Acknowledge your other commitments.
- Make realistic plans.
- Think strategically.
- Create a structure by making aims and objectives, goals, or more urgent and less urgent priorities.
- Evaluate and reflect on your learning.
- Be prepared to seek and accept help and advice from other people.

REFERENCES

NORTHEDGE A (1990) *The Good Study Guide*. Milton Keynes, The Open University.

2

Learning Skills and Learning Styles

Sian Maslin-Prothero

INTRODUCTION

The overall aim of this chapter is to build on the previous chapter and develop your learning skills. This will be achieved by identifying what learning is and how we do it. There will be an explanation of different learning styles and how they can affect your studying. There will be an opportunity to identify your personal learning style. Knowing how you prefer to study can help guide you through your course, however you need to be aware that your preference can change according to what you are studying.

Key Issues

The sections in this chapter will look at the following points:

- Responsibility for your own learning.
- Learning styles.
- Your existing learning skills.
- Learning from life experiences.
- Learning contracts.
- Support networks.
- Self-assessment.

BEING AN ADULT LEARNER

One of the points which will be emphasised on any course of study is the importance of taking responsibility for your own learning. Further education is very different from school. At school, it was your teachers who were responsible for identifying what and how you learned. As an adult learner, it is up to you to identify what you want to learn and how much effort you are going to give to learning. That is, only **you** can successfully complete this course.

This book aims to assist you in becoming an independent and self-directed learner. This means you will be able to identify what you need to learn and access the information you require, without the assistance of a teacher. There will be additional mechanisms in your place of learning to support and assist you during the course, but you need to recognise how you take responsibility for your own learning.

From personal experience, a key proponent to any success is motivation, or a sense of purpose; this is perhaps the most crucial aspect of learning. You must **want** to study. For example, if you are undertaking a pre-registration nursing course because you couldn't think of anything else to do, you are not increasing your chances of success.

 Briefly note down what has motivated you, either to commence a new course, or learn a new skill.

We undertake new things for a variety of reasons, because they help us to undertake certain responsibilities or deal with problems. The most powerful motivator to learning comes from ourselves and the desire for increased job satisfaction, self-esteem and quality of life. You might have identified some of the following:

- to get a degree;
- to get a better job;
- to earn more money;
- to learn new skills;
- to 'better' yourself;
- to keep up with colleagues.

The reason why motivation is so important when you are embarking on something new and challenging, such as a course, is that there are going to be times when you find the course difficult. Regardless of what you have identified as motivating you at the start of a new course, you will find that your motivation changes during the course. Sometimes your motivation is going to be high, sometimes lower. This might be for a variety of reasons.

On a separate sheet of paper, jot down some of the concerns you have anticipated experiencing. Keep this so you can refer to it as your course progresses.

Some of the concerns you have identified may include:

- financial insecurity;
- meeting new people;
- reduced time available for family and friends;
- making time for study;
- not understanding the course and/or the academic language used by your teachers and fellow students.

A new course is exciting, however it is going to bring about a change in your life. This change might cause stress. Stress is not always a negative thing; only when you are experiencing too much pressure does stress become a problem. A certain amount of pressure stimulates us and can be a very positive thing. However if not managed correctly, this pressure can become too much and we are unable to cope. It is important to be able to recognise these signs and symptoms in yourself and others. Only through recognition and then doing something to create a change will you adequately address the problem. Chapter 1 identified some positive strategies that can be used to resolve some of these issues.

LEARNING STYLES

Learning underpins everything we do, for example learning to drive, trying out a new recipe or learning to rock climb. We rarely stop and think how we have learned a new skill. During the course your teachers will support your learning through a variety of teaching and learning strategies, including lectures, seminars, tutorials and practice.

Too often both students and teachers believe that the teacher is the 'expert' and knower of all things. First of all, this is untrue: we are all constantly learning new things and developing new skills. Becoming dependent on teachers will stifle your creativity, and your ability to make independent judgements and utilise new information. You will find that your teachers will expect you to take responsibility for your own learning, through making the most of every opportunity offered you.

See Chapter 1

What you will find is that we all learn in different ways. This will be based on your previous experiences, and how you have learned to learn in the past. In order to be successful you need to identify how you learn best, and develop your learning style so that you can optimise any learning situation as it presents itself.

Honey and Mumford (1992) identified four basic learning styles: the activist, the reflector, the pragmatist and the theorist. The following summarise each of these different styles.

The Activist

- Enjoys new experiences and challenges.
- Enjoys an environment of changing activities.
- Likes being the centre of attention.
- Appreciates the chance to develop ideas through interaction and discussion with others.

The activist will thrive and develop in an environment which utilises some of the following teaching and learning strategies: group work, seminars, discussions, debates and workshops.

The Reflector

- Appreciates the opportunity to reflect prior to making a decision or choice.
- Preference is to listen and observe others debating and discussing issues.
- Would choose to work independently of others.

The reflector is someone who prefers to work on their own, through individual study and project work. They are likely to prefer lectures.

The Pragmatist

- Likes linking theory with practice.
- Enjoys problem solving.
- Appreciates the opportunity to develop practical skills.

The pragmatist will enjoy those learning experiences which involve problem-solving activities, practical sessions, clinical experiences and work-based projects.

The Theorist

- Enjoys theories and models.
- Thrives on problem solving which involves understanding and making sense of complex issues.
- Likes structure and making the link to theories.

The theorist will benefit and enjoy those sessions which use problem solving, evaluating material and discussing theories with colleagues and teachers.

From what has been listed you can probably begin to identify your preferred learning style, and this will help guide you and help you recognise those situations from which you might learn more effectively. You will benefit from developing new skills, which may help you to learn effectively from different situations you encounter. The following are suggestions on how you might develop a new learning style.

- Developing an activist style
  - Diversify. Learn to divide up your time between activities. For example, read an article, then prepare for tomorrow's lecture etc.
  - Contribute in discussions and debates. Let people know what you think.

    See Chapter 7
  - Group participation will help you develop your arguments (excellent practice for essay writing). It will also increase your confidence and self-esteem.

    See Chapter 10
- Developing a reflector style
  - Spend time thinking things through. Develop plans for assignments.

    See Chapter 9
  - Read around subjects being studied. Think and plan carefully what you are going to write. Discuss these plans with both your teacher and fellow students.

    See Chapter 8
  - In discussions, observe what is going on. What are other people saying? How do they react to others in the group?

    See Chapter 7
- Developing a pragmatist style
  - Have a go at linking the theory to practice. For

example, do a literature review using the CD-ROM; have a go at practising your basic life support skills on a manikin.
  - Get yourself and others to observe what you are practising, and offer/receive constructive feedback.
- Developing a theorist style
See Chapter 9
  - Develop your analytical skills. Compare and contrast two conflicting articles. What are the pros and cons of each of these articles?
  - Discuss your findings with colleagues. What did they find?

You will find that your preferred learning style might change depending on your needs or who is facilitating the session. The important thing is to learn to be flexible and develop your skills.

In your learning diary record some of your learning preferences for different aspects of your course, or based on previous study. Note down if your preference changes. Are these changes according to what subject is being learned? Have your preferences changed since you were at school?

LEARNING FROM LIFE EXPERIENCES

Your attitude to learning will be affected by your previous experiences. The knowledge, skills and attitudes you have will have been gained in a variety of ways, and it is important that you recognise the part informal learning has to play in your development. However these experiences need to be structured and organised, in order that learning becomes a conscious activity.

By using the four stages of the learning cycle shown in Fig. 2.1, and asking yourself the following questions, you can be conscious and structured about your learning. This is referred to as **reflecting**.

- What have you done today?
- What have you learned from what you have done today?
- How did you learn from what you have done today?

This is both common sense and a critical aspect of learning and self-awareness. Chapter 3 is devoted to developing reflective skills and their significance to you both as a student and as a nurse.
See Chapter 3

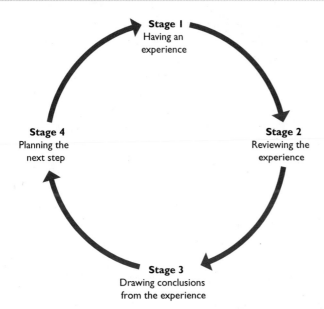

Figure 2.1   The learning cycle (adapted from Richardson 1995 and Kolb).

LEARNING DIARIES

As identified earlier, we all learn in different ways. We are able to learn more quickly if the material is relevant and interesting to us. By drawing on your own personal knowledge and life experience you can try out and test new ideas and concepts. That is learning by doing, practising and occasionally making mistakes. Through feedback from others (as well as ourselves), absorbing what has been said, and making sense of what has been said, we then progress. It is important to see this as a continuous process. We might not think of it consciously, but when we stop and think 'How did I get here?', we are able to follow this process.

One way of assisting this process is through a learning diary. Keeping a learning diary will enable you to:

- record details as they occur;
- remember things that happened;
- organise and clarify thoughts;
- apply your experiences;
- assess your development;
- take a longer term view.

This learning diary will be your own personal record, to record your thoughts and feelings about colleagues, teachers and clients.

You will find expressing your thoughts and feelings very therapeutic, and throughout this book you will be encouraged to record your experiences in a learning diary. However, you need to be sure that confidentiality is maintained and that individuals cannot be identified, should anyone else read your learning diary.

How to go about developing your learning diary

■ Set aside 5–10 minutes a day.
■ Consider and record your responses to the following questions:
  – What have I done today?
  – What have I learned from what I have done today?
  – What am I going to do differently as a result of this new learning?

You will find that developing a learning diary can also help you develop your profile for the United Kingdom Central Council for Nursing, Midwifery and Health Visiting (UKCC) requirements (UKCC, 1995). At the end of each chapter in this book there is a section encouraging you to reflect on what you have learned, and how you are going to use the new information.

LEARNING CONTRACTS

A learning contract is an agreement between two or more people. We are making informal contracts with people all the time, for example 'If I look after the children while you go for your tutorial today, can I go climbing later in the week?' A learning contract is used when there is an exchange of something; this can be skills or knowledge. In this context a learning contract is a more formal, written agreement between a teacher and a student, or a group of students.

Learning contracts are being used more frequently in education institutions. The philosophy goes hand in hand with students taking more responsibility for their own learning. Once you embark on any course you enter into a variety of informal, unwritten agreements, such as attending the course and completing the required number of assignments.

Learning contracts are particularly useful when you have specific learning outcomes, or need to negotiate how you are assessed. They can also be used when you want accreditation for prior learning (APL) or accreditation for prior experiential learning (APEL).

See
Chapter 11

Learning Contract

Learning Contract: Su Lin

Name of tutor/practice supervisor: Liam Bryant

Individual learning objective(s):
   1) To develop my Team working skills – both clinically
      and when in The college.

Plan of action
   - Identify aT least four skills I need To develop, making me
     a more effective Team member
   - UnderTake an analysis (with a colleague) of my present
     sTrengThs and weaknesses when working in a Team

Resources for help
   - RevisiT noTes on group work (see chapTer 7)
   - A colleague (either from The deparTmenT or pracTice
     area) who will help with The analysis

Evidence (i.e. objective(s) achieved)
   Self assessmenT
   Willingness To parTicipaTe in a Team
   ConsTrucTive conTribuTion To The Team
   CommiTmenTs To The Team achieved

Date of contract	Date to be completed by
25.4.96	19.5.96

Signature of student	Signature of tutor/ practice supervisor
Su Lin	L. G. Bryant

Figure 2.2   Learning contract.

Figure 2.2 shows a worked example of a learning contract. Learning contracts enable the student to identify, plan, manage and evaluate their own learning. The learner and their supervisor discuss, agree and record what the student wants to achieve and how it is going to be achieved. This document is then signed by both parties.

Learning contracts have a number of benefits.

- Everyone is clear about what the goals are and how they will be achieved.
- Everyone knows what is expected of them.
- Negotiating your contract not only helps you recognise your needs but also enables you to take responsibility for your learning.
- Learning contracts can recognise prior learning, for example APEL and APL.

Learning contracts are useful for both the learner and the supervisor, and can help reinforce their commitment to the learning experience. This form of contract can be used in conjunction with a placement or workplace experience, where more than two people are contributing to the process.

There are a number of points you need to consider prior to agreeing your contract.

Learning contracts

- What do you want to get out of this experience (your objectives)?
- What skills and knowledge will you gain?
- How will you reach/achieve these objectives?
- What are the deadlines?
- How will you know you have achieved your objectives?

It is important to see the learning contract as something important to you, a way of you achieving your goals, with help and support from your supervisor.

Some of you might have experienced undertaking an individual performance review (IPR). This is a form of appraisal that is frequently used in the NHS. It is a form of learning contract, and is a way that you can ensure that things that are important to you, as well as the organisation, are achieved.

SUPPORT NETWORKS

Chapter 1 referred to your expectations and fears when embarking on a course of study, and emphasised the importance of managing your time. This leads to a more balanced life where you are able to include socialising and successfull studying.

Having identified your preferred learning style, you also need

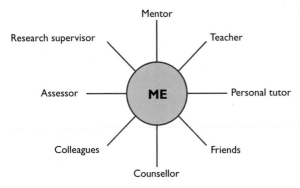

Figure 2.3 Supervisors and you.

to recognise how to get the most out of your supervisors. Supervisors come in a variety of shapes and forms; they can be your teacher, personal tutor, mentor, friend, colleague or research supervisor. A supervisor is an experienced individual who facilitates the development of a colleague both educationally and professionally.

Your supervisor is there to help you learn. This can be in a variety of ways, including helping you get the most out of your practice placement, or acting as role model, a resource, a counsellor or as a teacher (Fig. 2.3).

The following are characteristics of a supervisor:

- a good listener;
- constructive;
- a resource;
- a role model;
- competent.

However, supervision is not a one-way relationship; your supervisor will have certain expectations of you as a student.

- Supervisors are not only responsible for you, they are usually busy and will have other commitments.
- Make appointments to meet your supervisor, and turn up prepared and on time.
- If you are unable to make an appointment, telephone and let them know you won't be attending.

The emphasis is on you being prepared to listen to the constructive feedback and act on recommendations made. This will require both commitment and work from you. Be prepared to assess yourself and your progress; your learning diary will help you do this. As mentioned previously, your supervisor is not a god (and omniscient), they are there to guide your learning. You are responsible for how well the tutorials proceed by being prepared and focused for them.

Most practice placements will have a mentorship scheme. The mentor/supervisor is an experienced nurse who is there to help make the clinical experience a positive one for you. As with teaching supervisors, you need to establish your relationship and identify your expectations for the practice placement. Your mentor should know what stage you are at in your course, and will help you to get the most out of your placement experience. It is important that you work with your mentor as much as possible. The same things apply as with your tutor: organise regular meetings, and come to them on time and prepared. There are additional points you need to consider with your mentor, including identifying your learning needs whilst on this placement, and any assessment and when this will take place. You will be responsible for any assessment documentation, so look after it.

What to do When it goes Wrong

It is still the case that the majority of students are allocated to a mentor, rather than being able to choose their mentor. Sometimes the relationship does not work. This can be for a variety of reasons, which may include not liking each other, your supervisor being unavailable, or your requirements changing. The most important thing is to do something about this. First, you should talk to your mentor and discuss how you are feeling. This might be embarrassing, but it will be constructive and allow you to carry on learning. If it is not possible to resolve any difficulties between you and your supervisor, then you need to identify a replacement mentor.

Study Networks

Another way of improving your learning is to form study networks with other students. Study groups are a form of self-help group, and can provide additional support to that which is provided by your teachers.

Advantages of Study Networks

- Share resources.
- Pool ideas.
- Brainstorm.
- Meet and make more friends.
- Share tasks.
- Develop group working skills.

You might find you have to initiate the development of a study group. If you are unsure how to do this, approach your teacher for assistance. The following points might help you.

Developing Study Networks

- Organise a meeting.
- Explain the purpose of the group.
- Decide when, where and how often you will meet.
- Keep in touch: exchange addresses and telephone numbers.
- Meet regularly.

ASSESSING YOURSELF

Throughout your career in nursing there is an expectation that you can assess yourself, including:

- your personal skills and qualities;
- your strengths and weaknesses;
- your learning requirements.

You will also be expected to learn to evaluate your own work, as well as others. The ability to accurately assess yourself will be useful in your professional career, as well as a valuable skill from a personal viewpoint. Self-assessment fits well with writing a learning diary. It will help you recognise what your learning needs are and identify how to achieve them, subsequently supporting feedback received from supervisors, teachers and colleagues.

CONCLUSION

In this chapter you have looked at a variety of essential points necessary to help you with your learning. By identifying your preferred style of learning you can use this information to enhance your studying. In addition, there are costs to learning; these are not only financial. Support networks are available to make your experience less painful. Finally, the use of learning contracts with supervisors can help you make the most of your learning, and ensure that you remain in control and pace yourself through the course.

- It is important to take responsibility for your own learning.
- Acknowledge your hopes and fears, and use them to your advantage.
- Recognise stress in yourself and others and know what to do about it.
- Write a learning diary and use this to guide your learning.
- Identify your strengths and weaknesses – enhance the positive, eliminate the negative.

Before moving on, consider the following:

- What is your preferred learning style?
- How will you use this preferred learning style to your advantage?
- List the requirements of your ideal supervisor. What do you think they might expect from you?
- Identify a supportive friend with whom you could develop a study network.

- Talk to your teacher about learning contracts, and developing a learning contract to meet your specific learning needs.

REFERENCES

HONEY P and MUMFORD A (1992) *The Manual of Learning Styles*, 3rd edition. Maidenhead, Peter Honey.

RICHARDSON A (1995) Preparing for learning. In: Richardson A (Ed.) *Preparation to Care: A Foundation NVQ Text for Health Care Assistants*. London, Baillière Tindall.

UNITED KINGDOM CENTRAL COUNCIL FOR NURSING, MIDWIFERY AND HEALTH VISITING (1995) *PREP and You: Maintaining Your Registration; Standards for Education Following Registration* (factsheet). London, UKCC.

Reflective Skills

Elizabeth Anne Girot

INTRODUCTION

Much has been written in the nursing press recently on the subject of reflection. Indeed, after considerable consultation with the profession, the UKCC (1995) has included reflection as an integral part of each practitioner's post-registration education and practice (PREP) requirements. Every practitioner is now required to complete a personal professional profile, a personal record of individual development and learning from both study (e.g. courses, study days, conferences etc.) and practice (learning from experience), in order to reregister. Reflective practice is therefore an obligatory part of your personal professional profile and necessary for reregistration.

First, this chapter sets out to explore the role of reflection in learning from your personal life experiences. Second, the chapter examines how you can develop the skills of reflection further to help you in the study process and gain more from the experiences you are exposed to, both personally and professionally.

Key Issues

- The meaning of reflection:
  - personally;
  - professionally.
- The process of reflection.
- Reflection as an aid to study:
  - theory;
  - practice.

- Types of reflection.
- Where to start:
  - critical incident analysis;
  - learning diaries/journals and portfolios;
  - developing a learning culture within the workplace.
- The need for reflection as essential to the development of care.

WHAT IS REFLECTION?

Jot down what you understand by the term reflection.

People make decisions and act as a result of two types of action: routine action and reflective action (Dewey, 1933). Routine action is carried out by 'taking for granted' everyday realities of life. This 'taking for granted' then allows you to concentrate on developing other aspects of your life in order to make you a more effective and efficient decision–maker. It is easy to move on to 'automatic pilot' in terms of what you do and how you do it. For example, think about what you did between waking up this morning and arriving at work/college. Do you ever think about what you do in your routine activities? Perhaps it is as well that you have such a thing as routine action, otherwise, if you had to think about what you did and rethink all your decisions every day, you would be worn out! You would certainly have no energy left to make the important decisions or make decisions when faced with the unexpected. If you have learned the 'best' way of doing something, e.g. dressing yourself, driving etc., then having the capacity to use this learning in an automatic way is an important facility you need to make use of.

Reflective action, on the other hand, is concerned with weighing up all aspects of the situation and making a conscious and informed decision what to do. It means taking active control over what you do and how you do it. Some aspects of your everyday life depend on your use of this reflective action. However, when something works out well for you on a few occasions, this may then become a routine action. However, if changes then occur, you may need to reconsider your automatic decisions.

You need therefore to use both your reflective action and routine action selectively. When much of your action is routine, then you can afford to spend time evaluating other aspects of your decision-making through reflective action, and once you are satisfied with your choices, these can then become 'automatic action' in the future. This has important implications for developing your study skills, and also for developing your expertise in professional practice, which we will examine later.

Think of something significant that happened to you recently in your everyday life that did not work out as well as you had hoped. Jot down what happened and why you think it happened the way that it did.

It is often said that we learn from the mistakes we make. Life can be seen as a series of hurdles: each time we meet new experiences, we try to fit them into our already existing understanding to make sense of them. However, learning from our experiences does not always happen. Some people are particularly self-aware and sensitive to their own response in certain circumstances, while others never seem to learn from their experiences and continue to make the same mistakes over and over again. Alternatively, you can learn to forget the experience – the experience can be too painful to explore, or your feelings can be too strong to dissect. So, when you meet a similar situation in the future, it is easy to make the same mistakes over again. The learning has been one of forgetting.

There are two important issues here. First, that feelings are extremely important aspects of the learning process, and the way you feel can dictate whether you learn from a particular experience or not. Feelings of anxiety or uncomfortable feelings can be a barrier to learning. Second, it is crucial that you do not learn to forget too many experiences, otherwise making mistakes repeatedly may be extremely problematic for you, especially when there may be the opportunity of making life easier for yourself.

So, it may be argued that whether you think about what you do and decide to forget the experience altogether, or whether you do in fact learn from the experience, reflection is occurring to some degree.

Often when you 'reflect' you acknowledge it happened. You describe it to yourself, perhaps over and over again. Perhaps then you share it with someone else and this helps you see it in a different light. However, often your 'reflections' stop there. You do not allow yourself the opportunity of making sense of the situation for another time; rather you seem to recall it numerous times to 'get it off your chest'. Merely thinking about what you did is not in itself true reflection, certainly not at a level that requires you to make sense of it and change what you do the next time.

Already you have explored some aspects of what is meant by reflection and how you can relate it to your everyday life. It is not a complicated activity; you are doing it to some degree all the time. It is a natural part of your development. However, perhaps it would help to explore the notion of reflection in greater depth, and how you can get the best out of your reflections for your professional practice.

REFLECTION IN A PROFESSIONAL SENSE

Reflection in professional terms takes on a particular meaning. This relates to both your study skills development and to your professional practice.

There are numerous definitions of reflection. In essence, they all seem to be suggesting that it is a way of thinking about what you do, in some sort of objective way. From a process of exploration, it then encourages you to make sense of that experience and learn from it to help you in the future. The most important aspect of reflection is *learning from the experience.* As already mentioned, feelings are a crucial element in terms of allowing you to learn from the experience or not.

Reflection consists of:
- thinking about an experience;
- exploring that experience in terms of feelings and significant features;
- processing the significant features and identifying **learning**;
- effects on future practice.

THE PROCESS OF REFLECTION

The process of how you learn from your experience may appear complicated. Trying to put into words the way you processed the experience and finally learned from it is a complex activity. Much has been written about the need for reflection, but it is less clear as to how you should go about it in practice. There are several frameworks available that different theorists have developed to enable you through the process. Some are fairly detailed, others simplistic. Whatever the approach, the important factors are that you analyse your experience and learn from it. One of the most popular frameworks to help you gain the most from your reflective action is that described by Boud *et al.* (1985). Their framework has been further modified to make it easier to remember in practice. Essentially, it requires you to ask yourself three questions about your particular experience:

- What? (Returning to the situation and describing it – what were the key aspects?)
- So what? (Understanding the context – feelings and effects of the different actions.)
- Now what? (Modifying future outcomes – what would you change?)

Each of these three questions can be subdivided into further questions, as shown in Fig. 3.1 (Driscoll, 1994).

Take the last reflective exercise, when something happened to you in everyday life that did not work out as well as you had hoped, and use Driscoll's (1994) questions to help you analyse the situation and learn from it. Does this framework help you to alter your decision-making in the future?

A worked example of this may be your meeting with six friends to complete a joint study (agreed at a previous meeting) required for your course, and finding that you failed to achieve what you set out to do.

What? (Returning to the Situation)

The second meeting was arranged to complete some work as a group, that you were required to present at your next study day. You personally had completed some reading and written notes but were not quite clear as to what was expected from your contribution. At the meeting there was a great deal of argument among you, as some had completed work and others had done nothing. You were angry as you felt no one really appreciated what you had done.

The key issues as you see the situation are that:

? WHAT (Returning to the situation)	? SO WHAT (understanding the context)	? NOW WHAT (modifying the outcomes)
■ is the purpose of returning to this situation?	■ were your feelings at this time?	■ are the implications for you, your colleagues, the patient, etc.?
■ exactly occurred in your own words? (describe or write)	■ are your feelings now? Are there differences? Why?	■ needs to happen to alter the situation?
■ did you see? did you do?	■ 'good' emerged from the situation, e.g. self, others?	■ are you going to do about the situation?
■ was your reaction?	■ troubles you, if anything?	■ happens if you decide not to alter anything?
■ did other people do, e.g. colleague, patient, visitor	■ were your experiences in comparison to your colleagues etc.?	■ might you do differently if faced with a similar situation again?
■ do you see as key aspects of this situation?	■ are the main reasons for feeling differently from your colleagues etc.?	■ information do you need to face a similar situation again?
		■ are the best ways of getting further information about the situation should it arise again?

Figure 3.1 The WHAT? format of structured reflection – a retrospective view of practice. Based on the seminal work by Boud *et al.* (1985)

- an amount of work was completed by three members of the group only;
- the other three had done nothing;
- no one was quite clear as to what had been actually agreed at the first meeting, and most had a different interpretation of what was decided at that meeting.

So What? (Understanding the Context)

Personal reflection: I felt angry at the time of the second meeting, as my own contribution did not seem to be valued by the others in the group. I also felt angry and felt resentment at others who had not completed any work. I felt I had wasted my time.

After questioning, the three members of the group who had not completed any work were quite adamant that at the first meeting it had been decided that everyone should read around the subject matter in order to formulate a plan of action at this second meeting.

Once everyone had had the oppportunity of expressing how they were feeling, it was decided to elect a group leader for this particular work so that some clear decisions could be made and documented and everyone's contribution could be clearly identified.

Learning: I now feel that we should have made this move at our first meeting. However, I am glad that we felt comfortable enough with each other to express ourselves, and it seemed to clear the air. I can now see that some of us felt quite differently from others in the group simply because of the vague discussions and decisions that were made at the first meeting. I don't feel so angry now, some time after the event, and it does not seem surprising now that we got ourselves in such a muddle. The need to elect a leader and identify a clearly documented action plan for future work was a lesson well learned.

Now What? (Modifying Future Outcomes)

I now see that when we are faced with a similar activity in the future, a spokesperson should be identified and each decision that is made at the meetings should be clearly documented, so that everyone knows and understands what is expected of them. I now realise that if we ignore this learning experience, we are very likely to land in a similar disorganised situation again and not be fortunate enough to have the time we had available, this time, to achieve our expectations. In addition, I realise that the rapport that is required to work closely together is jeopardised and the final presentation is not so likely to be successful. This is really important as I know that we will have many similar exercises to completed for other subjects. Also, I know that if everyone knows what their contribution should be for the group presentation, I personally will feel much more motivated to complete my side of the bargain.

So far, you have been concerned with decisions that have not gone according to plan. However, reflection is not just about making sense of situations when they go wrong. It is important to examine why some decisions you make are successful. You need to make sure that good decisions are repeated, rather than just changing decisions that have gone wrong.

> Think of a situation in your everyday life that you felt you handled particularly well. This may be the way you handled a particularly sensitive situation with a friend who sought your advice, or it may be how you mastered a skill you have recently been working on. Why do you think you handled the situation so well? What did you say/do? What other aspects were involved that made it a success?

Again, you may like to use Driscoll's (1994) questions to help you analyse your situation in some depth. The questions should help you probe different aspects of the situation, perhaps aspects that have not readily come to mind, that you felt were not significant.

This brings us on to applying what you have done so far – reflection as an everyday activity – to your study development and to learning from your professional practice. The three key stages in the whole reflective process can be summarised as follows:

> **1)** Reflection seems to be triggered by the element of surprise (when situations turn out better than you had hoped) or by an uncomfortable feeling or thought.
> **2)** Critical analysis of the situation, involving feelings and understanding.
> **3)** Development of a new perspective on the situation.

REFLECTION AS AN AID TO STUDY

Studying Theory

As we have already discussed, merely thinking about what you do is not in itself true reflection, certainly not at a level that will help you learn from it. It is all too easy to switch yourself onto 'automatic pilot' as far as studying is concerned, and not consciously think about how you study and how you can get the best out of the time you spend studying. Devoting 3 hours of your evening to sitting over your books may give the appearance that you are deeply involved in study, whereas you may in fact be totally involved in thinking about how you hope to spend your next weekend off, what shopping you need to do, what might be on the television etc. Routine action where study is concerned can often be time wasted. Time is precious and you need to make the most of the time you allocate to studying.

Think of the last time you sat down to study. How much time did you spend overall? What time of the day was it and did that affect your ability to learn? How much did you feel you achieved? How could you have made better use of your time?

We all learn differently and in different ways: what might be suitable for one person is not always suitable for another. Before embarking on a programme of study, you need to identify and clarify for yourself the best way for you to learn. Ideas that might help you are developed more fully in Chapters 1 and 2. There is no right or wrong way to learn overall, but after analysing your own past experience of study, it may become clear to you what opportunities you gain from most. This is extremely important, particularly when you have to study at the same time as undertaking shift work. Knowing when, where and how you best study will help you make the most of your time.

See Chapters 1 and 2

To get the most out of your study time and the activities of reading and notetaking, you need to read Chapter 6. This will help you examine how your own pattern of study, reading and notetaking has helped or hindered you in the past. Reflecting and examining your own experiences can now help you to improve your study for the future.

See Chapter 6

Learning Practice

Learning is not just about poring over books and learning from the written text. Much of nursing is learned in practice. Theory and practice are closely linked; each supports the other and both are vital for successful patient care. Therefore, it is important to know how you can get the most out of your experiences in practice and learn from them.

Nursing practice is complex and uncertain. You are constantly being reminded of the need to develop holistic care, yet traditional textbooks are full of prescribed care that you should be offering patients. The complexity of nursing is often not recognised by the very people who do it! Often experienced nurses when teaching colleagues 'nursing care' spend little time on the actual care aspects and much more on technical, procedural and medical treatments. Once it is mastered, it is as if nursing care is self-explanatory and requires little thought. With the enormous amount that you are expected to learn in both pre- and post-registration programmes, some part of your programme occurs directly in practical experiences and you are required to learn from these experiences. Rather, there is much that can be learned and taught about both the art and science of nursing and in particular from the experiences you are exposed to in practice during both pre- and post registration programmes. It is important therefore to consider how you can get the best out of these. So, to continue developing your care skills, in spite of the increasing pressures of work, consider the following questions.

- How can you make the most of your experiences in the different contexts you find yourself in?
- What is it that actually turns the experience you are gaining into learning?
- Why is it that some learners appear to benefit more than others in the clinical setting?

Recent research by the English National Board for Nursing, Midwifery and Health Visiting (ENB, 1993) suggests that reflection needs to take a much more important role in all pre-registration courses. All practitioners need to develop much stronger links between theory and practice, and encourage a positive response to the above questions for all learners of professional practice. In addition, the recent factsheets from the UKCC

(1995) for the fulfilment of the PREP requirements involve reflection as an integral part of the mandatory updating process in an attempt to encourage each individual to gain from their experiences, both clinically and educationally.

There has been a move in recent years away from the traditional approach to education (giving you information and encouraging you to apply this information to a variety of circumstances) towards a much more problem-solving approach, where you are expected to learn from what is happening around you. The process of 'learning how to learn' has become much more important than simply the acquisition of knowledge itself. The value of reflection has become a crucial element, and both pre-registration students and qualified practitioners are encouraged to learn from the 'real life' situations faced in daily practice. Whether you are engaged in a pre-registration programme or studying on a post-registration programme, you need to have a clear understanding of why you are there in the first instance. This may seem self-explanatory; however, it is very easy to feel so much part of the team of carers, part of the team that is required to 'get the work done', that it is easy to lose sight of what you hope to gain from the experience.

What responsibility do you personally take to learn from the experiences you are faced with in the clinical settings? Do you expect to 'be taught' or do you 'actively seek to learn'? How can you improve on this?

Returning to the two types of action mentioned at the beginning of this chapter, it is very easy to switch to routine action when practising clinically. It is easy not to concern yourself with what happens, or with whether decisions have been taken well or badly, especially if someone else takes the responsibility for the key decisions. However, every student and practitioner has a professional responsiblity to learn to improve practice. In addition, nurse educationalists are determined to find new and innovative ways of delivering education programmes for practice, rather than encouraging the traditional theory/practice divide.

LEARNING FROM OUR MISTAKES

You will have met practitioners who have been in practice some years and have developed their practice, kept themselves up-to-date and become expert practitioners. However, you may also have had the misfortune to work with other practitioners who have been in practice for a number of years but have simply repeated their experience over time and have not learned from it.

With the introduction of healthcare assistants into nursing practice areas, the boundaries between professional work and non-professional carers have become blurred. Dewar (1992) found that first level nurses could not differentiate easily between their own work and that of healthcare assistants. You may be quite clear in your own mind what the differences are, but if challenged can you put them into words? Perhaps the development of reflective skills will enable the profession, as a whole, to articulate the value of the professional carer. In turn, this may allow us to distinguish between a professional and their assistant, and encourage us to articulate it in practice.

TYPES OF REFLECTION

As the concept of reflection has developed in relation to professional practice, a number of different types of reflection have been identified, i.e. in relation to reflecting before, during or after an event.

Reflecting before action: this is concerned with the variety of approaches available to you when offering patient care, planning care and anticipating the possible outcomes of a particular plan of action. Here you should be thinking about what you are about to do before you do it, and should link your already existing theoretical knowledge with the practice you are planning or implementing.

Reflecting in action: this relates to thinking on your feet, working out what you are going to do as you are doing it. This is distinguished from routine action, as you are consciously making decisions, and adapting care to suit individual needs. This is sometimes called active reflection. The link between theory and practice here is much more complex, although most 'expert' or experienced nurses are doing this all the time.

Reflection on action: this aspect of reflection is what we have mainly been concerned about so far in this chapter. Here, you look back on your experiences and consider the success of particular interventions and decisions. The link between theory and practice may be made much more clearly some time after the event, once you have the opportunity of analysing the situation either alone or with others, and considering the deeper meanings and different perspectives of what was done.

As you develop your skills in reflecting for learning, all three types of reflection will be used.

In addition to the different types of reflecting, there are different levels of reflecting. These levels are of particular importance clinically, especially when you engage in a group discussion of an incident that happened in your work. Also they are of importance when developing your skills of reflection for academia. These are considered briefly below.

Learning from practice is very important in any programme of professional development, whether pre-registration or post-registration. After all, the whole purpose of learning is to gain practice and to develop standards of care. Otherwise, learning and study become sterile activities.

WHERE TO START

What can you do in a practical way that will help you develop your reflective skills more formally? There are three main areas that will be considered here.

1) The use of critical incident analysis.
2) Learning diaries/journals and portfolios.
3) Development of a learning culture within the workplace.

1) The Use of Critical Incident Analysis

Critical incidents are a way of examining a particular situation in your practice and identifying what you have learned from it. 'Critical' here refers to your critical examination of the situation. Critical incidents have been utilised in nursing for some years. More recently they have been developed for assessment purposes and for use in developing your personal professional profile. Although critical incidents have been associated with crisis situations or with mistakes that have been made or poor decision making, they can and should be used for all situations. As already mentioned, learning from what has gone well is as important as learning from what has gone badly.

The use of critical incident analysis is similar to any reflective analysis but is clearly related to practice. The format for working through the analytical process can be wide and varied. Indeed you can devise your own way of analysing the situation. Alternatively, the framework that was described earlier (Boud *et al.*, 1985) may be helpful, or additionally, the following might be more helpful.

1) Describe the situation.
2) Examine the components of the situation – the key issues/roles.
3) Analyse your feelings about the situation – how you felt then, how you feel now.
4) Analyse what you know of this aspect of practice – the alternatives available to you.
5) Challenge any assumptions you have made.
6) Explore how you might change or confirm your approach for the next time.

Nature of Knowledge

It is important to recognise that knowledge gained for practice does not just come from textbooks. The different sources of knowledge have been explored by a number of theorists; Robinson (1991) identifies three main sources of nursing knowledge:

■ personal experience;
■ social groups;
■ formally, from theory or research.

Think of a situation that occurred in your own practice recently. It may be a routine activity that you felt you handled particularly well or something that sticks out in your mind as special in some way. Using the framework identified for critical incident analysis, identify any new knowledge you have gained from the experience and where you obtained this knowledge from.

The skill of integrating new knowledge with previous knowledge is important in all our development and helps us individualise the care we give and improve the standards of care overall. It is an important skill, enabling reflection to help us to adapt care in new situations and change our thinking about the way we do things.

2) Learning Diaries/Journals and Portfolios

As mentioned earlier, since April 1995 all qualified practitioners are obliged to complete their own personal professional profile in order to reregister. An integral part of that profile is the development of your reflective accounts of practice and the study you do. These need not be lengthy tomes, but short, analytical accounts of what you gained from the experience. As you become more adept at documenting your experiences and what you learned from them, you will become more skilful at getting down to the point of:

See
Chapter 11

- describing your experiences;
- identifying the learning (from a variety of alternatives available);
- making changes in how you might approach the situation again.

Increasingly, programmes of study encourage students to complete reflective diaries of learning experiences. Here you are expected to identify the learning you gain from the theoretical component and also from any practical component. However, as has already been discussed, reflection is more than just thinking about your situation and more than just describing it. Examining your learning more objectively, by identifying the context of the situation, influencing factors that encouraged you into one particular course of action, and the feelings of yourself and others involved, are all important when unravelling the complexities of your practice. The more you examine and explore your practice, the easier it should become to probe deeper into understanding all the issues involved.

3) Developing a Learning Culture Within the Workplace

Reflection need not be a solitary activity. In fact, it could be argued that there is only so much you can learn when reflecting on your own. As reflection is now an integral part of each practitioner's development, everyone is expected to reflect and show evidence of reflection. Reflection can be extremely time consuming and laborious, or it can be pleasurable and profitable. It is up to you to make the most of the opportunities that present themselves and gain from your experiences. Part of that may be finding the right person to help you through your thought processes. Driscoll (1994) refers to a learning culture within the workplace. This simply means that enjoying and sharing learning within your workplace becomes part of the 'norm'. Then, in turn, you might document some of the most meaningful reflections in your personal professional profile.

One of the greatest qualities you can have to aid someone in their reflections is the skill of listening. It is easy to interrupt a colleague or friend when they are exploring a situation that happened to them with a similar experience that you have had yourself. Resist the temptation and encourage your colleague to explore the situation deeply. It can be satisfying and fulfilling to participate in others' reflective activities, as well as to share your own experiences. When several of you have been involved in the same situation, you should consider finding the opportunity of sharing the different perspectives of the situation together. It may surprise you to discover the different perspectives and lessons that have been learned by each of you.

More emphasis seems to be placed recently on the importance of sharing your reflections in practice. Formal roles have been devised and formal structures implemented to aid the process.

Think of the formal roles and structures that are in progress in your own area of practice, or that you are aware of, and identify whether they are successful or not. You might now explore why they are so successful (or not!).

Formal roles such as mentoring, preceptorship and clinical supervision are recent innovations within nursing in the last 20 years. The success of the roles and structures is dependent on the ability and commitment of the individuals themselves, as well as the preparation and resources available to fulfil the roles as they were designed. Shared reflections within a trusting relationship are an important ingredient to the success of these roles. However, short placements, resource constraints and sometimes a misunderstanding of each other's roles are causes for concern and preventing their greater success. Individual performance appraisal is another structure in progress that allows the opportunity of reflecting on your experience over the last year with your manager and identifying your aspirations for the coming year, in line with departmental/trust policy. To get the most out of this appraisal, you need to work hard at your reflections and encourage positive discussion about how well you are progressing and how your manager can help you fulfil your aspirations.

WHY REFLECT?

We have explored the difference between routine action, and reflective action and how each can help you get the most out of your experiences. It is important to clarify when it is appropriate to use each of them. You cannot survive without some routine action, but neither can you survive effectively without reflective action. The two combine to help you along the road to expert practitioner. Studying and learning from practice must be balanced. It is important to remember that reflection is a natural activity that you carry out every day. However, reflection in relation to study and professional practice is concerned with a more analytical process and encourages you towards a more in-depth examination of your practice. This exploration and examination allows you to take control of your practice and makes you a more informed practitioner.

Much has been written about the theory/practice gap in nursing, but little headway has been made as to how the gap can be narrowed. Perhaps the recent response from the profession towards developing the reflective practitioner (where learning has its foundation in practice and theory is developed out of practice) will provide a more united approach to this elusive issue.

Palmer *et al.* (1994) discuss 'emancipation through critical reflection'. This emancipation can be both personal, for you as an individual, as well as professional, for the profession as a whole. Perhaps through the development of shared reflections, where trusting relationships are encouraged and learning from different perspectives are recognised, the profession can begin this emancipation. It is hoped that the subsequent shared and supportive environment will enrich your practice, and in time, the profession will be better enabled to articulate its value, as well as to draw together the theory and the practice of nursing for the development of care for clients.

CONCLUSION

In summary, this chapter links closely with the previous chapters, and will help you to develop your understanding of how reflection can be used to help you study, and in particular to gain as much as you can from both your study and your clinical practice.

- You need to distinguish between automatic action and reflective action, and consider when each is appropriate in both your study and your practice.
- Reflection can be valuable both personally and professionally. You need to reflect on how you can make the most of your reflections for successful learning.
- There are different ways of reflecting. You need to find the best way for you.
- There are different types of reflection. As you become more skilled, you will find yourself developing the skills of each type of reflection.
- Different ways have been identified to get you started.

1) Discuss with your friends what they mean by reflection and how they go about it.
2) Discuss with your colleagues/mentor how you could share your reflections about aspects of care that several of you are involved in. Perhaps there is a time in the day/week that you could find to undertake this.
3) When something out of the ordinary happens, reflect on it and see what you have learned. Discuss it with someone else involved. Write it down.
4) Read some of the References to find other 'ways'/structures to help you examine your practice more easily and learn from it.

REFERENCES

BOUD D, KEOGH R and WALKER D (eds) (1985) *Reflection: Turning Experience into Learning.* London, Kogan Page.

DEWAR B (1992) Skill muddle? *Nursing Times,* 12(88), 24–27.

DEWEY D (1933) *How We Think.* DC Health and Co., Boston.

DRISCOLL J (1994) Reflective practice for practise. *Senior Nurse,* 13(7), 47–50.

ENGLISH NATIONAL BOARD FOR NURSING, MIDWIFERY AND HEALTH VISITING (1993) *The Current Teaching Provision for Individual Learning Styles of Students on Pre-registration Diploma Programmes in Adult Nursing.* London, ENB.

PALMER A, BURNS S and BULMAN C (1994) *Reflective Practice in*

Nursing: The Growth of the Professional Practitioner. London, Blackwell Scientific.

ROBINSON K (ed.) (1991) *Open and Distance Learning for Nurses*. Harlow, Longman.

UNITED KINGDOM CENTRAL COUNCIL FOR NURSING, MIDWIFERY AND HEALTH VISITING (1995) *PREP and You: Maintaining Your Registration; Standards for Education Following Registration* (factsheets). London, UKCC.

Using the Library

Kym Martindale

INTRODUCTION

Both this chapter and Chapter 6 are about gathering information from a variety of sources. The emphasis is on your
role in the process: how you can make the material and
resources work for you.

Gathering information can be broadly divided into two
stages:

- locating the material;
- using the material.

This chapter deals with the first, while Chapter 6 looks in
detail at the second.

Key Issues

- Using libraries, indexes and abstracts to find the right material.
- Information sources.
- Accesssing library resources.
- Literature searching.
- Obtaining literature.

CRITICAL PROCESS

Finding and using information is a process which involves critical
thinking, understanding and constant interpretation. It is a questioning process and good foundation for the reasoning skills you
need to present a written argument.

See
Chapter 10

GUIDING PRINCIPLE

Gathering information is done more effectively if you have
defined your purpose. Whether you're deciding which index to

search or which article to read, keep your purpose clearly in mind. For example, whilst preparing for an essay keep the essay question clearly visible (a useful tip for when you come to write it), to prevent you from straying down interesting but irrelevant avenues.

There is a huge amount of sources of material available and it is easy to be overwhelmed. Knowing your purpose keeps you focused and enables others, e.g. library staff, to help you.

INFORMATION SOURCES

As a student (and professional) you can expect to use the following:

- **Libraries** for:
  - books (general and specialised texts);
  - journals (professional, academic or specialised);
  - audiovisual material, e.g. videos;
  - CAL (computer-assisted learning) packages;
  - reference material (dictionaries, etc.).
- **Professional associations/specialist information centres** for:
  - contacts;
  - specialist information;
  - patient information.

This chapter will concentrate on how to access the information sources generally found in libraries. The aim is not to turn you into an expert, but to give you the confidence to use the expertise of the resources and staff.

LIBRARY RESOURCES

Most libraries will have the resources in Table 4.1, which offer material appropriate to different search needs. How do you know which to use when, and how do you access them?

Table 4.1 gives a general picture of sources, means of access and purpose, but it is not meant to be exhaustive. Your own library may hold other sources. There is an activity at the end of this chapter to help you explore your own library thoroughly.

Table 4.1: **Library resources**

Source	Access	Access route	Purpose
Textbooks and government publications	Library catalogue	Computer or card index	Core course material; skills and guides; general and historical; official
Reference: Dictionaries Encyclopaedia Yearbooks Directories Atlases	As above	As above	Definitions; further reading; contacts; statistics
Videos and audiovisual material	As above; special list	As above; depends on library	Instructive; visual; documentaries and/or TV programmes; current and contemporary
Computer-assisted learning (CAL)	As above	As above	Interactive learning; visual and/or diagrammatic
Journals	Indexes and abstracts; current awareness publications	Printed; computer, e.g. CD-ROM or online	Current and specific material; research; current professional news; jobs; information exchange; professional development events; contacts
Newspapers	Indexes	As above	Current and contemporary 'lay' material; factual; statistics

You can probably begin to see how the type of information you need, i.e. your purpose, determines which source to use. Take the two following questions and, referring to Table 4.1, think (for about 5–10 minutes) where you would look for the material for each. *There could be more than source.*

■ Describe the structure and function of the skin.
■ What causes the skin condition psoriasis and how is it now treated?

Both questions deal broadly with the skin. The first concerns basic anatomy and physiology, factual information that is unlikely to change greatly. Textbooks and visual material, i.e. CAL and videos, would probably provide excellent information for this question.

The second question deals with a *specific* skin condition, and requires *current* information. Textbooks would provide some material, and a medical dictionary would give an introductory definition, but you would use journal literature to discover up-to-date treatment and care, and any research, findings or discussion/controversy concerning them. There may also be recent TV documentaries (recorded and held in the library) or newspaper reports which are relevant, current, and which might aid your understanding of the more clinical material in the health journals.

The questions shared a broad subject base, but had different information needs. The needs were met in both cases by using a *range of sources*, but with the *emphasis* on established and journal literature, respectively.

WHAT RESOURCES DOES YOUR LIBRARY OFFER?

If you don't already know what your college and/or professional library holds, and how and where books, journals and indexes, etc. are kept, **find out**! It is best to familiarise yourself with such things early in your course before you need them. College libraries usually offer induction and tuition in the first few weeks of a course. Make the most of such opportunities, seek them out. If you don't have such opportunities, or they were not useful, the library orientation activity at the end of this chapter may help.

THE LIBRARY CATALOGUE

This resource must be mastered as soon as possible. The catalogue tells you what stock the library has and where it is shelved. The type of material listed will depend on the library, but will certainly include books and government publications. Videos, models and CAL programs may be in the catalogue, but journals generally are not.

Most libraries now have computerised catalogue access, often known as OPACs (online public access). OPACs can tell you what material the library holds by author, subject or title, where any item is shelved, or whether it is out on loan. Other facilities are dependent on the system used by the library. (See the library orientation activity to help you to discover the benefits of your library's system.)

JOURNAL LITERATURE

What is a Journal?

Essentially, journals are a way of communicating with your fellow professionals nationally and internationally. All professions and trades have journals: the medical and health professions have thousands, and your library will not therefore have all of them.

You may come across journals referred to as 'serials' and/or 'periodicals', because they are published periodically, and because each issue is part of the whole. A journal may come out monthly, weekly, bi-monthly, quarterly (four times a year), or occasionally less. Generally, the issues appearing in one year will be described as one volume, each year having a volume number. For example, *Nursing Management* is published monthly. All 12 issues for 1991 comprise Volume 22, 1992 Volume 23, and so on. Within that, each issue has its own number, e.g. the February 1991 issue will be Volume 22 Number 2. The standard way of writing this is 22(2); the volume number precedes the issue number which is in brackets. (See Appendix A.)

How is the Material in Journals Different from that in Books?

In four important ways:

1) **Currency**: books can take 2–4 years to reach publication; journal literature is usually published within months, depending on the frequency of the journal itself.

2) **Specificity**: articles are condensed material and therefore focused on specific areas. When you search the literature, your subject headings can be correspondingly precise.

3) **Ongoing**: reports of long-term research projects are to be found in the relevant journals, information otherwise unavailable for perhaps years.

4) **Contemporary**: literature from journals published in the 1960s will directly reflect the tone, attitudes and knowledge of the time, unmuddied by hindsight.

What Sort of Material do the Different Journals Have?

You can expect the more frequent (weekly, monthly) journals to contain current affairs, jobs and listings, and articles which are informative and wide-ranging, but not necessarily research based. The name of the journal is a fair indication of its broad aim, standards and content. So, *Nursing Times* or *Nursing Standard* aim to inform the nursing profession and will cover anything they consider relevant. The journal *Cancer Nursing* clearly has a narrower remit; articles are longer, specific and often research based. Published bi-monthly, its material is less immediate and more analytical.

Journals are regular sources of material which is valuable for its specificity, currency and contemporaneity.

ACCESSING THE JOURNAL LITERATURE

When you need to find out whether a book contains information on a topic you use the index at the back. This tells you if the topic is covered, on which pages, and in how much detail.

The principle is the same with journals, i.e. you use an index. It tells you what articles are available on a subject and in which journal you will find them. The chief difference is that journal indexes are separate publications from the journals themselves; they also index many different journals simultaneously.

There are advantages to this. Remember, there are thousands of health and health-related journals, hundreds in nursing alone. If these were indexed individually instead of collectively, searching the literature would be an enormous task, and you would be restricted to the journals your library held. (The flip side is that using journal indexes means you will require articles not held by your library; most libraries recognise this and will request articles from other sources via an interlibrary loans system.)

What is a Journal Index?

Indexes, like the journals themselves, are published monthly, bi-monthly or quarterly in volumes and issues. Again, like the journals, they vary in their subject coverage, purpose and origin. Several are now also available in computerised format, either on CD-ROM (compact disk – read only memory) or online, and this makes them a powerful, flexible search tool. This chapter will look more closely at both these formats.

Indexes, whatever their format, can be produced by anyone from large single-purpose commercial concerns to institutional libraries as a marketing sideline. Their aim is roughly the same, i.e. to scan a discrete area of literature and list the bibliographic details of the items under subject headings. In most cases these items are journal articles, but dissertations may be included. Some indexes cover unpublished material, leaflets/pamphlets, or even audiovisual material. However, most of the literature is journal based.

How Much Information does an Index give About Articles?

Index information consists of the basic bibliographic details about any one item. For a journal article these details should be:

- title of article;
- author(s);
- journal name;
- volume and issue number;
- date;
- page numbers.

This information makes up the **citation** or **reference**. Depending on the index, you may be told more about the article, e.g. how much further reading it includes or references it cites, and whether the content is research based, statistical etc.

> *Below is an example of a citation*
> Promoting nursing research. (Hancock C) NURSE
> RESEARCHER 1993 Dec; 1(2): 72–80 (7 ref)
>
> *This is what the different parts of the citation mean*
> Title of article. (Author) NAME OF JOURNAL Date;
> volume (issue): page numbers (number of references to
> other articles, books etc. cited by author in this article)

Abstracts

Some indexes go further and provide a summary of content. This
summary is called an **abstract**. Indexes which provide such
information often include the term 'abstract' in their title. For
example, *Nursing Research Abstracts* and *International Nursing Index*
are two publications which clearly indicate the type of literature
they cover and how much information they give about the items
they list.

Abstracts help you to make a more informed decision about
the value to you of an article, paper or report. They are not a
substitute for the original text and must not be treated as such.
You must not quote them as if you had read the original full-
length work.

Which are the Best Indexes/Abstracts?

There are so many health journals and other types of health
literature that no one index can cover all the material. You will
find that many specialise in a subject area, e.g. *Palliative Care
Index*, or a type of material, e.g. *Nursing Research Abstracts*. Others
are more comprehensive and cover broader areas, e.g. CINAHL
(*Cumulative Index to Nursing and Allied Health Literature*), INI
(*International Nursing Index*) and ASSIA (*Applied Social Sciences
Index and Abstracts*). It is your information needs that determine
which indexes are best. Table 4.2 lists *some* of the different indexes
available in the health information field; there are many others.

CD-ROM

As we have seen, there are several media on which information
can be stored: paper (books, journals, indexes/abstracts), audiovisual (videocassettes, audiocassettes, slides and films) and com-

Table 4.2: **Indexes and abstracts**

Index/abstract	Coverage
ASSIA (*Applied Social Sciences Index and Abstracts*)*	Social aspects of health; international, but strong on UK material
CINAHL (*Cumulative Index to Nursing and Allied Health Literature*)*	Nursing, health-related and allied health; international, but US bias in coverage and origin; US spelling and terminology
Health Service Abstracts	Management, quality assurance and administration issues; UK origin
INI (*International Nursing Index*)	International in coverage, content and language; nursing with some allied health; US terminology and spelling
Medline* (*Index Medicus* is the name of the printed version)	Highly clinical and medical, allied health and some nursing, also dental and veterinary; international in content, coverage and language
Nurses' and Midwives' Index	Strong UK coverage; community, nursing and midwifery, some psychology and sociology, and health service generally
Nursing Research Abstracts	Research, published and unpublished, relevant to nursing; strongly UK in content
PsycLIT* (*Psychological Abstracts* is the name of the printed version)	International in content and language, relevant to psychology and related disciplines, and US in origin; covers journals, books and specific chapters
Social Services Abstracts	UK material, social policy, services and welfare in practice

* Available on CD-ROM.

puters (floppy disks, hard disks). With the exception of the paper formats, these need equipment with which to read the information on them, e.g. tape machines, viewers and projectors for audiovisual material; terminals/VDUs, keyboards and drives/modems for electronic information. A CD-ROM is a compact disk and requires access via a computer. (The 'read only memory' means the data stored on the disk can only be read, and not altered or added to in any way.)

Almost anything can be stored on CD-ROM, but it is probable

See Chapter 5 for techno-logical details

that those in your library will hold journal indexes, dictionaries, encyclopaedia or perhaps back copies of newspapers. The computerised format facilitates swifter and more flexible searching by allowing:

- a combination of subject headings, e.g. 'insulin dependency' and 'adolescents' and 'diabetes mellitus';
- other combinations, e.g. author and subject, subject and type of material such as statistics or research, subject and specific journal or type of journal, subject and specific years of publication.

Some searches which the CD-ROM format can deal with more effectively than the printed counterpart are shown below. The terms which would be used in the search are in bold type.

- **Research** on the increase of **asthma** in **children** in the **UK**.
- **Reflection** in **nurse education**: an **evaluation**.
- Articles on **PREP** (post-registration education and practice) from **Nursing Times** during **1992–1995**.
- **Case studies** of **breast cancer** sufferers with particular reference to **post-operative care**.
- Any articles by Philip **Burnard** on **interpersonal skills**.
- Articles on **evaluation** of **management methods** from **nursing** journals published in the **UK**.

All of these searches would be possible using the appropriate printed indexes, but you would be hampered by only being able to use one search term at a time. For example, in the above search concerning breast cancer, you would look up 'breast cancer', then check the citations given to see, as well as you could, if they were also case studies looking at post-operative care. The CD-ROM would however allow you to state all those search terms in combination, e.g. 'breast cancer' *and* 'case studies' *and* 'post-operative care'.

The advantage of the CD-ROM format is that it gives you more means of access to the information, and therefore greater control over your search. There are other benefits, such as being able to print out your search results, and the greater detail available about the articles indexed; you will discover these as you use different CD-ROM facilities. Again, find out now what your library offers and start using it.

You find literature on a chosen subject, whether in journals, dissertations or reports, by looking up that subject in the appropriate indexes. Different indexes cover different types of material, subjects and journals; deciding which indexes to use is determined by your information need. Indexes can be printed or in computer format, the latter being most widely available as CD-ROM. Computer searches can be swifter and more effective than their printed counterparts.

STARTING THE LITERATURE SEARCH

Consider your search/information needs.

1) What sort of information do you need: statistics, research, recent material, specifically UK or international?

2) Are you working to a deadline? Leave enough time to search for, order if necessary, and read material. Don't forget, you still have to *write* your essay.

3) Have you thought about your search terms/subject headings? Think carefully about what headings you might use and how the indexes might express your subject. It is useful to brainstorm this, creating a spider map of your subject area (Fig. 4.1). This helps to identify specific and broad terms, and provides a rough, visual hierarchy of the subject.

Purpose

All these considerations are about defining and sticking to your purpose. Points 1 and 3 above are particularly important, and getting them right will help you achieve the deadline mentioned in Point 2.

Which Index?

You will have realised by now that your search needs dictate your choice of indexes. Below is an exercise (maximum 10 minutes needed) which allows some practice at this.

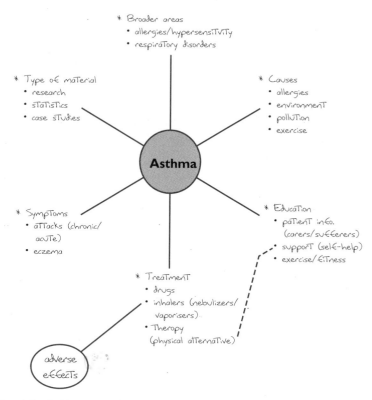

Fig. 4.1   Spider map of search terms.

   The exercise involves matching search needs to the right
.indexes. Use Table 4.2 (p. 63) to decide which indexes might
be most appropriate for finding the necessary material for these
searches. There isn't a right or wrong choice exactly, but clearly
some indexes are better than others.

As you match search and index/es, note the reasons for the
choices you have made. This may help to clarify the thinking behind
your decision.

Examples

1)   What effect does a hip replacement have on the
     patient's self-image, and how might that influence their
     recovery?
2)   Does nurse education equip students to cope with the
     emotional stress of nursing terminally ill patients?

> 3) What, if any, relation is there between inequality in health and social class?
> 4) What effect have the recent NHS reforms had on staff morale, and how has management responded?

1) This question encompasses two issues: the psychological and social effects – psychosocial factors – of a condition, and the role of the carer in recognising and dealing with these effects. There is a clear nursing angle so the indexes CINAHL, *Nursing Research Abstracts*, INI or NMI would all be useful sources. A combined search on the CD-ROM CINAHL under 'hip surgery' *and* 'self-image' (or whatever the correct search terms might be) would swiftly reveal what, if any, material is available.

    The nursing indexes are the obvious source for the caring angle. However, you might want to read current material on the subject of self-concept, and explore its psychology. Psyc-LIT or *Psychology Abstracts* would then be a useful source.

    It is probably immaterial whether the articles you find are American, British or Australian since there is no particular cultural slant to the search. Your main concern is the subject, which is universal.

2) Again, this is clearly a nursing issue. CINAHL, NMI, INI and *Nursing Research Abstracts* would be appropriate routes to the relevant material. However, the question is also about stress, death and education. The educational element needs you to be aware of the country of origin of the material you might find; it could well still be relevant for the sake of contrast or proposed change, but if you only require UK material use the UK indexes first.

    You may search Medline/*Index Medicus* for information on how effective medical education is in this regard. General material on occupational stress could be found in any of the sources mentioned, but add *Health Service Abstracts* for a management angle.

3) This question is primarily sociological. ASSIA is the most appropriate source. *Health Service Abstracts* might provide information on the monitoring of the quality of delivery of health across society. *Social Services Abstracts* could be equally useful for material outside the remit of the NHS, e.g. the effects of the inequalities. Again, country of origin

might be important, although American material (for example) could be useful for comparison.

4)   Since this question is based around the NHS, British sources are more directly relevant. The subject itself concerns management, change, stress and staff motivation and development. *Health Service Abstracts* would be a good starting point. NMI is a less obvious choice, but its strong UK bias and broad range of health journals makes it a useful source for NHS material generally. ASSIA would be effective for material on wider aspects of the reforms.

The reforms are relatively recent, and realisation of their effects even more so. This would determine how far back you search.

All the searches in this exercise required:

■ identification of the key element, e.g. nursing, education or psychological;

■ an awareness of the importance of country of publication;

■ consultation of more than one source, especially for the wider or background material.

Other Sources

Table 4.2 is not a complete list of indexes/abstracts. There are many smaller, monthly publications which are often subject specific, e.g. *Palliative Care Index*, *Diabetes Contents*. Their particular strength is their currency, i.e. they aim to keep their audience abreast of new material which is too recent to have been indexed elsewhere. They are referred to as *Current Awareness* bulletins or services.

There are also several other health- and medicine-related indexes available online. These are computerised databases whose benefits are much the same as those of the CD-ROM databases. However, the cost of using them is prohibitive since they are accessed via computer and modem, i.e. telephone, and the searcher is charged for the time spent online. The facility for such searches is entirely dependent on your institution's resources.

Which Subject Headings?

Having identified the appropriate indexes, you need to clarify your **subject headings**. These are the words you use to look up your subject in the indexes. They may also be referred to as **search terms** or **keywords**.

Identifying your headings is done in two stages:

- highlighting the key terms in your essay question;
- ensuring they are the terms used by the indexes you intend to search.

For the first stage, look again at the questions in the exercise on p. 66. Take 10 minutes to identify what you consider to be the keywords for the search (then check them against those below). See p. 66

1) hip replacement   self-image   recovery
2) nurse education   students   stress   terminally ill
3) inequality   health   social class
4) NHS reforms   staff morale   management

It is possible that your keywords are not exactly the same as those used by any of the indexes. It is helpful at this stage to brainstorm for alternatives:

> **1)** hip replacement: hip surgery/hip prosthesis/artificial hip
> recovery: rehabilitation/post–operative care
> self-image: body-image/self-concept/self-esteem

It is also likely that in some cases the headings you use will be different depending on the index, despite the fact that you're looking up the same subject.

Both factors are due to cultural differences in terminology and spelling, and diversity of language. For example, look at the two lists below, of terms related to their subject:

Cancer	**Ageing**
cancer	ageing/aging
oncology	aged
neoplasm	elderly
tumour/tumor	old age
growth	geriatric
carcinosis	gerontology
melanoma	
canker	

An index could use quie a different term to the one you have chosen to search. If your search terms do not match the index headings you are wasting your time. If you look up 'geriatric nursing' in an index and find no material, there are two possible explanations:

- there may not be anything published/available;
- the index has used the heading 'care of the elderly'.

But, how do you know which explanation is the case?

It is essential when you are searching an index, particularly a printed one, that you speak its language. It is also important when using CD-ROM versions, although there is greater flexibility. The problem is finding out the correct terminology for the particular index you wish to search.

Most indexes try to help by providing a list of their terms for you to check before you begin to search. Called a **thesaurus** or **subject headings list**, it has two functions:

- to provide you with the correct search terms for that index (see first entry in example below);
- to introduce you to narrower (more specific), related or broader search terms, i.e. to alert you to other headings which may be equally or more relevant (see second entry in example below).

Example: **thesaurus entries**

Nurse education
    see Education, nursing

Education, nursing
    see also
    Education, nursing, Baccalaureate
    Education, nursing, continuing
    Education, nursing, post-registration

Such a list is essential, not only to you the searcher, but also to those compiling the index. They need to standardise their headings so that related material is clustered under the same term ensuring that you will find all the material available on a subject. Every year, with each new edition of the index, there is an updated thesaurus; this reflects the growth of information, the need for more specific terms, and changing language. Consulting an index's thesaurus informs you of the best search terms. If your terms are wrong you will not find the material. Subject headings/ search terms really are **key** words.

A thesaurus is not infallible. It will not always list your original search term and therefore alternatives. In this instance, you need to be your own thesaurus. This is where brainstorming possible subject headings (see p. 67) is helpful. Another source of help is, See p. 67 of course, the librarian.

Spelling and terminology are especially tricky if the index is American as are CINAHL and INI. Library staff accrue a healthy vocabulary of American terms and spellings over time – tap into it. Accurate spelling is essential when using CD-ROM databases. If you type in the UK spelling of a term while searching CINAHL on CD-ROM, you will retrieve far less material than the database holds on that subject. This can be advantageous if the subject is large and you only want UK material, but you will also miss much good material.

- Identify your search terms from your essay question, or write down your search need in a way that helps you to highlight the keywords. Brainstorm for alternative keywords/search terms.
- Use the thesaurus (if the index has one); it ensures you are using the correct search terms, and those most appropriate to your search.
- American indexes use different spellings and terminology; some indexes have no thesaurus at all. Consult library staff and your own brainstorm list.
- Identifying your search terms properly will retrieve relevant material, or confirm its absence.

How Useful is a Reference?

It is difficult to deduce the potential value of an article from the basic information given in an index, i.e. the citation. However, there are indicators.

- Is there an abstract? Check CD-ROM, the journal itself if possible, or another index.
- Check the authors' credentials – they may be well known in their field, or have written other material.
- Is the cited journal academic, scholarly, research based or more news based?
- How long is the article? If it is long, consider the time necessary to read and understand it; if short, how informative will it be?
- How many references does it cite? These may lead to other

material on your subject, and may indicate the authenticity of the authors' work.

- Is the article itself cited by others? Check a citation index if possible (ask your library staff); this will tell you if, and how often, this particular article has been referred to by other published authors.
- Peer discussion/sharing information – tutors and fellow students or colleagues may have read, seen or know of certain work.

This is a skill which will come with practice. You will make mistakes, because you cannot be 100% certain of any material until you have read it. There won't always be an abstract; and both authors and journals are numerous and many will be unknown to you. But if your search terms are accurate and thought out, you are more likely to retrieve relevant material.

What if You find Little or Nothing?

Information retrieval is a frustrating business. There will be times when there appears to be nothing published on your subject. However it is also true that failure to locate any material can never be attributed with certainty to the fact that there is nothing. There will always be a niggling doubt that you didn't seek hard enough or in the right places.

Certainly, there will be times when you have to accept that there is no published information on your subject, and re-adjust your search (or do some research and get it published to fill the gap!). But don't give up straight away: first be resourceful and adaptable in the following ways.

- Check your search terms – use the thesaurus, library staff or fellow students.
- Are you using the most appropriate source (printed vs CD-ROM indexes, textbooks vs journals, general vs specialist libraries/information centres)?
- Is there comparable information available? For example, question 1 in the exercise on p. 66 could use research material from studies on breast cancer or AIDS – the key element is the patient's self-perception and response to their condition.
- Talk to colleagues, fellow students, tutors and library staff – they have expertise, contacts and knowledge not available via established channels.

See p. 66

- There are twists and turns in the literature search, but you are not alone. You are not expected to struggle on without help. Professional help and expertise is to hand – use it! But, help them to help you by being clear about your purpose.

Below is a checklist which condenses the main points of this chapter and the steps of a literature search.

Preparation

1) Define your purpose: why do you need this information and what precisely do you need? Write this out.
2) Plan your time: allow for search setbacks, for obtaining items from elsewhere, and for reading the material.
3) Familiarise yourself with your library's facilities as soon as possible – e.g. opening hours, CD-ROM access, photocopiers, and journals in stock.

Defining your Search

1) Identify your keywords from your search statement/ essay question.
2) Brainstorm your keywords for alternative headings.
3) Identify appropriate sources.

Ask for help at any point

Starting the Search

1) Check your search terms in the thesaurus/subject headings list for each index you use.
2) **Record**:   search terms used, sources searched, e.g. NMI 1993–1995 under 'nurse education' or CINAHL 1993–1995 under 'education–nursing' and 'death–education'. This saves you repeating parts of your search and can inform library staff in giving you further help. CD-ROM databases often allow you to print your search giving you an excellent record of terms used and how, i.e. your search strategy.
3) **Record**:   full citation details of items, articles etc. which you wish to locate and read. This information is necessary for swift location *and* for your own final reference list. Noting each citation separately on index

See Appendix A and the section on plagiarism in Chapter 12

cards enables easy filing with space for annotation, i.e. brief notes on its usefulness and content.

4)   Locate/order and read your material noting further search needs and ideas.

5)   Adapt your search as necessary – modify search terms, explore related subject areas, use comparable material. This is **developing your strategy**. Record such developments.

6)   Stick to your time plan and your purpose; literature searching is time consuming and full of distractions. Your time for searching and reading is limited. Be realistic and have a clear cut-off point (although you can note items of interest for another time).

CONCLUSION

In this chapter we have discussed and tested the process of information finding. At all stages, you have had to make decisions based on your needs, acting critically and reflectively. In order to do so, you have had to keep your purpose to the fore. In Chapter 6 we will see how knowing your purpose also applies to *using* the information you acquire during your studies.

- Get to know your library and its resources.
- Ask for help whenever you need it.
- Make full use of any library tuition.
- Allow time for library and literature searches.
- Identify your information needs.
- Define and stick to your purpose.
- Your best sources of information will change according to your needs.
- Spelling and terminology differ according to origin and source.
- Journals contain much more current material.
- Your library is unlikely to hold everything you will need.
- Your library can obtain material from other libraries.
- Allow time to order material.
- Keep references and records.
- Practise these skills.

GLOSSARY OF TERMS

Abstract   Summary of article/paper.

Audiovisual   Material which needs to be viewed or heard.

Bibliographical   Information detailing particulars of book, article etc. which enables your reader to locate the material.

Citation   The giving of bibliographical information.

CD-ROM   'Compact disk – read only memory': retrievable information stored on disk which is updated at given intervals.

Current Awareness   Bulletins which provide information on recently published work.

Index (journals)   Collective list of work (usually published in journals) arranged by subject.

Journal   Regular publication, e.g. monthly, weekly, bi-annually; forum for articles, research papers and professional exchange of information.

Literature search   Search of mainly journal and research literature for material relating to your topic.

OPAC   'Online public access catalogue': system which gives you access to library computer catalogue – replaces the old card catalogue system.

Online   Live database being constantly and simultaneously used and updated.

Periodical   See **Journal**.

Reference   Unit of bibliographical information.

Serial   See **Journal**.

Thesaurus   List of alternative/correct subject headings used by particular index.

Library Orientation

Essentially, these are checklists to help you identify the facilities and services your library offers, and where they are located. Before you begin, find out whether your library offers any tuition, and if so in which areas and at what level. Personal tuition is always preferable: you can ask questions on the spot, and the teaching will be geared towards your institution, resources and needs. These activities are substitutes and must of necessity be general, although they may complement any tuition offered by your library. They also apply the underlying principle of Chapters 8 and 9: specific questions, i.e. purpose, help you focus on what you need to know.

Library Facilities

What	Where/how	Notes
e.g. Private study area	e.g. **B Floor**	e.g. **Must book**
Toilets		
Lockers		
Enquiry desk		
Issue counter		
Books: how are they arranged?		
Other material: Videos/government reports/ pamphlets/ models Offprints/exam papers		
Quick reference: Dictionaries etc.		
Library catalogue: OPAC card? Includes books, videos, other? Tells you loan status (if book is on loan or not), numbers of copies, how many items you have out? Can you search by author, title or subject, make reservations?		
Journals: are they listed anywhere, how are they arranged, are some held in the stack?		
Private study areas		
Groupwork areas		

What	Where/how	Notes
Journal indexes		
CD-ROMs: what databases, need to book, tuition available?		
Computer facilities: what packages, need to book?		
Photocopiers: cash or card or both		
Staff availability: professional, identified subject librarian?		
Hours of opening: Term/vacation		
Membership: entitlements, duration, special needs		

Library Services

There may be handouts or leaflets available detailing extent, costs, availability and instructions on how to use any of the services listed. Don't hesitate to ask the library staff.

Service	Details/leaflet available
e.g. Literature searches	e.g. **Leaflet: online must be requested**
e.g. Inter-library loans (requests for journal articles not held by your library)	e.g. **15 max per year**
Loan periods: Books (long/short-loan) Other items Vacation/placement allowances	

Service	Details/leaflet available
Reservations: 　　Via OPAC/request form 　　Waiting lists 　　Pick-up point	
Inter-library loans: 　　Cost 　　Waiting time 　　Pick-up point 　　Conditions of use	
Use of other libraries: 　　At other sites 　　At other institutions 　　At local hospitals 　　On placement	
Tuition: 　　Resource 　　Level 　　When	
Literature searches: 　　Help available? 　　Cost 　　Conditions	

Each library will differ in the services it gives. Those listed above are standard and can be expected from most educational libraries, but many will offer additional services. Consult with your library staff over these checklists (which can be photocopied for your use). They will inform you of any extras.

Using Information Technology

Jansci Sketchley-Kaye

The computer will always do exactly what you tell it to do: this may not always be what you want it to do.

Anon.

INTRODUCTION

This chapter is about how information technology (IT) can help you to study more easily and more effectively. This chapter assumes no knowledge of computers. If you are already using a computer or word processor, then some of the material will already be familiar and may be skimmed through or omitted altogether.

The anonymous quote above emphasises that a computer is merely another tool – a means to an end – and also that you need to be aware of what a computer *cannot* do for you, as well as what it *can* do.

Key Issues

- What information technology is.
- What a computer does.
- Hardware and software.
- Uses of a computer (word-processing, databases, spreadsheets, graphics).
- The Data Protection Act.
- Using computers to communicate.
- Useful addresses.
- Glossary of terms.

WHAT IS INFORMATION TECHNOLOGY?

The essential word is *information*. The facts and figures (**data**) that we use in everyday life only make sense and impart knowledge, i.e. provide information, when arranged in a particular way or given in a particular context. For example, the sequence of numbers and letters M123XOU becomes meaningful in the context of a car registration number: M123 XOU. In a similar way, letters in a sequence are data, but organised into words and arranged in particular patterns they convey information. Information is the foundation of all activity.

The role of *technology* is to help with the management of the information: one of the reasons for the rapid expansion of computer use is the way in which computers have made information management easier, faster and more efficient.

 When did you last use a computer?

If you have answered 'never' to the above, ask yourself when you last used a cash dispenser or an automatic washing machine, or programmed a video recorder, or used a calculator. All of these are 'computers' of a sort:

> **computer** n. automatic electronic apparatus for making calculations or controlling operations.
>
> (*Concise Oxford Dictionary*)

If we take the cash dispenser as an example: when you go to take some money out, the two things which you tell the computer are your personal identification number (PIN) and the amount you wish to withdraw (this is often called the **input data**). You do this by putting your card in the slot and pressing the buttons on the keypad. The computer checks that the card and the PIN match, that the card has not expired, and that there is enough money in your account to cover the withdrawal (the term **data processing** is used for this bit). The computer then carries out a calculation, tells you the balance of your account, and operates the mechanism which counts and issues the money. This final stage is called the **output**, and can take the form of information and/or activity or a product. The process is illustrated diagrammatically in Fig. 5.1.

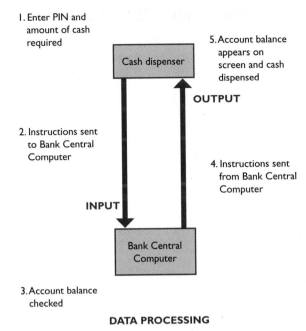

Figure 5.1

Can you think of another example from everyday life?

- The machine.
- The input data.
- The data processing.
- The output.

As we have seen, computers come in many shapes and sizes, and do many different things. The example you gave above may have been about using a computer in the course of your clinical work: over the past 10 years computers have become an accepted tool at ward level, and are used for a variety of purposes, e.g.

- ordering stock;
- keeping a duty roster;
- planning patient care;
- pathology results.

You may be able to think of other uses. In all the above examples the computer is used as a tool, one which (hopefully) makes your work easier.

THE PARTS OF A COMPUTER SYSTEM

Although you don't need any special technical knowledge to work a computer, it is helpful to have a basic understanding of what the components of a computer system are and what they do.

Computers come in many shapes and sizes, from large machines the size of filing cabinets and bigger (**mainframe computers**), through **mini-computers** (as big as a night storage heater), to **micro-computers** which are small enough to sit on a desktop, or even fit inside a briefcase. The main difference between the various types is the amount of data that they can handle and the speed at which they work. The type of computer which you are most likely to encounter and use is the **personal computer** (PC), which sits on a desk or workstation. Computer technology is still developing extremely quickly. The micro-computer of today can do the work of a mainframe computer of 20 years ago.

A computer system consists of three elements:

Hardware: the bits of the computer which you can actually touch: keyboards, monitors, printers etc.

Software: the instructions or programs which a computer needs to make it work.

Liveware: the human computer operator.

HARDWARE

Input Devices

Any method of feeding data into a computer can be called an input device. Some typical input devices are described in the box below.

- **Keyboard**   Basically like a typewriter keyboard, but with some additional keys.

- **Mouse**   A handheld device used to move a small pointer on the screen and select items from a menu of choices.

- **Scanner**   Similar to a photocopier in some ways: a picture or page of text can be copied into the computer's memory and changes made using special software.

- **Bar code reader**   Used to read information in a bar code (a label carrying an arrangement of black and white strips of varying thickness). You may have seen a bar code reader being used at a supermarket check-out, either held in the hand or built into the top of the check-out desk.
- **Touch-sensitive screen**   Some large shops and building societies use these. The user chooses options by touching different parts of the screen.

The Processor

The central processing unit (CPU) is the heart, or perhaps more accurately the brain, of the computer, since it controls everything which the computer does and carries out the data processing. The CPU and various other electronic components are located within a metal or plastic case.

Output Devices

An output device is anything which produces information from the data processing in a usable form. Examples of output devices are given in the box below.

- **Monitor**   Sometimes called the VDU, this looks like a television screen and comes in a range of sizes. The screen display may be colour or monochrome.
- **Printer**   These come in many shapes and sizes, but all do essentially the same job, producing printed text, pictures, diagrams etc. onto paper.

Information Storage

An important element of any computer system is information storage and retrieval. It would clearly be very inconvenient if, for example, you were using your computer to write an essay, and had to type the whole essay in each time you wanted to alter it or print it, so various methods of storing information have been devised. Most of them work by recording data in electromagnetic form on a plastic disk or tape coated in metal oxide, much as a tape recorder does. More recently the compact disk (CD) technology used to record and play back music using a low-power laser beam has been adapted to record and store other sorts of information. Most machines have what is called a **hard disk** inside the case, on which information can be stored in chunks as named files. Files can also be stored on **floppy disks**, which fit into a slot in the computer and may be taken away and used on another machine of similar type which is **compatible**, i.e. able to run the same programs. This is very useful if you are using a machine in a college or at work, and want to take something home to work on using your own machine. Floppy disks need to be handled with the care you would use for a CD or a vinyl record.

SOFTWARE

Software can be divided into two main groups: **operating systems** and **applications**.

Operating system software contains the basic instructions which the computer needs to work. The average user does not need to know much about the operating system, and the computer industry generally tries very hard to make life as easy as possible for the majority of users who are not technically minded.

You will, however need to know about the application software which you will be using. Application software is the general name given to the programs which carry out the various jobs which the computer user wants to do: writing letters, reports, essays, keeping accounts, keeping records etc. Applications fall into various groups, the most important of which will now be considered in turn.

Word-Processing

Many courses of study will require you to produce written work: in your career to date you will probably have been asked to write some or all of the following: essays, care studies, reports, journals, literature reviews.

 Think about the process you go through when preparing written work: identify and jot down the various stages, from being given the title or assignment guidelines to handing the work in. You will use your answers to this question later in this section.

Word-processing software is probably more widely used than any other group of applications, and will probably be the first thing you will be interested in as a student. Word-processing software is produced for use with PCs, but it is also possible to buy a word-processor. These machines look very like a typewriter, but have a small screen and are able to store and retrieve information like a PC and also print out. If all you wish to do is word-process, then this kind of machine may suit your needs.

There are many different makes of word-processing software: you may recognise tradenames such as WordPerfect, Word, WordStar, and LocoScript, but there are many others. All have certain similarities and some individual features: it is not possible to recommend one above another.

Functions of a Word-Processor

- **Text entry**   Text is usually entered from the keyboard, but may be read in with a scanner. The keyboard is used like a typewriter, and the text appears on the screen as it is entered.

- **Editing**   Spelling and other mistakes are easy to correct: single letters and words may be deleted and replaced with ease. Most word-processors now include a feature which checks spelling.

- **Formatting**   Any alterations to the layout and appearance of the text fall under this heading. Words, sentences, whole paragraphs and more can be printed in bold type, underlined, put in italics, or in larger or smaller type. Margins can be made wider or narrower, line spacing increased and decreased. These changes can be made as the text is typed in, or afterwards.

- **Cutting and pasting**   Using this feature, chunks of text can be moved or copied elsewhere.

- **Word count**   When you are asked to produce written work for a course you will often be set a word limit. The word count feature gives a quick and accurate total.

Look back at your answers in the reflective question above. Where might a word-processor be useful?

The chief advantage of the word-processor over other methods is that the basic text of an essay only needs to be typed in once: thereafter the text may be edited, formatted, added to and printed out without the need for tedious retyping or rewriting in longhand.

Debbie is undertaking a course in nursing research: as part of her course she has to write a 3000 word essay on research-based practice.

Her initial search in the library turns up a number of useful looking articles. She writes some brief notes on each. Using a word-processor she then writes the full references for the articles (see Appendix A for details on this) and under each reference writes further notes about the content of the article, how she reacts to it and how it might be used in her essay. She makes sure that she saves her work frequently and, at the end of the session, copies the file onto a floppy disk in case the hard disk in the computer gets damaged, or somebody else accidentally deletes her files.

She then uses the word-processor to produce an outline plan of the essay. She shows this plan to her tutor and as a result of the discussion adds some extra headings to her plan and revisits the library. New material is summarised as before.

The revised plan looks good, and Debbie begins to write the first draft of her essay. She refers to her notes as she goes, and is able to copy some of her quotes straight into her essay using the 'cut and copy' feature of the word-processor. She remembers to save her work every 5 minutes or so: that way, if the power supply fails for some reason, or the machine breaks down, she won't lose too much of her essay. Once again, she also makes sure she copies the file onto a floppy disk. She uses the spelling checker to correct her spelling mistakes and typing errors, and the word count feature to make sure she is not going over the word limit for the essay.

When the draft is complete, she prints a hard copy and discusses it with her tutor. The tutor suggests some alterations, which Debbie is easily able to make by typing in new text in some places and cutting and pasting existing paragraphs in others. She checks the length of the essay again, and finds that she needs to delete one or two unnecessary paragraphs.

The instructions for the assignment say that work needs to be double spaced, so when Debbie is happy with the text, she increases the line spacing. She also adds page numbers, and changes the section headings to a bold typeface. She sorts her reference list into alphabetical order. One final spell check, and the essay is ready to print out onto good quality paper.

On the way home that night, Debbie leaves her bag (with the essay in it) on the bus, and is unable to recover it. Fortunately, she has remembered to copy the essay onto a floppy disk, and is thus able to print another copy very easily.

Databases

Sometimes your work as a student will involve listing and sorting information; for example you may carry out a research study which involves asking questions and recording answers, or you may wish to create a list of names and addresses of useful contacts for later reference. Both these tasks could be carried out manually, but if you are handling more than a small amount of information the process of checking your records by hand could become lengthy and tedious. Imagine, for example, that your list of contacts has a hundred names on it. For each person you have the following information: surname, forenames, address, job title, place of work, telephone number, birthday. You could order the surnames alphabetically, using a card index, and thus easily find the record for any given surname. But imagine that you wished for some reason to make a list of all your contacts in a particular hospital, or who hold a particular post. You would have to look at each card in turn, which would take some time.

Database software provides an easy solution to the above problem. The best way to think about a database is as an electronic filing system where any one of the pieces of information stored can act as a base for sorting and retrieving the records within the filing system.

Let us take the example of names and addresses from the illustration below (Fig. 5.2).

For each person you want to record:

- surname;
- first names;
- address;
- job title;
- place of work;
- telephone number;
- birthday;
- date of last contact.

These are called the **field names**. Next to each field name is a space (the **field**) into which the appropriate data is entered. All the fields together make up a **record**, which is unique to the individual concerned. A group of records is a **file**, and one or

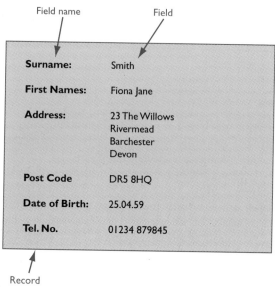

Figure 5.2

more files together make up a **database**. You might find it helpful to think of the database as a filing cabinet, the files as drawers in the cabinet, the records as the documents in the suspension pockets of each drawer and the field names as the pre-printed headings on each record card.

Once you have created your database, you can then sort and retrieve groups of records using any one of the fields. For example, you could call up all the records where the surname was Smith, or all the records of people with a birthday in July. This type of operation is called a search or a query.

The setting up of a database needs some thought: you must think about how you want to use the database, and the sorts of information you wish to be able to extract. If, for example, you wish to be able to group your records according to the county in which your contacts live, the county part of the address needs to be set up as a separate field.

Most databases are able to print out a report, so that you have a paper copy of the results of your search, and most are able to perform some basic statistical calculations, which may be useful if you are carrying out certain kinds of research. If, however, you will be dealing with a lot of figures, you might do better to use a spreadsheet, or purpose-designed statistical software.

Can you think of any other ways in which a database might help your work or study?

You might use a database to store and organise details of book and journal references; to keep track of clinical contacts and medical sales representatives; to keep staff records; and for stock-keeping.

CD-ROM

A specialised form of database are the catalogues and indexes which many libraries now hold in compact disk form. CD-ROM stands for compact disk – read only memory. This means that the data stored on the disk can only be read, not altered or added to. The CD-ROM can be very useful if you are looking for journal articles on a particular topic. You search the database by entering keywords about your chosen subject, and the system will produce a list on screen of any articles which match these search terms. This list contains such information as the author's name, the title of the article and the journal in which it was published, the volume, issue and page number on which it can be found and often a brief summary of the content of the article. This list can be printed out if the CD-ROM machine is connected to a printer, or even copied to your own floppy disk for later use.

See Chapter 4 for a list of indexes and more information on searching literature

Spreadsheets

A spreadsheet is a piece of software which enables you to record and process numerical information, and carry out arithmetical and statistical operations on this kind of data.

	A	B	C	D
1				
2				
3				23
4				12
5				35
6				16
7				

Figure 5.3

The basic appearance of a spreadsheet is illustrated above. Each column of the grid is identified by a letter, each row by a number. A spreadsheet may have dozens of columns and hundreds of rows. The intersection of a column and a row forms a **cell**; each cell is identified by a unique address made up of the column letter and the row number. In the illustration the number 16 is in cell D6. Cells may contain **text** (titles, headings etc.), **values** (numbers) and **formulae** for mathematical and statistical calculations. It is this last feature that makes the spreadsheet so useful, and gives it a huge advantage over an electronic calculator. Consider the column of figures below:

12
4
20
15

There aren't very many, so you could use pencil and paper to total them up, or perhaps a calculator if your maths isn't very good. Now consider the following column of figures:

56.89
92.35
45.67
23.09
107.34
237.74
126.01
45.67
34.79
23.32
44.56
23.12
67.09
23.59
16.96
115.32

There are many more, and they are quite complicated, so using a pencil and paper would take a long time, although you could still use a calculator. A spreadsheet can be used like a calculator: you could type in 56.89 + 92.35 + 45.67 etc., and get a total. However, if one of the figures in the column changes for some reason, the sum at the bottom no longer produces the correct answer, and has to be rewritten. What a spreadsheet allows you to do in this example, is express the sum in terms of the *contents of the cells* in the column, rather than in particular figures. The sum thus becomes (D3 + D4 + D5 . . . + D16) and you get the correct total in cell D18.

	A	B	C	D
1				56.89
2				92.35
3				45.67
4				23.09
5				107.34
6				237.74
7				126.01
8				45.67
9				34.79
10				23.32
11				44.56
12				23.12
13				67.09
14				23.59
15				16.96
16				115.32
17				
18				1083.51
19				

Figure 5.4

If you later change one of the figures in the column, the spreadsheet notices this, and recalculates the total automatically.

The basic principle described above applies to all other mathematical and statistical operations.

Can you think of any ways in which a spreadsheet might be useful at work or at home?

Spreadsheets are typically used for things like keeping accounts, planning budgets and dealing with wages. Because of the way in

which they work, they can also be very useful in making projec-
tions, e.g. a manager might wish to look at how a 4% increase in
nursing salaries will affect the total wages bill, and therefore the
profitability or otherwise of the unit.

At home a spreadsheet could be used to keep a bank account,
or record the income and expenditure of a club.

A specialised form of the spreadsheet is the statistical package,
which is able to handle very complex statistics and large amounts
of data – perhaps from a large-scale research project – with ease.

Graphics and Drawing Packages

You have probably seen some of the clever title sequences and
logos which television companies use. These are produced by
designers using powerful graphics software, but smaller and
cheaper programs are available which you can use to add diagrams and pictures to project work or reports, or to produce
posters and brochures for work or home.

The term graphics covers everything from simple black and
white shapes like that in Fig. 5.5 to complex colour images.
Many of the illustrations in this book will have been produced
using graphics software.

Graphics packages can be used in several different ways: you
can produce your own drawings from scratch, and if you have
time and skill enough, these may be very detailed and complicated. Or you can make use of clip-art: these are pre-drawn
images supplied by a software company, which you can retrieve

Figure 5.5

from a disk and use as they are, or alter further. Usually they are free of copyright, which means that you don't need anybody's permission to use or reproduce them. A third alternative, mentioned above, is to scan in an image from a paper copy and use it, but in this case you need to be careful not to infringe copyright. These can be used to enhance a presentation you give to colleagues.

See the section on plaigarism and copyright in Chapter 12

See Chapter 12

THE DATA PROTECTION ACT 1984

Anybody in the UK who uses a computer to store and process personal information on other people needs to be aware of the Data Protection Act. The Act was passed by the UK Parliament in 1984. Its aim was to lay down standards of practice for people and institutions holding potentially sensitive data on individuals in electronic form. The Act sets out the responsibilities of those holding the data (data users), and the rights of those on whom data is held (data subjects). A copy of the Act should be available to any person working with personal data.

The Act provides that data users must register with the Data Protection Registrar, and must comply with data protection principles laid down in the Act. These principles are summarised below.

Personal data should be:
- collected and processed fairly and lawfully;
- held and used only for specified and lawful purposes;
- adequate, relevant and accurate;
- held no longer than is necessary for the registered purpose;
- protected by proper security.

Failure to comply with the provisions of the Act may lead to prosecution.

For further information, contact the Data Protection Registrar at the address given at the end of this chapter and ask for the Student Information Pack.

USING THE COMPUTER TO COMMUNICATE

As well as being a very useful tool on its own, the computer can also be used as a means of communicating with the next room, the next town, or across the world. Computers within a building or on a hospital site can be physically connected with electronic cables to form a **network**. A network enables users to share information, and send messages from machine to machine (this is usually called electronic mail or e-mail). You may already use a network where you work.

Computers thousands of miles apart can also communicate, either down telephone lines or using a satellite link. For example, a ship at sea can communicate directly with a home port, or an explorer in the Antarctic with a colleague on the other side of the world. In order to use a telephone link, a computer needs to be connected to the telephone system through a **modem**: this is a device which translates the outgoing information into a telephone signal, and decodes incoming information.

As well as local networks a much wider network has grown up around the world, the so-called **Internet**. This started off as a means of communicating and sharing information between academic institutions, but more recently businesses and governments have begun to make use of it as a way of making information more widely available.

BUYING A COMPUTER

This section is intended as a brief guide only.

Before you part with any money, before even you start looking at computer magazines or in computer shops, ask yourself a few questions.

What do I Want a Computer For?

If you have already worked with computers before, or if you have read through this chapter, you will already have some idea of what a PC can do, and just how useful a tool it can be in the home or office. However, before you go any further, write out a list of what you want to be able to do with the computer – the more specific you can be the better. For example, instead of saying 'I want to sort my finances out', say 'I want to be able to manage two current accounts, one personal, one business, a Building Society deposit account and a small portfolio of investments.' Instead of 'I want to do a bit of writing', 'I want to write short articles for the Parish magazine, and I would like to be able to do posters for Church events.' In either case, your requirements will be rather less than someone who writes 'I want to manage all the accounting for a national company, and produce a monthly newsletter with colour pictures for distribution to all our branches.'

How Much Can I Afford?

Work out how much you are willing and/or able to spend on your computer system. If you want to buy a printer, a CD-ROM drive or other 'peripherals' as they are sometimes called, don't forget to allow for this. Remember also that as well as hardware you will need to buy software. Very often software is included, or 'bundled' with the purchase price of the computer, and it is possible to pick up software at greatly reduced prices by taking advantage of this tendency – you should remember, however, that something is only a bargain if you were going to buy it anyway.

Where am I Going to Buy?

This can be a hard question if you are new to computers. As a rule of thumb, buying through a large warehouse will be cheaper than a small dealer, but the smaller dealer may be able to offer valuable advice before you buy, and good after-sales service. Buying through mail order from an advertiser in a computer magazine is probably not advisable unless you know exactly what you want. Shop around and ask for advice from friends and colleagues who know about computers.

New or Secondhand?

Computers become obsolete faster than any other item you are likely to buy. The pace of technological change is such that this year's latest model is next year's reduced bargain buy. However, if you buy a machine that is adequate for your requirements, it will give many years of faithful service: there are plenty of people using computers which are 5 or 6 years old, or older still, just as there are many people still driving cars which have been out of production for many years. The moral is, don't try to keep up with the neighbours just for the sake of it.

Buying secondhand is not advisable unless:

a)   you know what you are doing and/or
b)   you know and trust the person you are buying from.

Avoid auctions too, unless a) applies.

The computer which you buy this year will be half the price

next year. This also relates to the pace of technological change, because as new technology is developed and put on sale, manufactures and dealers still have lots of older equipment which they wish to unload. The computer marketplace is also extremely competitive. However, this fact can work to your advantage, as companies compete for business by offering special deals.

Questions to Ask Yourself

■ What do I want a computer for?
■ How much can I afford to spend?
■ Which peripherals are essential, which only desirable?

Questions to Ask the Computer Dealer

■ Is this machine able to do what I want it to?
■ Are there other/cheaper machines which would do the same jobs?
■ How much is it?
■ Do I get any software included in the price?
■ What warranty and after-sales service do I get for my money?

Computer magazines (you will find shelves full of them in most newsagents) from time to time print articles or small free booklets aimed at the beginner. These can be worth watching out for, as they explain the technical terms in a way which is easy to understand. You should be aware, however, that such booklets are sometimes sponsored by companies which produce computers and will, undoubtedly, tend to push their brand in preference to any other.

CONCLUSION

This chapter has given a brief overview of information technology and how it may be able to help you as a student. Using a computer can speed up many of the study tasks you will undertake. However, IT is not an end in itself, merely a tool. As with all tools, you need to learn how to use it appropriately and effectively.

- Information technology is primarily about handling information: the technology is secondary.
- You can use a computer without understanding how it works.
- You can use a computer to write, draw, calculate, store information and communicate.
- It may take a little while to learn to use a computer, but it is a worthwhile investment of your time.

Investigate the computer facilities which are available to you locally, within your place of work, or at nearby colleges.
- What hardware is available?
- What software is in use?
- What introductory courses are on offer?
- What help and support is available for inexperienced users?
- Do you have to pay anything to use the facilities?

GLOSSARY OF TERMS

Applications   The programs which enable the user to make effective use of the computer to carry out various tasks – word-processing, keeping a database, working with figures, drawing diagrams etc.

CD-ROM   Compact disk – read only memory. Data stored on the CD can only be read, not altered, deleted or added to.

CPU   Central processor unit. An electronic component within the computer case which controls and co-ordinates the working of the computer system.

Data   Raw facts and figures.

DOS   Disk operating system. An operating system controlled through the computer keyboard.

Floppy disk   A flexible plastic disk coated in metal oxide, on which data can be stored in electromagnetic form. It is contained in a light plastic shell for protection.

Hard copy   A printed version of a letter, essay, spreadsheet etc.

Hard disk   A rigid metal or plastic disk coated in metal oxide on which data can be stored in electromagnetic form. Usually a permanent part of the computer.

Hardware   The physical components of a computer system.

Modem   Modulation–demodulation. A device which converts information held on a computer into a telephone signal and vice versa.

Network   A group of computers connected together by cables which can share programs and information.

Operating system   The software which gives basic instructions to the computer. Part of this is semi-automatic, but the user is also able to give instructions to the computer by using a keyboard or a mouse.

Peripherals   The hardware which is not essential to using the computer (i.e. everything except the processor, the keyboard and the screen).

Software   The programs which give instructions to the computer.

User-friendly   Easy to learn and use.

Windows   The tradename of a popular operating system produced by Microsoft Corporation which uses a mouse pointer to give instructions to the computer.

USEFUL INFORMATION

The Data Protection Act

Contact:

The Data Protection Registrar
Wycliffe House
Water Lane
Wilmslow
Cheshire SK9 5AF
UK

Computer Users' Group

Nursing Specialist Group of the British Computer Society
1 Sanford Street
Swindon
Wiltshire SN1 1HJ
UK

Tel./Fax 0171 7904817

The NSG publishes a quarterly journal *Information Technology in Nursing*.

Nursing Informatics Courses

For details of centres which offer these courses contact:

The English National Board for Nursing, Midwifery and Health
Visiting
Victory House
170 Tottenham Court Road
London W1P 0HA
UK

Tel.   0171 3883131
Fax   0171 3834031

The Welsh National Board for Nursing, Midwifery and Health
Visiting
Floor 13
Pearl Assurance House
Greyfriars Road
Cardiff CF1 3AG
UK

Tel.   01222 395535
Fax   01222 229366

National Board for Nursing, Midwifery and Health Visiting for
Northern Ireland
RAC House
79 Chichester Street
Belfast BT1 4JE
UK

Tel.   01232 238152
Fax   01232 333298

National Board for Nursing, Midwifery and Health Visiting for
Scotland
22 Queen Street
Edinburgh EH2 1JX
UK

Tel.   0131 2267371
Fax   0131 2259970

Getting the Most from Reading and Lectures

Kym Martindale

INTRODUCTION

Understanding information demands effort from you, the reader/listener. Your role is not passive; for example, good note-taking skills make all the difference in the ultimate value of any material to you. Nor is it confined simply to the time spent in the lecture or reading that article. Both of these activities are part of the process of involving yourself in your learning.

This process is greatly helped by you knowing what you want. As in Chapter 4, the rule is 'define and stick to your purpose'.

Key Issues

- A critical approach.
- Reading skills.
- Reviewing and recording.
- The role of the lecture.
- Note taking.
- Engaging with the material.

A CRITICAL APPROACH: SUBJECTIVITY AND INTERPRETATION

Employing a critical approach means first of all recognising that all information is presented in edited form. No matter what the medium – an article or book, a TV programme or radio broadcast – the contents and presentation are chosen by authors, editors or producers. This is not generally from cunning on their part. More often it is a response to the constraints any medium imposes, and the understanding that any material needs to be shaped for the reader/listener.

However, this does mean that those presenting and editing material do so from within their own *frame of reference* (Giroux, 1978 cited in Baron and Sternberg, 1987). A frame of reference is an individual's beliefs and values and the factors which go towards forming them. It is unique to that person, although it is probably similar to others'; it can change, but as a teacher cited by Baron and Sternberg (1987, p. 113) states, 'at any one time, it still functions as a finite lens through which some experiences are filtered and beyond the bounds of which other experiences simply do not register.'

Two obvious examples of frame of reference influencing information are politics and newspapers. You are aware of the values and beliefs through which that speaker/journalist operates so you listen/read in a questioning light. But, politicians and newspapers hold stated positions (officially or not). Most authors are firstly professionals in their field, operating through a complex system of values, beliefs, ethical concerns and cultural influences. These factors are not easy to detect or define. Combined with the air of authority which the media (especially print) seem to bestow, they can lull you into a false sense of acceptance.

The Great Eskimo Vocabulary Hoax

A wonderful example of how print can establish error as fact is related by Stephen Pinker in *The Language Instinct*. The Great Eskimo Vocabulary Hoax, i.e. the claim that Inuit peoples have dozens, even hundreds of words for snow, has been widely propagated in print. The claim, originally a modest, if inaccurate, seven, was published in an article early this century. Successive publications inflated the claim and with each publication cemented the error. Only recently have linguists returned to question the source, i.e. the original author's frame of reference and credentials.

An 'amateur scholar of Native American languages' with 'leanings towards mysticism' (Pinker, 1994, p. 63), Benjamin Lee Whorf's theories were based on shaky research and clumsy translations. But, the Great Eskimo Vocabulary Hoax was compounded by a 'patronising willingness to treat other cultures' psychologies as weird and exotic compared to our own' (Pinker, 1994, p. 65). In other words, social attitudes allowed Whorf's theory to flourish without question.

How do you Know Who to Believe?

Approaching material critically recognises that 'she's right, he's wrong' won't always be the case. A critical approach involves you saying 'what made her reach that conclusion when he decided this?' The subject may have been differently researched, differently experienced and differently interpreted.

In considering material you have to weigh these factors and how they could affect the information you're given. You are questioning the author/editor/producer, bringing their frame of reference to the fore. In Chapters 8 and 9, deciding which material might be of use to you involves examining the author's credentials. This is similar but in greater depth.

See Chapters 8 and 9

Your Questions won't All have Answers

It is important to realise that your questions won't all have answers. You won't be able to find out everything you'd like to know about a piece of research or an editor's influences. But, the *questioning* is the critical act. It shows that you can look beyond the text or the lecture. So, you won't always know who to believe. You must appraise the evidence, both stated and implicit, and decide for yourself.

- Being a critical and active learner involves questioning:
  - who is giving you your information?
  - what is their purpose?
  - what are their sources, and methods of research?
- Our individual frame of reference influences our work. Nothing is truly objective. This is true of all presented information, including scientific, factual research reports or articles, the news and documentaries.
- You won't always be able to provide answers to the questions you raise, but raising them demonstrates that you have thought around the subject.

Question . . . Concentrate . . . Understand

We have spent several pages addressing this issue, but it is important preparation. A questioning reader/listener is thinking and concentrating on the material. It follows that such a student stands a better chance of understanding and, in the long run, remembering.

READING: BEING PRACTICAL, REALISTIC AND PREPARED

This section will look at how reading skills vary depending on the material and your need, how to be selective, and how to ensure you focus on your information need while reading.

Different Skills for Different Material

You already have sophisticated reading skills and apply them every day to the various types of material you encounter. Table 6.1 lists some examples, their possible purpose, and the level of reading skill you would require.

Table 6.1:   **Material types and the skills involved**

Type of material	Purpose	Reading skill
Travel guide	General information	Use of index/contents to locate relevant information
Encyclopaedia	Specific definition and information	Specific search under heading
Anatomy textbook	Informed, factual understanding	Slow and concentrated, re-reading, making notes and diagrams
Technical instructions	Accurate completion of task	Step-by-step reference
Article on inequalities in health	Understanding and knowledge of the issue, relevant theories and views	Slow reading and re-reading, noting own ideas, linking to other reading, questioning the material
Library opening hours	Factual information	Note/memorise for future reference

Consider Table 6.1 for 5–10 minutes. Note in your learning journal roughly:
- what types of reading you have done this week;
- how you went about them, i.e. how did your approach differ?

From Table 6.1 and the notes in your learning journal, you can see how you, perhaps unconsciously, employ a range of reading skills. However, you might not be using them as well as you could. For instance, how selective are you in your reading? Do you try and read as much as possible or give close attention to carefully chosen material? When you've finished reading do you understand the content? If not, what do you do about it? Reflect on this in your learning journal for 5 minutes.

The Active Reader

Look again at Table 6.1. Most of the reading tasks require some active involvement from the reader. But, the two whose purpose is *understanding*, i.e. the article and the textbook, require several readings, notes/diagrams and an intelligent personal response. Within that, you would consciously have to apply different levels of reading skills.

- **Skimming/scanning** the material for the gist. You can quickly decide what parts you need to concentrate on, i.e. which sections contain the information you need. Use the layout of the material, i.e. contents page, headings, index, tables/charts.
- **In-depth reading/re-reading** the denser material. Be prepared to spend time on this with reference books, e.g. a dictionary for unfamiliar words, and with pen and paper to hand for your notes.
- **Infer** as you read, i.e. read between the lines and be aware of context. You already do this when you read anything; no written material is without context and the same statement in different contexts can have different intent (see box below). Inference and context are related to **subjectivity** and **interpretation** discussed earlier.
- **Paraphrase** important or difficult points and ideas in your notes. In this way you are recording your own understanding of, and response to the material. Paraphrasing involves you interpreting the material and making sense of it, and this is far more effective than simply highlighting passages of text – not only do you achieve better understanding of, and concentration on the material, you are also honing your writing skills; the notes you make at this point may also be the germs of ideas for your essay.

> ### *How context can change intent*
>
> Statement: 'I blame the parents'
>
> Context 1: Letter to local paper complaining about vandalism.
>
> Context 2: Slogan on T-shirt worn by rock singer with known anti-establishment views.
>
> In Context 1, we have a straightforward reference to the decline in family values and its effect on society.
> In Context 2, the statement becomes ironic and subversive.

Preparation and Purpose

Remember: *define and stick to your purpose.* The active reader does this by identifying what they need from their material. Writing these needs down as a series of questions both clarifies and keeps them visible so you don't stray from your purpose. If you're clear about the answers you need, you are less likely to waste time on irrelevant material. The activity below (10–20 minutes) asks you to read a passage of text, firstly without and secondly with identified information needs, i.e. questions. You may then reflect on the effectiveness of your readings in each case.

The passage below is from *Health* by Peter Aggleton and defines one current way of thinking about health. Read it through as you would any text for study.

Bio-medical Positivist Explanations

*Towards the end of the eighteenth century, a major change took place in the organization and provision of health care in Europe. The transformation first began in France in response to demands for better health care from the poor, but it soon spread to other countries. Hitherto, in times of sickness and disease, health care had for the most part been provided within the home by household members and non-professionals as well as by physicians. The early 1800s, however, saw the growth of what Norman Jewson (1976) calls **hospital medicine**, as institutions were created in which the sick could be administered to on a grander scale. For most people, these early hospitals were not places to be visited by choice, rather they catered for the homeless and those who could not afford to be looked after at home.*

For doctors though, they provided a ready supply of research material (Waddington, 1973) and this, together with development of positivist research techniques by natural scientists, led to the emergence of bio-medicine as it is known today.

Positivism is a view of the world which suggests that the most important things around us are those which are observable and measurable, and positivist researchers are those who believe that by careful observation it is possible to identify the relationships between observable and measurable things. The relationships they are particularly interested in are those in which one variable can be said to cause another one – **cause and effect** relationships as they are generally known.

In the natural science, positivists go about their work by observing events, by noting what preceded them, and by identifying what follows them. They begin from tentative ideas or **hypotheses** about the relationship between variables and they then repeatedly **test** these ideas against the available evidence. This process of testing, and the observations that are made from it, eventually leads to the development of **theories** about the ways in which variables are related to one another.

Ideas such as these very much influenced the work of nineteenth- and twentieth-century European doctors. The observation and the dissection of corpses, for example, led physicians to locate disorders and pathologies within particular organs. It also encouraged the development of medical specialisms such as dermatology (skin), neurology (nervous system), obstetrics (childbirth), cardiology (heart), and haematology (blood), each of which focuses on a particular part of the body or a particular system within it. Because of this emphasis, bio-medical positivism came to concern itself largely with the presence of disease and illness, working from negative rather than positive definitions of health (see pp. 6–12).

Positivist inquiry also led to the development of new ideas about the origins of diseases. The doctrine of **specific etiology**, as it came to be called, suggested that specific diseases have specific causes, and it identified a key role for germs such as bacteria and viruses in this process. Prior to this, it had been widely believed that one cause could give rise to many different diseases. Thus miasma, or bad air, was thought to be responsible for diseases as diverse as cholera, typhus, measles, bronchitis, and pneumonia. Finally, positivist bio-medical thought led to the widespread adoption of **allopathic** kinds of treatment, which use drugs as a kind of 'antidote' for the diseases they are used to treat.

To summarize, bio-medical positivism suggests that illness or distress arises from a malfunction in some part of the body, that malfunctions can be detected by appropriately trained experts using appropriate scientific aids, and that once detected, malfunctions can usually be treated by administering drugs or by removing or surgically modifying the part of the body that is no longer working properly (Open University, 1985b).

The scientific medicine, to which bio-medical positivism gave rise, is far from a neutral activity. Indeed, it has had wide-ranging social consequences. According to Lesley Doyal and Imogen Pennell (1979: 30), it is **'curative, individualistic and interventionist'**, it objectifies patients, and it denies **'their status as social beings'**. No matter what doctors working within this tradition may say to the opposite, people in their wholeness are rarely the subject of the medical interest in the way that they are with other systems of health care. Instead, diseased organs and unbalanced physiological systems become the major focus of medical attention.
(Aggleton, 1990, pp. 61–3; reproduced with permission from Routledge)

Now re-read the passage with the following questions in mind.

1) What is positivism?
2) How does its application in medicine affect the patient–doctor relationship?
3) In what regard is this way of thinking held today?

The above activity should have helped you to concentrate on the passage in the following ways.

1) You are looking for an explanation of positivism so, while the historical information is interesting background, your real reading begins at the second paragraph 'Positivism is . . .'. Important terms are highlighted, and positivism and its role in the development of bio-medicine are thoroughly explained and summarised.

2) The effect on the patient–doctor relationship is implied in these paragraphs, especially in the summary. The author talks of 'malfunctions . . . parts of the body' whilst treatment is 'drugs . . . removing or surgically modifying the part . . . no longer working . . .'. The patient has become a broken machine, no longer a person.

The phrase 'social consequences' in the paragraph following the summary should have alerted you to further discussion on this.

3) Current regard for bio-medical positivism is critical, as the phrase 'far from a neutral activity . . . social consequences' should indicate. The author goes on to cite other criticism, and agree in essence, that the patient as a person is not medically important. By spotting the key phrases and the citation you could see that this paragraph dealt with your last question.

Identifying your information need has meant you could select and concentrate on the relevant sections of the passage. Being selective, i.e. focusing on a few well-chosen readings, is essential.

- Your time is limited – you can't read everything.
- In-depth reading is time consuming, but you will understand material better by giving it close attention.
- Quality not quantity!

REVIEWING AND RECORDING YOUR READING

Reviewing your reading is a useful way of summarising what you have learned and ensuring that you have answered your questions as fully as possible. Your review could be recorded with the bibliographic details.

See Appendix A

See section on plagiarism in Chapter 12

Recording the bibliographic details, i.e. the citation, is necessary for your end of essay reference list and to enable you to locate that material in the future. This also applies to audiovisual material, e.g. radio/TV/video. Brief notes on content and usefulness may be helpful towards future essays. In this way, you will build up an annotated bibliography of material you have used throughout your course. Such a database can be stored and arranged as you like, but the cheapest, most effective way is on index cards.

The box below shows the possible content of such a record.

AGGLETON, P. (1990) *Health*. London: Routledge
pp. 61–63 clear explanation of positivism with refs – used for holistic health essay (but rest of book good for inequalities in health)
Related reading – see Doyal/Smith/Wiggins
Library no. 361 AGG

As an active reader you recognise that:
- reading is work – to be done at a desk, not in an armchair;
- you read to learn; keep a dictionary to hand for new terms;
- you read at different levels: **select** material, **scan** for relevance, read the relevant material **in-depth**;
- purpose and preparation help concentration and understanding;
- understanding means time spent re-reading, and referring to other works;
- understanding means engaging with the material, paraphrasing, and re-interpreting in your notes;
- you must read critically, always aware of context and the author's frame of reference;
- you keep records of your reading, recording the bibliographic details, and reviewing the contents and value;
- your responses and ideas from your reading are the beginning of your essay.

Plagiarism

Keeping records of your reading is essential for your reference list. If you quote or refer to the work or ideas of another person, whether published, broadcast or spoken informally, you *must acknowledge your source*. To claim, even accidentally, the ideas of others as your own is intellectual theft. If discovered you could fail your course.

See Chapter 12

Several referencing systems exist. Your college should give you guidelines on which to use in your written work.

See Appendix A

LECTURES

This section looks at learning effectively from lectures. Many of the principles from reading still apply, but some of the techniques are different.

The Role of Lectures

You could be forgiven for seeing lectures as the most important part of your course. They are given by the 'experts' and have an air of authority.

It follows that you may also see lectures as being wholly the responsibility of the lecturers. Their job is to package and impart information to you.

Neither of these perceptions is the case.

Lectures are certainly important, but their aims are:

- to introduce material (terminology, ideas, theories, a line of argument);
- to explain the above;
- to complement your reading.

Time spent in lectures is often far less than that used for private or group study.

Lectures are of little use unless you participate. As in reading, you must be active. During the lecture this entails:

- asking questions;
- effective note taking.

To get the most out of lectures you should:
- **prepare**: get some idea of the content of the lecture, and read some background information (see box below);
- identify the **purpose** in your preparation, note areas on which you want to concentrate; be clear about what you want;
- **summarise** the content of the lecture briefly in your notes – this will help your review;
- **review** from your notes and handouts whether you achieved your purpose, and plan further reading/discussion.

You will probably recognise the similarity between being an active reader and an active listener. The key is taking responsibility for your own learning. You are being an active student.

Preparation can help understanding and concentration

Think back to a TV documentary you have watched recently. In your learning journal reflect on:

- what, if any, pre-programme knowledge did you have?
- either way, how did this affect your understanding and concentration?

Note Taking in Lectures

Lectures can be stressful because you cannot control the pace as you do when reading or watching a video. You end up trying to do several things at once:

- listen;
- understand;
- take notes.

Unfortunately, this is impossible. You cannot listen and take notes continuously. You cannot understand without giving thought to something, and if you're thinking you're not listening. So don't try!

This is where you need to have identified areas for your concentration. You can focus on what is being said and summarise the content in your notes when the lecturer moves on. The act of summarising means you interpret and this will help your understanding. It is similar to **paraphrasing** in your reading notes.

> Whatever you do in lectures, don't try and write down everything. It simply is not possible, nor is it the purpose of the lecture.

Styles of Note Taking

There are as many different ways to take notes as there are students, but they fall broadly into two categories:

- visual;
- linear.

How you take notes depends on you. A visual approach might look like this:

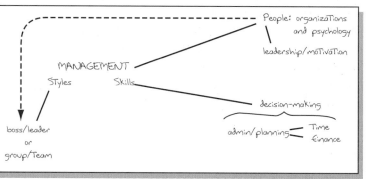

Figure 6.1

See Chapter 4 You are creating a map of the subject, as you did in Chapter 4. This organises it in your mind and you can note areas for further reading. You can code or highlight areas with different coloured pens so that their importance is obvious.

A linear approach might use headings, indentations and personal shorthand. It might look like this:

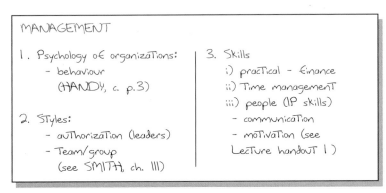

MANAGEMENT

1. Psychology of organizations:
   - behaviour
     (HANDY, c. p.3)

2. Styles:
   - authorization (leaders)
   - Team/group
     (see SMITH, ch. III)

3. Skills
   i) practical - finance
   ii) Time management
   iii) people (IP skills)
   - communication
   - motivation (see Lecture handout I)

Figure 6.2

Again you are arranging the subject, organising it for your own understanding. This approach can also be highlighted and marked visually.

See Further reading, p. 114 Experiment with styles, and adopt the one which suits you, your subject and your needs.

As an active listener you recognise that:
- you need to **prepare** for lectures;
- identifying your **purpose** helps you to focus on the relevant areas during the lecture;
- you will need to **ask questions** during the lecture;
- you take notes to **understand**;
- lectures must be supported by **reading and discussion**;
- **reviewing** your notes and handouts will help to identify areas for further reading;
- **summarising** a lecture is part of the review.

CONCLUSION

Both this chapter and Chapter 4 stress the importance of your role in seeking and using information effectively. Learning takes place not only in the lecture, or from reading masses of titles from your reading list. Nor is it solely the responsibility of your tutors. Your involvement is the key.

Main Points to Remember

- Be critical.
- Be selective.
- Different reading needs require different levels of study and skill.
- Prepare for lectures.
- Engage with the material.

Lecture Preparation

Look at your timetable for a lecture which will cover a subject new to you. Note in your learning journal:
- the lecture title;
- the subject to be covered.

The day before/of the lecture read briefly round the subject (a chapter/article). You may not understand it – don't worry. Note in your learning journal:
- the reference for the material read;
- the time spent on it;
- your understanding of it, e.g. poor, OK, good.

After the lecture consider in your learning journal:
- did your pre-lecture reading familiarise you with terminology, concepts?
- was your understanding of the lecture enhanced?
- were you able to make clearer notes?
- were you able to ask questions of the lecturer from a more informed position?
- did you have a better idea of which points you needed to be explained further?

You should have answered positively to some of the above points. It is surprising how a little reading can lay the groundwork of understanding for a lecture on a new subject.

Finally, re-read your pre-lecture material. It should now begin to make sense. It may even round out your lecture notes.

REFERENCES

AGGLETON P (1990) *Health*. London, Routledge.

BARON JB and STERNBERG RJ (1987) *Teaching Thinking Skills: Theory and Practice*. New York, W.H. Freeman and Co.

PINKER S (1994) *The Language Instinct*. London, Penguin.

FURTHER READING

FAIRBAIRN GJ and WINCH C (1991) *Reading, Writing and Reasoning: a Guide for Students*. Buckingham, Society for Research in Higher Education/Open University Press.

NORTHEDGE A (1990) *The Good Study Guide*. Milton Keynes, Open University Press.

ROWNTREE D (1988) *Learning How to Study: a Guide for Students of All Ages*. London, Macdonald and Co.

Group Work and Presentations

Sian Maslin-Prothero

INTRODUCTION

The aim of this chapter is to develop your skills for group work so that you can get the most out of seminars and tutorials. Group work is frequently used as a method of learning in education. This chapter aims to introduce some ideas about groups and how they work.

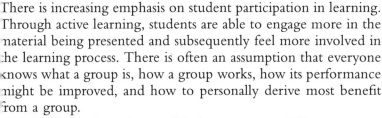

Key issues

- Characteristics of groups.
- Group work and group dynamics.
- Participating in group discussions.
- Action in groups.
- Tutorials.
- Seminars.
- Giving presentations.

There is increasing emphasis on student participation in learning. Through active learning, students are able to engage more in the material being presented and subsequently feel more involved in the learning process. There is often an assumption that everyone knows what a group is, how a group works, how its performance might be improved, and how to personally derive most benefit from a group.

If you think about it, we all belong to many different groups, e.g. family, aerobics, skittles team, voluntary association, or trade union. Being in a group is part of being human, and therefore working in groups is a part of all our lives. Groups consist of two or more people who meet regularly to follow a chosen activity. Some groups are more personal and voluntary than others, e.g. a hobby group compared with a workplace group. Groups may be formed to achieve a specific task, and are expected to work collaboratively.

One of the most effective ways of learning is through interacting with other people. It not only gives us the opportunity to hear other people's ideas and thoughts, but it also gives us the opportunity to try out and share our own opinions. A group will bring together a wide range of attitudes, knowledge and skills that cannot be created alone. This is one advantage of a group for problem solving or decision making. If all members of a group feel valued and can participate, then there is greater commitment to, and support of, the group and its decisions. Group discussion can help you think. However, to be an effective member of any group, you need to understand the process of group work.

CHARACTERISTICS OF GROUPS

Groups have a number of common characteristics.

- A definable membership.
- Group consciousness.
- A shared sense of purpose.
- Interdependence.
- Interaction.
- Ability to cooperate.

ADVANTAGES OF GROUPS

 Reflect on your own experiences of working in a group. What do you think are the advantages of working in a group?

There are a number of advantages to working in a group, and you might have included some of the following points.

- Sharing the work load:
  - thinking;
  - problem solving;
  - understanding.
- Increased efficiency.
- Increased effectiveness.
- Social support.
- Allows active participation.
- Purposeful activity.

DISADVANTAGES OF GROUP WORK

However, there can also be disadvantages to working in a group.

Can you recall an experience of where a group activity failed?
What do you think was the reason?
What do you think might be some other disadvantages of working
in a group?

A group might be unsuccessful for a number of reasons, some of
which are listed below.

- Poor group dynamics.
- Lack of communication.
- Task is not completed.
- Not all members of the group participate.
- Feeling isolated.
- Comparing yourself with others.
- Gossip.
- Dominance by an outspoken member.

Therefore you need to understand why groups need to exist, and
strategies for ensuring they work. As highlighted in the advantages of groups, a group can bring together a range of skills and
knowledge, which an individual on their own would not have.
This can be used to the advantage of the group in achieving tasks.
In order for the group to be successful all the group members
need to feel a part of the group and that their contribution is
valued by the group.

GROUP DYNAMICS

In order for a group to be both effective and efficient, you need
to have a mix of personalities. There are a number of different
roles within groups. The role you play in a group will depend on
your personality and on the reason for the group existing. Belbin
(1981) identified eight key roles for an effective group.

- **Company worker** – practical person who organises the
  group, and makes any tasks manageable.
- **Chair** – co-ordinates the group and ensures all contributions
  are heard.
- **Shaper** – pushes the group and encourages the group to
  complete the task.

- **Plant** – the creative source; provides the group with ideas.
- **Resource investigator** – liaises with people outside the group, and explores new ideas.
- **Monitor/evaluator** – the critic who finds the faults in arguments.
- **Team worker** – the individual who holds the group together, and supports group members.
- **Completer/finisher** – the perfectionist who ensures the group meets any deadlines.

One person can take on more than one role in a group. It is important that there is balance between each of the roles in the group if the group is to remain effective.

Having looked at the different roles in a group, which would be your preferred role?

MANAGING A GROUP

The last section examined the roles of individuals in a group. Prior to looking at how you can contribute to a group discussion, you need to understand about managing a group. A successful group will be purposeful, without the need for teacher intervention. The two main factors in managing a group are:

- group tasks;
- group maintenance.

Group Tasks

The task or tasks of the group relates to its purpose, structure and activities. These need to be clearly defined, for example, group composition, members' roles and tasks, group management, ground rules (see below), study requirements (seminar presentations, assignments, assessments), deadlines and preparation for meetings.

Maintenance of the Group

This is all about creating a climate which encourages discussion and debate. This can be achieved through the group members being accepting of and co-operative towards each other, particularly when there are conflicts of opinion or personality clashes.

Through active participation group sessions can be enjoyable, as well as an excellent opportunity for learning.

The amount of time spent on the maintenance of a group will vary; it is particularly important in the early stages of a group's formation.

GROUND RULES

As mentioned above, participating in group discussions enables us not only to learn from others, but also to develop our own thoughts and beliefs about a subject. In order for the group to be successful it is important that the group meets and agrees ground rules. Ground rules are a set of guidelines which the group acknowledges and adheres to each time it meets. Having ground rules allows each member of the group to know what is expected of them.

> Imagine you are meeting in a group for the first time. Jot down the sort of ground rules that would be important to you. Keep these and refer to them when you are asked to identify ground rules.

You might have identified some of the following as important.

- Confidentiality.
- Be tactful, considerate and respect others' opinions.
- Punctuality.
- Supportive
  - share knowledge;
  - don't 'put down' others.
- Do not distract
  - keep noise levels down;
  - don't interrupt;
  - stick to the point.

The use of ground rules allows each member of the group to know what is expected of them as well as other members of the group. There may also need to be agreed sanctions for members who break any of the ground rules.

GROUP MEETINGS

See
Chapter 6
In order to be effective, everyone needs to be committed to the group. This means attending group meetings. By not turning up for a pre-arranged meeting, you are letting your colleagues down.

The group needs to have a focus, a 'frame of reference'. That is the subject the group is going to discuss or a task the group has to achieve. For example, imagine your teacher has asked you to find out about asepsis. In order to develop your understanding of asepsis you have to expand your knowledge, either through thinking, brainstorming ideas, reading or discussion. Through sharing the topic with others you will be able to keep sight of the frame of reference, and move forward, utilising the opinions of others as well as cultivating your own.

If a group meets on a regular basis then it can build on the information gained at previous meetings, thus enabling the conversation to become more advanced and sophisticated. Groups go through stages of development before performing successfully. They will also change and develop over time, from their initial formation, through conflict, co-operation and final task completion.

GROUP DISCUSSION

Many students gain support from a group. Not only are you developing your academic skills, but it can be comforting to find that other students feel the same as you. For example, imagine you have been asked to read a complex article in preparation for a group seminar. You read the article but you only really understood the abstract; the rest of the article makes no sense to you. When you meet for the seminar, you discover that some of your colleagues were equally baffled. However, some of the group understood some of the article. Through group discussion, and co-operation you will be able to grasp and make sense of the article.

The group can provide moral support in other ways, such as sharing articles, or skill tips. We all experience difficulties in our lives and through sharing these difficulties we can help each other, and make the ordeal of learning less stressful.

What do you do if you don't want to participate in the discussion, possibly because you are too shy, or afraid that your colleagues might think what you have to say is daft? Remember that discussion is there for everyone's development, not only those who appear to have no fear of expressing their thoughts and feelings. Don't be afraid to make an observation – what appears quite simple to you might be just what another colleague needs in order to make sense of the subject. Another important point to remember is that we all feel anxious about expressing ourselves; even experienced people feel inadequate and anxious about contributions they make to debates.

As discussed at the beginning of the chapter where we talked about group dynamics, we all have different roles in a group, and as long as you participate by actively listening you are contributing to the group discussion.

WHEN THINGS GO WRONG

There will be times when things go wrong. The most important thing is to maintain a climate of co-operation. This can be achieved by involving the whole group in identifying the problem, and then how to resolve it.

Hostile Members

This problem can occur in small or large groups. Examples include overt hostility, aggression, point scoring and inappropriate humour, all of which can hinder the success of the group. It is important to acknowledge this when it occurs. If you feel you need support when you tackle hostile members, get other group members to support you.

Avoiding Difficult Situations

This is when members of the group avoid a specific issue by being disruptive, withdrawing from group activities or trying to change the subject. You need to recognise when this is occurring and vocalise your thoughts – remember communication is essential if the group is to be successful. The group may leave the same person to make difficult decisions.

Dominating Members

There will be occasions when some of the group dominate the conversation, and thus prevent others from participating. If the group is being facilitated by a teacher, you might see it as their responsibility to control the group. However, each member of the group has a responsibility for regulating the group, more so if ground rules were developed, so don't be afraid to manage unruly members. Your backing will be appreciated, not only from your colleagues, but also by any group facilitator.

SELF-HELP GROUPS

See also
Chapter 2 You can set up an informal group to achieve specific tasks, such as revision for examinations or writing an essay. Don't wait for someone else to do it, set up the group yourself.

- Listen to other group members.
- Appreciate others' contributions.
- Communicate.
- Don't let the group down.
- Give the group time to achieve its aims.
- Enjoy yourself.

ACTION IN GROUPS

There are other methods of learning used to help develop your understanding of a subject. Experiential learning means learning by doing, i.e. you can learn from living and working. This can refer to learning through everyday experiences – being aware of them, then thinking and reflecting on your experiences. Inter-See
Chapters 3
and 11 on
reflection
and critical
incident
analysisactive teaching and learning methods can include:

- one-to-one discussion;
- buzz groups;
- brainstorming;
- role play.

These interactive teaching methods involve active participation by group members. The thought of participating in these different methods of learning can be quite frightening, but in reality, they can be an excellent way of learning. Not only do you learn about the subject being covered, but also about members of your group.

One-to-one discussions are frequently used as ice breakers. A group is divided into pairs, and each pair is given a task. The task can be to find out about each other, and then to introduce your partner to the rest of the group. Or pairs are given a specific question, and then they have to feed back to the whole group. This activity helps you to develop your listening skills.

Buzz groups are often used when there is a large group. The group is divided into sub-groups of four or five learners. Each sub-group is given a specific topic to discuss, which it then feeds back to the whole group. This is a useful way of involving the whole group, and allowing quiet members to contribute to a discussion.

Brainstorming is a way of introducing creative and different ideas. The group is given a problem, and a few minutes to think of possible solutions. The group is then invited to contribute these ideas; all ideas are welcomed and recorded. The aim is to generate as many ideas as possible. Once these have been recorded, the group can use the points for discussion.

Role play is a teaching technique used for developing skills such as interpersonal communication and empathy, or for dealing with difficult issues. The facilitator sets the scene, and explains the exercise. Learners are invited to participate by acting out specific roles. The participants have their role explained; there may be even a script. Those learners observing the role play are asked to contribute, i.e. to observe what is going on in the role play, and when invited, comment on the interactions that occurred. Don't be embarrassed, and do have a go at participating in role play. You can reflect and comment on your experience of what you felt and understood. It is important that everyone is de-roled on completion of the exercise.

This can be linked back to Chapter 2, where you identified your preferred method of learning. You might prefer not to actively participate, and find it very threatening. And yet the very act of participating allows you to learn. Experiential approaches are far more interesting and stimulating than more formal methods of teaching and learning. See Chapter 2

TUTORIALS

Tutorials may occur on a one-to-one basis, or with a small group of students meeting with their tutor. The overall aim of a tutorial is to learn from a small group discussion, and develop your ability to listen, evaluate, criticise and argue. Therefore you need to be prepared for your tutorial; if you have been asked to read an article, do so.

Tutorials can end up becoming mini-lectures from your teacher. You are not going to learn much if this occurs, so don't be afraid to contribute and even challenge your teacher. Teachers don't know everything. Contributing will also help you argue your case and develop your skills.

SEMINARS

Occasionally you will be asked to present a seminar. This is a popular teaching and learning strategy in nurse education. This section will examine points you need to consider prior to undertaking a seminar. A seminar involves giving a short presentation on a chosen topic, either a book or an article, for approximately 10–15 minutes. Students may present on their own or in a small group. This is then followed by discussion.

Initially, this can seem overwhelming for many students; however, preparation is the key. First of all ascertain from the facilitator exactly what they want you to cover. Don't be tempted to do too much, do only what you are asked to do. You will be surprised how quickly 10 minutes goes. The function of your presentation is to start the exchange. You might find it helpful to have an overhead acetate or handout prepared with the main points you want to cover written down. Remember, the subject will be familiar to you because you have prepared the seminar. Keep it simple and be prepared to explain or illustrate certain components for your colleagues. Following the initial presentation it is your responsibility to engage your fellow students so that a discussion ensues.

Details on preparing a presentation are covered on p. 125.

Preparing a Seminar

- What?
  - What are you expected to present?
- How?
  - How long have you got for your seminar?
  - Is it an individual or group presentation?
  - How is it going to be assessed (formative or summative assessment)?
- Who?
  - Who are you presenting to?
  - Who will undertake the assessment (teacher, peer or both)?

Finally, do you need submit an outline of the seminar to your teacher?

If your seminar is as part of a group, there are further points which need to be considered if it is to go well, relating to group dynamics. You need to ensure that the work is shared equally See p. 117 between group members, and that everyone knows what they are supposed to be doing during the seminar presentation.

If there are key points you want noted from the discussion then write them down on a whiteboard or flip chart. These can be used to focus the discussion following your presentation. You also need to control the group and make sure that people do not wander off the topic. Finally, summarise the main points at the end of the seminar.

Seminars will allow you to participate in your teaching and learning. They will help you to learn how to organise and present information, and then receive feedback from your colleagues. The skills you develop from seminar presentations are transferable and can be used when preparing other assignments, such as essays.

PRESENTATIONS

Presentations are a way of sharing information with colleagues and patients. They can be used as a way of sharing factual information with a particular audience, and may be used as a form of assessment on many courses.

The following are characteristics of a good presentation.

- The information is clear and relevant to your audience.
- Progress is logical.
- There is visual as well as aural presentation.
- The audience is responsive.

For a successful presentation you need to be prepared. The following will provide you with the necessary information to prepare a presentation.

Preparing a presentation
- Why?
  - Why are you presenting?
- Who?
  - Who is your audience?
  - What is the size of the audience?
- What?
  - What is your aim?
  - What do they already know about the subject?

- At what level will you pitch it?
- What will you include?
■ How?
  - What learning method will you use?
  - What are the key points?
  - Are you there to inform, persuade or amuse?
  - How long have you got?
■ Where?
  - Where will you be doing the presentation?
  - Do you have any choice?

■ Understand what you are to present (know the topic).
■ Structure the presentation.
■ Prepare notes to guide you.
■ Identify visual aids to support your demonstration.

Structure

See Chapter 4 on using the library and Chapters 8 and 9 on writing skills

A presentation is similar to writing an essay. You need to know your subject through researching it. Once you have the information you need to structure your presentation. As with preparing an essay, you need an introduction, main theme and conclusion. The introduction informs the audience what you are going to be discussing, the main body expands and develops the topic, and the conclusion is when you pull the whole thing together and summarise the key points.

See Chapter 1 for definitions

You should have a main theme or idea that you follow – having aims and objectives can help guide you and your audience through the presentation. The development of the presentation should be logical. Your message should be clear and to the point. If you are going to change the subject, tell your audience that you are moving onto another area. Finally, you should conclude by summarising the main points, telling the audience what you have already told them, and linking it to your aims and objectives.

Delivery

Preparation, once again, is the key. You should be well rehearsed and know what you are going to be talking about.

The use of motivators can attract individuals to your presentation, encouraging them to attend. These can come in the form of a question, and will help the audience to identify the relevance of your topic to their personal experience.

Remember, you are going to be communicating with the audience using the spoken word, supported by non-verbal clues through the clothes you are wearing and your facial expression. You need to decide from the start whether you are going to present formally with little or no interaction with the audience. In this situation, request the audience to keep their questions for when you have completed your presentation. Alternatively, you may have an interactive, audience participation session with activities, group work or discussion.

With thorough preparation, and brief notes to guide you, you will interact with your audience by maintaining eye contact and using appropriate gestures. Use the clues they provide to guide your presentation; for example if they look puzzled, maybe the definition of an unusual term, or a more detailed explanation is required.

As anyone involved in public speaking will verify, it can be a nerve-racking experience. Ensuring the room is ready, with the correct equipment, will help you feel much better. Finally, be enthusiastic – it is contagious, and your audience will be eager to listen and engage.

Equipment

There are many audiovisual aids which can be used to support and enhance your presentation, for example:

- overhead projectors (OHP);
- slide projectors;
- television and video recorders;
- tape recorders;
- whiteboards;
- flip charts;
- computers.

Know what equipment is available, how you are going to use it, and make sure that it works. The use of tables or graphs can act as a focus for the group participants. However, it is important not to provide too much information for your audience because this will not give them the opportunity to understand what is being said, reflect and ask appropriate questions. Only use an

See Chapter 5 on information technology

audiovisual aid if it can enhance your presentation, not just for the sake of it.

Audiovisual aids

- Do be prepared.
- Do have the right equipment (and make sure that it works).
- Do know how to operate the equipment.
- Do use key words.
- Do use large, bold writing/print.
- Don't use too many audiovisual aids.
- Don't have too much information.
- Don't obscure the view.
- Don't write/print in small writing.
- Don't panic. If something goes wrong, take a deep breath, find your place, and continue with your presentation.

Questions

As mentioned above, let your audience know at the beginning of the presentation when you are prepared to answer questions. Be prepared for questions based on your presentation: you can anticipate and prepare for the most likely questions.

When asked a question, be sure you have understood what they are asking. If it is unclear, ask for the question to be repeated or rephrased. If you are unable to answer the question, be honest and say so. Invite other people in the audience to answer, if they have knowledge of the subject. When replying make sure the answer is clear, relevant and to the point.

CONCLUSION

This chapter has looked at group work, and the different types of group you might encounter when learning. It has looked at how groups are formed, how groups work, the role of different group members, how to organise group meetings, how to participate in a group and what to do if things go wrong. The last part of the chapter looked at presentations and how to prepare and present to colleagues.

Bear the following in mind.

- There is an increasing emphasis on group and team working.
- Group work involves active participation.
- To be successful, individuals have to adopt different roles in a team. You will have a preferred role.
- To be successful the group must communicate.
- Be prepared for the group to change and develop over time.

Before moving on, take some time and record in your learning diary:

- Which is your preferred role in a group (based on Belbin's eight key roles) and why?
- Have you experienced conflict of opinion in a group? If so, how was the conflict resolved?

REFERENCE

BELBIN RM (1981) *Management Teams – Why They Succeed or Fail.* London, Butterworth Heinemann.

SECTION II

DEVELOPING YOUR WRITING SKILLS

Researching for Assignments

Abigail Masterson

INTRODUCTION

Writing is perhaps the most challenging part of all learning and studying. Writing involves communicating ideas and information in a clear, unambiguous way that others will understand.

As students and practitioners we need to be able to communicate effectively in writing to meet the requirements of academic courses, in completing nursing notes and care plans, and to support and justify changes in practice to managers and other multi-disciplinary colleagues. Increasingly, we may even wish to write for publication in order to be able to share our ideas with a wider audience.

Remember, there is probably no such thing as a born writer. The successful writer is the one who regards writing as a skill, to be learned, refined and constantly improved. And as we will see, the secret is careful preparation, planning and practice built on a foundation of good reading and researching skills. In this chapter we will focus mainly on the planning and preparation stages of the writing process.

Key issues
- Preparation.
- Planning.
- Researching skills.
- Putting it together.
- Purposeful learning.

PREPARATION

Planning Your Time

Preparation is the key to success in everything. It is important to start work on assignments early. Think for a moment: do you find it easier and more productive to work in long intensive bursts or are shorter, more regular periods better for you and your circumstances? Do you work better in the mornings or the evenings? Do you find it easier working in the library or at home with a cup of coffee and the radio on?

If you leave your preparation to the last minute, you may find that your colleagues have all got there first, i.e. few of the key texts are left in the library and your lecturer has no free appointments.

The following is a useful checklist to work through in helping you develop a study timetable which will suit you and your own particular circumstances.

- Give yourself ample time to get the work done.
- Pace yourself; as stressed in Chapter 1, very few people can survive very long without sleep, and life gets very boring if you do not allow yourself any social time with friends and family.
- Be realistic but strict with yourself.
- Include some flexibility in your study plan so that you can alter it if for example your days off are changed at short notice, or you get a cold and are not able to concentrate well enough to study on the days you had originally set aside.
- Identify appropriate periods of study time: if your study sessions are too short you will not have time to get into the focused and disciplined frame of mind required, and if they are too long you will get very tired and not be able to concentrate properly.
- Find out when your lecturers are available for tutorials, and the opening times of the libraries that you will need to use. Remember that during holiday times tutors may not be available and libraries may be closed or have reduced opening hours.
- Consider all the other work you have to do for college, your off duty, and be reasonable about other priorities on your time like partners, families, hobbies and social outings for further

See
Chapter 1

discussion about how to manage the demands of home and work).

- Check your student handbook and course regulations carefully to find out procedures and penalties for late submission of work. In some institutions late work may be given a minimum pass grade or may not be accepted at all.

- Let your tutors know as soon as possible if you do get into difficulties and they will then be able to guide you on the relevant procedures for obtaining an extension.

- Manage your time effectively by developing a study timetable as soon as you have been set an assignment.

- Identify how long you will allow yourself for getting together resources, how long for reading, and how long for writing and editing. It is often easy to get completely caught up in reading and gathering together more and more references, and not leave yourself time to actually write the assignment.

- Save time for 'sitting on' drafts. Revising and editing is crucial: leaving something aside for a few days or even a week allows you to look at it again with a fresh view, and your subconscious has probably been working on it in the meantime helping you develop new points and ideas.

- Allow time for getting your work typed or printing it out: most typists like a minimum of a week to type a 3000-word essay, and unless you have access to a very fast printer it will take you probably at least an hour or two to print out two copies of an essay of this length.

Look at your course handbook and note assignment submission dates. Work out a realistic timetable for your assignments (refer to timetabling in Chapter 1).

Your timetable might look something like this.

- Week 1 – read title and assignment guidelines carefully, check I understand them and am sure what is expected of me, brainstorm ideas and talk them through with lecturer.
- Week 2 – literature search of databases in college library.
- Weeks 3 and 4 – gather together references, read them, take notes and develop an essay plan.
- Week 5 – discuss plan with lecturer.

- Weeks 6 and 7 – write first draft.
- Week 8 – discuss first draft with lecturer.
- Weeks 9 and 10 – edit, redraft, type and submit.

Making the Best Use of Your Resources

See Chapter
4 for more
details

It is always worth taking some time to identify the most appropriate and relevant resources. Such resources should include people who may have an interest in the area or who it would be useful to talk your ideas through with. For example, if you are working on an essay about the nursing care of a patient with diabetes it might be useful to talk through your ideas with a patient who has this problem and the diabetic nurse specialist; or if you are writing on a professional issue such as accountability then you might find it helpful to make an appointment with the senior nurse in your clinical area or your mentor to get their perspective. If there are several of you who are all working on a similar topic or area it may be helpful to work together. You can then share resources and try out your ideas on each other. Also, you will not have to individually spend so much time in the library searching the literature and photocopying articles.

PLANNING

Thinking

It is important to spend time thinking about your assignment before you start your literature search, or talk to your patient/client if it is a case study. This thinking should involve clarifying the topic, jotting down your thoughts, and listing all the questions and issues which occur to you. This should ensure that your reading becomes purposeful rather than haphazard. It is crucial to focus on exactly what is required. It is often tempting to read things just because they are interesting rather than being absolutely clear that they are relevant. Equally, if you are not sure of your focus you may waste time going off on tangents, and getting together lots of material which is not really relevant.

Imagine you have been asked to produce a review of the nursing literature in relation to health and the implications for health promotion in children's nursing practice. Note down the key issues you would want to include.

Your list might look something like this.

- What is health?
- Models of health.
- Attitudes to and perceptions of health in children and their families.
- The influence of culture on health and health beliefs.
- Developmental needs in relation to health.
- Health education and health promotion strategies for children and their families.

This list would give a useful framework to help you select what sorts of resources you need to use, what key words you need to use for your literature search, and some of the points you may want to make in your discussion. You may find it helpful at this point to refer back to Chapter 4, where getting the most from your library is discussed in more detail.

See
Chapter 4

RESEARCHING SKILLS

Researching, or collecting material and resources together for your assignment, involves being systematic and organised. It is vital to record accurate details of what you are reading, however time consuming or irritating this may seem initially. When carrying out literature searches it is particularly important to note down the full reference, including the year of publication and the name and place of the publisher. In edited books it is necessary to record the names of the editors and the names of the authors, page numbers and titles of the individual chapters you wish to refer to. Some journals do not include details such as year of publication and volume and issue numbers on every page, so that even though you have a photocopy of the article you may waste valuable time relooking for these details later.

Recording References

Index cards are often used to record this sort of information because they are small enough to be carried around easily but large enough to contain the essential information that you need. In addition, they can be sorted into alphabetical order which saves time when you come to write up your references and bibliography. Each book, chapter, article or report that you

See
Chapter 5

read should be recorded on a separate card. Increasingly, people are using personal computers to store this type of information and there are now several software packages available to help you do this.

For example, the information which should be recorded for a book is:

■ Author's and/or editors' surnames and initials	Gough P, Maslin-Prothero SE and Masterson A
■ Year published	1994
■ Title	Nursing and Social Policy: Care in Context
■ Edition	1st
■ Number of chapters/pages	Chapters 1 and 2, pp. 9–56
■ Place of publication	Oxford
■ Publisher	Butterworth Heinemann

and for a journal article:

■ Author's surnames and initials	Smith P, Masterson A and Lask S
■ Year of publication	1995
■ Title	Health and the curriculum: an illuminative evaluation – Part 1: Methodology
■ Journal title	*Nurse Education Today*
■ Volume and issue numbers	Vol. 15, No. 5
■ Page numbers	pp. 245–249
■ Date of publication	October

In addition, it is often useful to note down where the reference is kept, for example a particular library or if it was borrowed from someone. Noting down the class number and accession number can also help speed things up if you need to find the same reference again. The subject matter of the reference should also be noted, along with the key points of argument or information it contains.

Read this excerpt from Cabell (1992) and identify the key points she makes about the role of an advocate and the argument she puts forward regarding nurses' suitability to be patients' advocates.

The role of the advocate has been defined in many ways, which can be categorised under two broad headings. First as a defender of human rights or as a 'social' advocate. This social description endorses the guarding of individual values, rights and justice [2,3], and advocates a redistribution of power and resources to those with a demonstrated need. Second, on an interpersonal level, it has been suggested that advocacy involves providing patients with relevant information and supporting their decisions [4]. Clark [5] specifically defines this role as one which 'means informing the patient of his or her rights in a particular situation, making sure that he or she has all the necessary information to make an informed decision, supporting the decision made, and protecting and safeguarding individual interests.' It is this definition of advocacy which provides the platform for this article. Melia [6] suggests that taking advocacy on board may be beyond nurses' competence. She believes that it provides an unrealistic view of the nurse–patient relationship as nurses may be too entrenched in the health care system to offer anything more than benevolent paternalism to a vulnerable patient. This view, however, may be overly pessimistic, and does not seem to recognise the influence brought by the advent of team and primary nursing. These organisational methods increase nurses' contact with patients and accentuate their responsibilities. The relationship that may form as a consequence of increased indivi-dual nurse–patient contact can give the nurse an opportunity to appreciate the unique strengths and complexities of the individual [7], which is liable to improve the likelihood of close therapeutic relationships.

Your notes should look something like this:

▮ Identifies two broad roles: (1) defender of human rights at a societal level and (2) providing patients with information and supporting them in their decision-making through an inter-personal relationship.

▮ Argues that team and primary nursing encourage the development of a therapeutic relationship which allows the possibility of true advocacy of the second type to happen.

PUTTING IT ALL TOGETHER

It is also helpful to note down any direct quotes which you may want to use in your writing. For example, if you were writing an essay about professionalism and nursing a useful reference which you might come across in your literature search is Hugman R (1991) *Power in Caring Professions*. Basingstoke, Macmillan.

Consequently your card on Hugman (1991) might look something like this:

> Hugman R (1991) Power in Caring Professions. Basingstoke, Macmillan.
> Royal College of Nursing Library 34AC HUG Chapters 1, 3 and 4 particularly helpful.
>
> Useful discussion on what is a profession and classic ideas in the area covering trait theory, occupational control, boundaries, social functions and links with power. Gives good illustrations of the issues in relation to nursing and highlights the conflicts between a professional desire for power and control and the philosophies of caring which involve supporting, enabling and empowering. Suggests an alternative model of professionalisation based on democracy which would '. . . recognise explicitly the aspects of power in caring professions, and from the questions which are raised by the consideration of power to seek the development of caring professions which increasingly are directed towards empowering their members and those who use their services' (p. 224).

Similarly an essay on the contribution of nursing theory to nursing practice might lead you to Sandra Speedy's article 'Theory–practice debate: setting the scene', and your card might look like this:

> Speedy S (1989) Theory–practice debate: setting the scene. *Australian Journal of Advanced Nursing*, 6(3), March–May, 12–20, RCN library.
>
> Defines the different ways that the relationship between theory and practice has been described in the literature, e.g. 'Practice is sometimes viewed as the "down-to-earth" action

carried out by the all-important "doers", while theory is viewed as somewhat esoteric, in some cases unnecessary or at best marginal. The outcome of theory may be perceived as vaguely useful, or the unintelligible mutterings of those in ivory towers. On the other hand, practice is sometimes viewed as routine and mechanical, while theory is considered a "higher" undertaking' (p. 12). Highlights the apparent gap between theory and practice and the implications of this gap for the development of practice. Explores the ways in which the gap between theory and practice could be reduced by practitioners, theorists and researchers. Advocates the development of new nursing roles and a new understanding of the preferred relationship between theory and practice.

The key to success then is being succinct but informative. You may find it helpful to keep the question and your initial brain-stormed plan close to you while you are reading to make sure that you extract only relevant information and do not get completely snowed under by notes.

Quality, not quantity, is what is required. There is no point in reading 50 irrelevant articles and books, it is far better to track down 15 relevant ones.

SELECTING SOURCES AND DECIDING RELEVANCE

It is much easier to read something if you have some idea about what it is going to be about and are sure that it is likely to be relevant or useful. Research reports are usually prefaced with an abstract which is a summary of why the study was done, what it is about and what the main findings and conclusions were. In journal articles and book chapters this sort of information is usually included in the first paragraph or introduction. In this book, for example, the introduction says quite clearly what the contents of the book are, in what order they are covered, and who is likely to find it helpful, and our suggestions for further reading provide a useful summary.

Imagine that you are doing a project on back pain in nursing. Read the following abstract through several times to make sure you understand it and note down the main contents and points which are being made about the topic of back pain.

The aim of this study was to examine current practices within the Lothian Health Board area in relation to reporting of occupationally induced musculoskeletal injuries, training in moving and handling, and use of mechanical aids. A sample of 5,184 nurses working throughout the health board was given a questionnaire containing both open and closed questions. The results showed a significant proportion of nurses had time off work due to musculoskeletal injury and that this was related to grade and speciality. There was also a significant proportion of the respondents who did not report injuries and/or who experienced pain/discomfort, but did not take time off work. Present moving and handling training appears to be inadequate and too infrequent for the needs of staff. These findings emphasise the need for review of both accident reporting systems and training, in particular in the use of mechanical aids. (McGuire and Dewar, 1995, p. 35)

You have probably noted that this was:

■ A research study, using questionnaires, carried out in Scotland, on a sample of 5000 nurses which investigated the reporting of job-related back injuries.

■ The findings indicated that a significant proportion of nurses had had time off because of back injury and that many nurses reported pain and discomfort but had not formally reported their injuries or taken time off.

■ The researchers concluded that current training is not meeting the staff's needs and that there was a need for a review of reporting systems and training in lifting and handling.

It would therefore seem that it is worth reading the whole article as it appears to be very relevant to the topic of your project.

If at this point, however, you are still not sure that a source is relevant, it is helpful to turn to the conclusion or summary and read it carefully.

If we did this with the McGuire and Dewar article we would find that:

The results of the survey indicate that about one third of the nursing population injure themselves at work through moving and handling and that a high proportion (51.4%) of these go unreported. There is clearly a need to examine further both the possible causes of such injuries and the most reliable method of reporting them. Training both in the use of mechanical aids and on lifting techniques needs to be reviewed since the survey showed that there were deficits in relation to the frequency of training and the appropriateness to the clinical situation. These issues together with a positive campaign to heighten awareness and change attitudes need to be seen as a priority. (p. 39)

This confirms our original conclusion that the paper is worth reading and likely to be useful for the assignment.

Similarly, well-constructed books will usually have a list of contents and an index. It is useful to scan both of these to see whether there is any explicit reference made to the topic you are studying. Then turn to the relevant pages and scan them quickly, focusing particularly on headings and subheadings in order to see whether there is anything useful there.

PURPOSEFUL READING

Once you have checked relevance and appropriateness, it is important to read the whole article right through, carefully and thoroughly.

This section builds on the reading skills which you worked on in Chapter 6

All the time you are reading, it is important to keep stopping and reviewing what you have read. The purpose of reading is to weave new ideas and information into your own thinking in order to reach a new level of understanding about a subject or topic. It is often useful to mentally ask yourself questions as you read.

'Is This an Account of a Research Study or Someone's Views and Opinions?'

There are many interesting, well-informed journal articles and books written by well-known authors, but if your assignment asks you to review recent research then it would not be appropriate to include them. If, however, you are reviewing the literature in order to ascertain the current understanding of a phenomenon, such as spiritual aspects of care, then such opinion articles, if well justified and referenced, would become relevant.

'How Recent is the Work/Ideas Being Discussed?'

There is often a gap between writing and publishing of as much as 2–3 years. Journal articles tend to reach publication more quickly than books, although the work they report on may be

a few years old. Some areas of nursing are changing very
quickly so the information may be almost out of date as soon
as it is published, or the recommendations may have been
superseded by more up-to-date knowledge. That alone does
not necessarily mean that it should be discarded. It depends
on the question or topic area which you are trying to address.
For some topics a historical context may be very important. For
example, if you were analysing a nursing model such as
Dorothea Orem's or Sister Callista Roy's, it would be important
to give depth and richness to your analysis to note how the
model had changed over time and the modifications and refine-
ments that have been made in response to the critique of other
theorists and practitioners. Similarly, if you were writing a
historical account of changes in the education and preparation
of nurses, or developments in nursing interventions, then quotes
from original textbooks and journal articles would provide a
rich source of examples.

'What Country Does the Author come from and What Country are They Writing About?'

Increasingly libraries stock books and journals from many other
English-speaking countries and many British journals contain
articles from authors working in other countries. Some things
will be common to all countries, others will not. Drug names, for
example, are different between the USA and the UK; the length
of education and the way nurses are taught is different in Australia; and the law is different in Scotland and England. Consequently, it depends what you are writing about whether such
contributions will be relevant. If you are writing about developments in the field of mental health nursing it may well be relevant
to draw some cross-national comparisons; if, however, you are
discussing the merits of different wound dressings, you need to be
sure you are comparing like with like, and a discussion of legal
issues in rights of people with a learning disability would need to
be confined to a particular country.

'Why is the Author/Researcher Writing What They are Writing?'

If a midwife researcher has been sponsored by a baby milk
company to research into patterns of breast feeding then they
may have been encouraged to show bottle feeding in a positive

ight. Similarly a patient/client education leaflet about the treatment of leg ulcers which has been sponsored by a wound dressing manufacturer will probably present their own products as being particularly helpful.

What are the Points the Writer/Researcher is Making; are these Points Validated and Justified by other Literature or Research?'

In many areas of nursing there are differences of opinion about the 'right' way to intervene or support patients/clients with particular problems or the right way to organise things. For example, in areas such as pressure area care and wound healing there is a lot of apparently contrary evidence; and there is a growing body of research and opinion articles supporting the use of primary nursing, but there are also some reputable studies which advocate team nursing.

Do you Agree with the Inferences and Conclusions the Writer has Made?'

In research studies in particular, it is extremely important to read carefully all the titles or captions which accompany tables, charts and diagrams. Well-constructed work should flow logically and the foundations for the conclusions which are eventually drawn should be apparent throughout.

Do you Understand It?'

The unclear or overwhelming will usually make sense if you take more time to read it. It is helpful to be able to change your reading speed so that you can read the easy bits fast and skim over them, but take more time with the difficult bits. This also depends on why you are reading. If there is a key resource it may be vital to spend a lot of time reading one article or book chapter to pick up every single point and nuance which it contains. Alternatively, if you are attempting to get a broad perspective on the range of opinion in a particular area then skim reading several sources may be more beneficial.

Unfortunately some of nursing's academic writing is very jargon ridden, is written in American English and is unnecessarily complicated, which can be very confusing, off-putting and frustrating at first. Specialists always develop their own language because it gives them extra power in analysing their subject in a detailed and systematic way. As you study subjects in greater depth and become a 'specialist' yourself, you will gradually find yourself using the same technical language without even noticing. For example, you may already find that you are beginning to talk about therapeutic relationships and 'obs', 'MIs' instead of heart attacks, and using words such as symbolic interactionism and dysphasia. Using technical language is not meant to annoy or be exclusionary and elitist, rather developing new ideas and fitting new words to them is part of the process of developing knowledge about a subject.

'How Does This Work Fit with the Rest of what You Have Read?'

It is important to be clear about the chronological order of developments. For example, there is no point in rejecting someone's work because it doesn't allow for some development which occurred 10 years later. Ideas are refined and developed over time. For example, good practice in care of the elderly settings in the 1970s in the UK involved a focus on maintaining safety and fostered dependence on nursing staff, whereas in the 1990s good care is seen as that which upholds the right of older people to be independent and to take risks. Similarly, some diversity of opinion is beneficial and informed debate is healthy and necessary, but it is important to be clear about what the differing stances are and the merits or otherwise of a maverick opinion or finding.

'How Does This Work Fit in with your Own Experience?'

It is often useful to think about occasions and events when you have come across similar patients/clients or problems to those you are reading about, and to consider how the author's point of view or description fits with your own.

'What Are its Strengths and its Limitations?'

Being able to evaluate the merit of a piece of work and the arguments or information which it contains is crucial. It is often useful to evaluate what you are reading both in relation to your own practice and to nursing as a whole.

NOTE TAKING OR PHOTOCOPYING?

You might be wondering whether it is most useful to take notes or just to photocopy everything which you need. Both are probably vital. Photocopying is quick and particularly useful for journal articles but can get expensive. With books there are restrictions about how much you are legally allowed to photocopy. Consequently, it is useful to learn how to take appropriate notes.

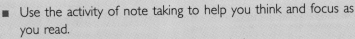

- Use the activity of note taking to help you think and focus as you read.
- Note down only key words, points and phrases.
- Diagrammatic notes can help conceptualisation of links and connections.
- Be careful if you develop your own shorthand that you can understand it later; do not use the same abbreviations for different things, e.g. pn for both primary nursing and postnatal.
- Keep your notes filed carefully somewhere safe so that you can find them again for exam revision and to use in future assignments.

If you are using photocopied articles then you may find it useful to highlight key words, points and phrases. However, if you are likely to use the same article again for something else it may be better just to underline the salient bits in pencil which can then be rubbed off when you are finished. If the book or article is your property you may find it helpful to jot down comments in the margins of the thoughts, questions and examples that came into your mind as you read it.

Note taking forces you to think as you read, because you have to clarify your interpretation of what you are reading and decide what to write down. Notes should not merely be a summary of what is in the text. The secret of note taking is to identify key words, points and phrases with regard to your purpose. The notes you require for a complex, key text will be very different from the notes you write to summarise an article that you just happened to read in passing. Different people acquire and store information in different ways, but generally you need to think 'what is this about?' and 'what do I need to remember?'

Effective note taking depends on identifying and arranging key points to suit your own logic pattern. Some people find that drawing spider diagrams and flow charts is helpful, others develop their own shorthand. The important thing is that your notes should make sense to you when you come back to read them several weeks or months later. Also, you may not be able to borrow that particular book again or get back to that library so you need to make your approach as effective as possible so that one reading is enough. Conversely, there is little point creating pages and pages of notes which just describe and reiterate what you have read. You do not need to take notes on everything that you read as some reading should just be about broadening your knowledge base and familiarising yourself with different ideas and different points of view.

You will need to develop some kind of filing system for your notes so that you can find what you want when you need it. It is also useful to record and remember which databases and libraries you have used, what you have already read, and any conversations with tutors/facilitators. It is important to keep your notes safe: don't carry them all around with you or you might lose them and have to start all over again.

If you are using a computer, it is a good idea to take a hard copy each time you finish working for the day, and to back up your disks.

CONCLUSION

In this chapter we have explored the process of planning an assignment. Preparation in terms of planning your time and making the best use of the resources available to you is crucial. Planning involves thinking carefully about the topic in order to direct your energy in the most useful way, and good researching skills require a systematic, organised and purposeful approach to accessing relevant and appropriate resources. Planning an assignment carefully is fundamental to good writing.

- Preparation is the key to success.
- Check your college's regulations regarding submission, presentation etc.
- Develop a realistic assignment timetable.
- Book appointments with lecturers well in advance.
- Think carefully about the topic and the expectations of the markers.

- Make the best use of your human and material resources.
- Work with your peers.
- Keep a good filing system.
- Take clear, relevant, appropriate notes.
- Read with a purpose.

Keep a diary about the process you go through when preparing your next assignment. Compare the process you go through with the suggestions in this chapter and reflect on how easy or otherwise it was to put the chapter ideas into practice, and any changes you would like to make in terms of preparing for your next assignment.

REFERENCES

CABELL C (1992) The efficacy of primary nursing as a foundation for patient advocacy. *Nursing Practice*, 5(3), 2–5.

MCGUIRE T and DEWAR S (1995) An assessment of lifting and handling practices among Scottish nurses. *Nursing Standard*, 9, 28 June, 35–39.

Literature Searching and Writing Skills

Abigail Masterson

INTRODUCTION

As nurses we must continually update ourselves on what is being done and discovered so that our practice is underpinned by the best knowledge available. As discussed in Chapter 8, good writing depends on preparation. In order to write meaningfully about a topic you need to be able to extract the right sources and review the available literature in a systematic, organised and purposeful way.

See Chapter 8

Key to a successful literature review is the ability to evaluate critically the work of others. You need to know what is asserted to be good practice, and to be able to judge whether the arguments that are being put forward are grounded in research-based evidence, and whether the research itself has been properly carried out. Evaluating the work of others is a difficult skill to learn. Deciding what are valid and invalid arguments, telling the difference between a good source and a bad source, seeing gaps in the literature and so on involves good analytical skills

Such skills do not come naturally but need to be learned and practised. Reviewing the literature is not just something you do as a student – being able to evaluate what you read in journals and books is fundamental to knowledge-based practice.

Key issues

- Evaluating the written word.
- Primary and secondary sources of literature.
- Developing an effective writing style.
- Getting started.
- Feedback.

Academic writing aims to be clear, logical and justified. In this chapter we will explore strategies that you will be able to use to develop your own style. We will focus mainly on the reading stages of the writing process. Having read and worked through the exercises in this chapter you should be able to:

- take appropriate notes and make decisions about the relevance and usefulness of different sources;
- understand the importance of writing clearly and concisely;
- begin to develop informed written arguments.

CRITICALLY EVALUATING WRITTEN MATERIAL

There is a tendency to be seduced into believing that if something is in print it must be true and the author's interpretation must be right. However it is healthy to develop a bit of scepticism about what you read, and to develop skills in evaluating the importance of a piece of work to your purpose, e.g. writing an academic essay or research-based report.

Books and articles are written for different purposes and different audiences. Textbooks are intended to provide general introductions to specific areas of interest, such as nursing care of particular patient/client groups, or subjects such as sociology and physiology. The intention of such books is to provide a straightforward, broad understanding. Specialist books aim to provide more depth and detailed analysis of defined areas.

The *Nursing Times* is the mainstream of popular nursing literature in the UK. It is written in an accessible style, has a huge circulation and is published weekly. The *Nursing Standard* aims to help nurses keep up to date with clinical developments and is also a popular weekly mainstream publication. Both the *Nursing Times* and *Nursing Standard* have panels of expert referees who review the articles submitted for publication to ensure that a particular standard is achieved, but the intention is not to produce academic, scholarly work. *Professional Nurse* is a monthly journal which also aims to provide articles which are informative but readable and practically orientated for clinical nurses. *Nursing Times*, *Nursing Standard* and *Professional Nurse* are all available to buy in most major newsagents.

Specialisms within nursing, such as care of the elderly, critical care and surgical nursing, also have their own journals which aim to provide more in-depth discussion about particular areas of practice. For example in the June 1995 issue of *Surgical Nurse* there were articles on intravenous therapy, the hazards of minimal access surgery, hand surgery, nutritional care, national guidelines and the health promotion role of the surgical nurse in cancer care. The *Journal of Psychiatric and Mental Health Nursing* is a relatively new journal which aims to focus on nursing innovation and the enhanced effectiveness of nursing practice within the area of mental health nursing. Potential contributions are sent to experts for review, and the focus is on a high level of scholarship. The *Journal of Advanced Nursing* aims to be an international medium for the publication of scholarly and research papers. It is available monthly on subscription only, is found in most nursing libraries and is a valuable 'heavyweight' resource for students on pre- and post-registration courses, educators and researchers.

Select one of the books or articles from your recommended reading list. As you read, ask yourself the following questions.

- Is the author providing me with the information I need?
- Who is writing (where do they work, what are their qualifications, do they know what they are writing about)?
- Who is the intended audience?
- Is the work published anywhere else?
- Is the topic dealt with in sufficient depth?

Compare your findings with those of a colleague.

When reviewing the literature it is usually sensible to start with the most recent article or book and work backwards chronologically if more detail about original works or significant changes in thinking is required. Some authors may have written on the same topic in many different journals or books, in which case even though you are able to access all of their publications you should be able to extract their key thoughts on the subject by only reading one or two of them. There is also a lot of repetition in the literature, so you may find if you do a very detailed search that you keep coming up with essentially the same ideas. If the source you are reading does not appear to be stretching you or enabling you to get a better grasp of the subject, it may not be worth reading it any further. Often it is best to restrict yourself to works that have been produced in the last 5–10 years. However, in most subjects there are also 'classic' or 'seminal' works which need to be considered. For example the work of Doreen Norton and others in developing a tool for the assessment of pressure sores in the 1960s was extremely significant in highlighting the importance of 'scientific' assessment in pressure area care. Similarly, the work of Kurt Lewin in the 1950s on change theory has influenced much of the contemporary writings on planned organisational change. Such works are milestones in the development of our understanding about a particular subject or phenomenon.

PRIMARY AND SECONDARY SOURCES

Primary sources are articles and books written by the original authors. Secondary sources are works where the writings of others are reported on and critiqued. For example Smith P. (1992) *The Emotional Labour of Nursing: its Impact on Interpersonal Relations, Management and the Educational Environment in Nursing* (Basingstoke, Macmillan) is an original report on a research study carried out by the author about the nature of nursing and caring, which explored how nurses care and learn to care and the effects of emotional labour on the nurses themselves and the people they care for. This book is a primary source. It has been referred to in many other pieces of work, for example, in Brykczynska (1992), where it is noted that Smith has identified emotional costs associated with caring.

Similarly Coutts-Jarman (1993) in her article 'Using reflection and experience in nurse education' quotes directly from Boud *et al.* (1985) in her description of the development of the reflective practitioner:

> *In recent years there has been much discussion in the nursing literature about the development of the reflective practitioner: 'Reflection is a form of response of the learner to experience . . . after the experience there occurs a processing phase: this is the area of reflection'* (Boud *et al.*, 1985).

Where possible it is always preferable to go to primary sources: the information is likely to be more accurate and informative than a second-hand paraphrased account or 'doctored' quote.

Reviewing the original also enables you to make your own interpretations of the content and conclusions rather than relying on someone else's which may or may not be accurate. So, after you have identified the range of references available in the area, it is usually better to concentrate on primary sources. However, if the primary sources are extremely complicated and difficult to read, then it may be better to start off with a description of the original in the introductory text and then to follow it up with the original once you have some idea of the content and key issues.

DEVELOPING AN EFFECTIVE WRITING STYLE

Academic Style

Academic style is important in the development of learning skills in two ways: you will come across it in what you are reading, and will be learning to develop it yourself through your assessed pieces of coursework. Therefore it is necessary to understand its 'rules'. Academic writing in its purest form is cautious and tentative in approach. The aim is to be as exact as possible and to say only what can be justified. Academic writing assumes a very critical reader who is interested only in whether the arguments make sense rather than appealing to the emotions. In your assignments it is important to justify and support the points you want to make with material that you have read. This does not mean however that you should cite 10 authors to back up statements such as 'many people experience pain following surgery' or 'maintaining patient/client dignity ought to be a high priority for nurses'. Make a clear distinction between what you know because you have read about it and what you know because of your own experience and reflections on those experiences. It is vital to try and express yourself as clearly and as succinctly as possible by using short sentences and straightforward language.

 Keep it simple. If you don't understand what you have written, it is unlikely that anyone else will.

For example, consider this excerpt from Farrington (1993), where a clear, logical and critical approach is taken towards the current unquestioning acceptance within nursing of the role of critical incident technique in the development of expert practitioners.

In nursing Benner (1984) made use of the critical incident technique while Schön (1983) considered that intuitive performances and reflection in action account for the manner in which expertise is achieved. Although such outcome knowledge is though to confer the wisdom of hindsight on our judgements, its advantages may be oversold and overvalued. Smith and Russell (1991) suggested that critical incident technique does not appear to be a useful strategy for heightening awareness of the complex skills of nursing and the dynamic interface between theory and practice. Despite this, Benner's (1984) work appears to have been widely accepted and introduced into curricula throughout the UK. It focuses on positive outcomes in nursing practice rendered by expert nurses in patient care scenarios. Discussion will continue to remain one-sided and unbalanced unless research addresses the old adage of learning from mistakes, especially regarding clinical decision-making and inappropriate or inaccurate judgements made by expert clinical nurses. With hindsight, people commonly exaggerate what could have been anticipated. Not only do they tend to view what has happened as having been inevitable, but also they view it as having appeared relatively inevitable before it actually happened. People often believe that others should have been able to anticipate events much better than actually was the case. As Fischoff (1975) pointed out: '. . . people even misremember their own predictions so as to exaggerate in hindsight what they knew in foresight.' If critical incidents and the notion of intuition are to be of any use in providing greater understanding of expert nursing practice, both the positive and negative aspects of decision making and judgements in clinical nursing practice need to be addressed and researched.

However clear and logical the argument, there can be a tendency to get frustrated with it very quickly if you do not agree with what the author is saying. When reading academic texts we are supposed to detach our thoughts from our feelings and put our own biases on one side in order to judge the validity of the author's arguments by their strength and soundness alone. This is practically impossible to do, however; if we were able to do this absolutely we would not have a position from which to think about, or to judge and criticise, what we read. Eventually we may or may not decide that the author has a point, but we need to give ourselves the chance to find out what is on offer and so must try not to reject opposing points of view too quickly. Instead we should use our feelings constructively by writing down our criticisms point by point.

Learning From Others

A valuable aid to developing your own writing ability is to look critically at the work of others. You may find it particularly helpful to read other students' essays and see what appears to work well and get good marks. Similarly, when reading books and journal articles try to sort out why you prefer one author's work over another. Critically judging other people's writing in this way is a good way of increasing your understanding of what you are trying to aim for in your own writing.

 Choose two journal articles that interest you. Read them thoroughly. Decide which is the better article and jot down the reasons why.

You have probably picked the article which is well structured, clear and straightforward to read.

Structure

All written work should include an introduction, where you set the context and outline the 'map' of what is to follow. This map should include what you are going to cover, why you have decided on this particular approach, and how your argument will develop.

If you have been given a formal title for an assignment, such as 'Discuss the contribution of nursing models to the development of practice', this gives some clues about what the structure and content of your essay should be. The key words in this title are 'discuss', 'nursing models' and 'practice'. 'Discuss' highlights that there are arguments for and against and indicates that your assignment needs to consider both sides. 'Nursing models' indicates that you need to clarify what a nursing model is. 'Practice' means that you need to confine your discussion to the impact on practice rather than education, research or management. The title thus can set out clear guidelines about the content that is expected. If, however, you have just been given a topic such as 'institutionalisation' you will have to decide what you think the key points and issues are. For example, you might decide that you want to explore the effects of institutionalisation on people with learning difficulties, and put forward the case for community care in small group homes. First of all you will need to define what institutionalisation is, discuss the contribution of people such as

Irving Goffman to our understanding of this concept, identify why people with learning difficulties may become institutionalised, and consider the importance of small group homes integrated into the normal social life of local communities in preventing institutionalisation.

In the main body you should outline the key themes and arguments. So, in our first example, you might have a paragraph defining what a nursing model is. Then you would outline the arguments from the literature and your own experience of the advantages and disadvantages of using models in direct nursing practice. This should take several paragraphs.

Finally you should end with a conclusion which pulls together and summarises the key points you have made. For example, the conclusion to the nursing model assignment could be as follows.

Nursing models were developed mainly in the USA in the 1960s and 1970s and were associated firstly with a desire to professionalise nursing and secondly to develop a knowledge base and way of thinking that was distinct from medicine. Nursing models provide us with images of different ways of focusing our interventions and practices. They provide a useful structure for assessment and help nurses make their goals of care explicit. Nevertheless, as most of the models were developed in North America they may not be readily translatable to nursing practice in the UK. Much of the language that is used seems unnecessarily complicated and is very difficult to understand. The depth of assessment that is expected may not be relevant for short-stay areas such as accident and emergency and day surgery, and as each patient/ client has different needs it may not be appropriate to use one model to plan care for all the patients or clients in one area. In balance, however, the potential benefits associated for both patients/clients and nurses of developing a focus for care which is complementary to but different from the bio-medical model is to be encouraged. Through the use and refinement of nursing models in practice, well-structured high quality care where the nursing contribution becomes explicit and valued should become the norm.

Using a spider diagram, plan what you will include in one of your assignments. Make an appointment and discuss your proposed assignment with your teacher.

See
Chapter 6

Each sentence in your assignment should logically lead on to the next, and there should be clear signposts to your reader when you are changing subject or introducing a new point of view. Paragraphs are collections of sentences on a particular theme. When you change tack it is time for a new paragraph. Clarity is crucial. There is often a tendency for students to use very long phrases and complicated sentences in an attempt to emulate what they read in the heavyweight journals and specialist books. However, ease of reading and simplicity are far more likely to impress.

For further discussion on constructing a logical argument see Chapter 10

Never assume anything. Your reader has not necessarily read the same sources as you and certainly does not know what is inside your head, so you need to explain all your ideas fully and give examples to illustrate the points you are making. Having your work typed is not usually essential but if you are hand-writing then it is important to write as neatly and legibly as possible. Write or type on one side of the paper only and leave a generous space between the lines – dense text is very hard on the eyes. Incorrect spelling, punctuation and grammar do not lose you marks as such, but may get in the way of the readability of your work and stop it making sense to others. If you feel that you may have a problem in these areas do seek help.

- Read the work of others. This will help you identify good and bad writing styles.
- Reading helps improve vocabulary and grammar.
- Practice makes perfect. Writing personal letters can help polish writing skills and boost your confidence.

PRACTICE

Getting Started

Most of the hard work should be done by now: you have collected your resources together and organised your thoughts. Your work does not have to be perfect. Students sometimes miss submission dates or do not start writing at all because of an unrealistic desire for perfection. Practice is important, but two or three drafts of any piece of work should be sufficient. Try not to write and edit at the same time as you may lose your capacity to think clearly as you get bogged down in the intricacies of spelling and grammar. Particularly when working on personal computers, there is a temptation and potential for wasting time by spell-checking practically every sentence and perpetually checking the word count.

> If you are working for a whole day, spend the morning writing and the afternoon editing.
> If working for part of the day, write for a couple of hours and edit for an hour.

Nothing is more off-putting than a blank page. If you cannot think of a punchy opening sentence or introductory paragraph, start somewhere in the middle and work backwards. Do not try and complete your task in one go: break the job down into manageable stages. If you get stuck on one bit, try another part and then go back to the first one once you have freed up your thoughts.

Finally it is important to trust your impressions and to have faith in yourself. There is usually no such thing as one right answer. You need to work out what your own thoughts are on the area. It is important to have your own opinion, but it must be based on reasonable evidence rather than gut feeling or prejudice. Finally, do not be constrained by fear of looking a fool or getting it wrong: have a go.

> Prior to submitting a completed piece of work check it against the following.
> - Is the right question/title at the head of your work?
> - Have you included all the relevant personal details, e.g.
>   - your name;
>   - candidate/examination number;
>   - course name;
>   - lecturer's/marker's name?
> - Is your work legible and ordered:
>   - neatly written or typed;
>   - only one side of the paper used;
>   - organised logically;
>   - pages numbered?
> - Is the spelling and punctuation accurate?
>   - Use spell checkers and dictionaries to help.
> - Have you kept a copy of the original, in case it is inadvertently lost?

Handing in your work and receiving a mark and/or comments is not the end of the process. If you want to progress and improve it is important to note the comments made by the marker and try to make constructive use of their feedback.

Accepting Feedback

One of the most useful ways of developing yourself, both as a student and as a nurse, is the ability to listen to others and to make the most of constructive criticism. You will receive feedback in practice placements, after doing presentations in class and on assignments.

As suggested in the introduction to this chapter, there is no such thing as a born writer: practice is essential. Often we compare our efforts with those of experienced writers rather than our peers, and get very disillusioned as a result. It is important to take every opportunity you are offered for feedback, and to try and learn from the feedback you are given, however painful this feels at first. It is always hard when you have spent a lot of time and energy on something not to get the mark you hoped for, or to receive pages and pages of criticism back from your lecturer or the editor of a journal. It is important to try and take such feedback as part of your development as a writer, rather than as a criticism of you as an individual or a nurse.

Nobody likes receiving negative comments about their work, particularly if they result in referral or failure of part of a course. When such things happen we often tend to try and blame others: the paper was hard, the marker didn't like us, the lecturer/our off-duty didn't give us sufficient time to revise. However, in order to grow and develop we need to acknowledge our own mistakes and take responsibility for our own performance.

If you get a mark that you are not happy with or are referred on a piece of coursework do not go and see your lecturer immediately. Give yourself time to adjust and get over the feelings of sadness, anger and disappointment. When you do go to see your lecturer, take along your assignment and any comments from the marker. The comments can act as a guide for the tutorial and can be useful prompts and pointers if you are required to rewrite the assignment.

See Chapter 2 for further discussion of the importance of taking responsibility for your own learning and development

I always keep a copy of the first essay I ever wrote for an academic course. If I ever feel disheartened by feedback, I can read through and remind myself how my style and competence has developed.

CONCLUSION

In this chapter we have explored the process of writing an assignment. You have been encouraged to be critical about what you read, and the importance of clarity and structure in your preparation and your writing has been emphasised. Successful writing, as with so many other things in life, perfectly illustrates the truth of the old adage 'practice makes perfect'.

- Just because it's in print doesn't mean it's right.
- Start with the most up-to-date literature.
- Use primary sources where possible.
- Read through the literature purposefully and critically.
- Use the literature to justify and support the points you want to make.
- Succinct, straightforward, structured writing is the ideal.
- Answer the question.
- Give yourself time.
- Presentation is important.
- Use feedback positively to help you refine your skills.

Take something you have written recently, e.g. an assignment, a formal letter or minutes from a meeting. Read it through carefully and 'mark' it against the following criteria.

- Has all the relevant information been included?
- Does it make sense?
- Is it simple and to the point?
- Is it legible and easy to read?

Having marked it in this way you should be able to begin to see where some of your strengths and weaknesses are, and where it might be useful to seek further help.

REFERENCES

BOUD D, KEOGH R and WALKER D (1985) *Reflection: Turning Experience into Learning.* London, Kegan Paul.

BRYKCZYNSKA G (1992) Caring – a dying art? In: Jolley M and Brykczynska G. (eds) *Nursing Care – the Challenge to Change,* pp. 1–45. London: Kegan Paul.

COUTTS-JARMAN J (1993) Using reflection and experience in nurse education. *British Journal of Nursing,* 2(1), 77–80.

FARRINGTON A (1993) Intuition and expert clinical practice in nursing. *British Journal of Nursing,* 2(4), 228–233.

SMITH P (1992) *The Emotional Labour of Nursing: its Impact on Interpersonal Relations, Management and the Educational Environment in Nursing.* Basingstoke, Macmillan.

Using Logical Argument to Develop Your Writing Skills

Jancsi Sketchley-Kaye

INTRODUCTION

This chapter considers the nature and purpose of logical argument. The ability to construct an effective argument is useful in both professional and personal life, and in the context of study. The term 'essay' will be used, but much of what follows is equally applicable to other types of work which involve putting forward a particular point of view or arguing a case.

> **Key issues**
> - What 'logical argument' is.
> - The usefulness of being able to argue logically.
> - Ways of persuading.
> - How arguments work.
> - How arguments go wrong.
> - Structuring an argument.

WHAT IS ARGUMENT?

To reason is to make a decision about what to believe or to do, on the basis of evidence about what is true or what is wise. To reason with someone is to try to influence a person's beliefs or behaviour by giving the person good reasons for preferring one belief to another or for choosing one course of action over another.

(Moore, 1993)

The ability to deploy a reasoned argument in support of an idea or belief is central to the academic process, and also to the vision of the nurse as a 'knowledgeable doer' expressed by the UKCC (1986); it is this skill which you are expected to display in your written work. An essay puts forward an opinion, and offers support for that opinion in the form of factual and rational evidence.

The academic use of the work argument must be distinguished from its popular usages. The definition which this chapter will use is that an argument is 'a **claim** or **proposition** put forward, with **reasons** or **evidence** supporting it'.

WHY BOTHER TO ARGUE?

Imagine that you are present in a court of law. If, at the start of the proceedings, the prosecution counsel were to stand up and say 'The defendant is guilty as charged: it's obvious, you can tell just by looking at him', it is, to say the least, unlikely that the jury would convict the defendant purely on the strength of this assertion.

What then is the missing element in the above example?

Just as a barrister needs to offer evidence in support of the case for or against the defendant and conduct the case according to the procedural rules of the legal system, so you, as a student writing an essay, need to put forward your point of view in a structured way and offer evidence which will persuade the reader that your point of view is the correct one.

 Reflect on some situations from clinical practice where your ability to put forward a good argument might be useful.

If you as a nurse were proposing to introduce a new method of patient care it is unlikely that you would be allowed to do it merely on a whim. You would need to persuade managers and medical staff of the benefits of the proposed changes, and that these would outweigh any costs involved. The skills of argument may therefore be of direct practical use in the clinical setting.

Domenica is the senior nurse on a respite/continuing care unit of a community hospital. She feels that the workload of the unit is increasing, and that she needs additional staff. To support her request to her manager, she gathers statistics about the numbers of in-patients and the average length of stay which show that the workload has been steadily increasing over the previous 18 months. The workload is particularly heavy in the winter months. On the basis of this information she requests, and is granted permission, to employ two extra part-time health care assistants.

IDENTIFYING AN ARGUMENT

In your reading as well as in your writing, it is important to be able to distinguish an argument from other types of writing.

Read the two passages below. Which is an argument?

1 The nurse pool in this hospital is stagnating. Nurses don't want to move sideways into other specialities, because they will probably have to drop a grade, and can't move up because there are no vacancies in more senior positions. Those who want to leave the profession altogether are put off by the current economic climate and employment market.

2 The nurse pool in this hospital is stagnating: in the year April 1992–93, of a nursing staff of 300, three F grade posts were filled and one G grade post. Only one of the posts was filled by an external applicant. The figures for 1991–92 were nine F grade posts and six G grade posts, of which five were filled internally. Figures for the year 1990–91 were broadly similar.

(Personnel Department statistics)

Using the definition above, paragraph 2 must be the argument, since it makes a claim ('the nurse pool . . . is stagnating') and supports that claim with statistics from the personnel department which show how the turnover of staff has slowed right down and that most posts are being filled by internal applicants.

Now read the two paragraphs again. What does paragraph 1 offer, given that the facts in paragraph 2 are correct?

Paragraph 1 offers an **explanation** for the facts given in paragraph 2. It seems, on the face of it, a reasonable explanation, but is is worth remembering that for any one set of circumstances there may be more than one explanation.

> A police officer arrives at a road junction and finds two dented cars and two angry drivers. The officer has no way of knowing who is at fault without looking at the physical evidence and taking statements from the drivers. Sometimes one explanation will seem more plausible than another, but this does not necessarily make it the correct one.

If you were the manager of the hospital in the example in the activity box above, what could you do to test the truth of the explanation offered for the slowing down in staff movement?

One possible way would be to carry out a survey of the staff and see if the reasons they give for reluctance to move tally with those suggested.

So far, then, we have two elements: the argument and the explanation. The third element in any discussion is **description** of facts and opinions. Description is a necessary part of any argument: in fact it is impossible to argue without describing various aspects of the subject you are arguing about. However, it is quite possible to describe without arguing. Take away the statement 'The nurse pool in this hospital is stagnating' in the second paragraph above and all that is left is a collection of statistics.

When thinking about subjects and questions, use a brainstorming approach. Write down anything and everything you can think of

FACT AND OPINION

When you are collecting the evidence which you will use to support your argument you must be careful to distinguish between objective facts and opinions.

In the sentence below, what is fact and what opinion?

There are over 100 000 nurses in the United Kingdom and most of them have suffered from stress as a direct result of their work.

The number of practising nurses in the UK is something which could be established with reasonable accuracy from published figures, and is therefore fact; whether the majority have suffered from work-related stress is more open to debate, however self-evident it appears. If you were to include a sentence like this in an essay you would either have to qualify your statement or provide evidence to support the opinion (the results of a survey, for example).

When preparing an argument, think of yourself as a lawyer getting ready for a court case and ask yourself:

- what is the charge (i.e. what is the subject of the essay or discussion)?
- am I prosecuting or defending (i.e. what is the claim I am making)?
- what evidence do I have which supports my case and will convince the jury that the defendant is innocent (or guilty)?

MEANS OF PERSUASION

How can you persuade another person to do what you want them to do or accept your point of view?

The means of persuasion break down into two main groups: **rational** and **non-rational** means.

Let us look first at some of the methods which may be used in place of reasoned arguments; these are sometimes called **argument surrogates**. In each of the examples below, try to identify where the argument fails to work. Remember the definition of argument given at the start of the chapter when you are thinking about this.

> We should bring back capital punishment: murder is a dreadful crime and murderers should pay the penalty for it.

A list of claims, eloquently made, can be very persuasive (politicians are generally very good at this), but it does not constitute an argument, because there is no **inference** or chain of reasoning.

 Look again at the above example: try crossing out any one of the statements. Does it make any difference to the other two?

It seems to make no difference: any one of the claims might be true or false, without affecting the truth or falsity of any of the other claims.

> ~~We should bring back capital punishment~~: murder is a dreadful crime ~~and murderers should pay the penalty for it~~.
> We should bring back capital punishment: ~~murder is a dreadful crime and murderers should pay the penalty for it.~~

This argument substitute may be called the **unsupported assertion**.

> Parent to child: 'If you don't stop teasing your brother, I will smack you.'
>
> Nurses who do not accept the new working practices will be deemed in breach of their contract of employment and subject to immediate dismissal.
> Hospital notice
>
> St Ignatius Hospital – the home of the truly professional nurse.
> Recruitment advertisement

Threats and seduction use physical or psychological coercion to cause a person to act in a particular way or adopt a certain point of view. The former uses the threat of harm of some kind, the latter, promise of reward. The first two examples above are threatening, the third seductive.

Consider your reaction to the following paragraphs. What factors might affect your reactions in each case?

The wholesale slaughter of helpless creatures in these animal Belsens, a direct result of this unnatural craving for flesh, represents an unjustifiable oppression of sentient beings.

Demand for increased quantities of meat has led to intensive 'factory farming' methods, where the welfare of livestock may take second place to economics.

The rights and wrongs of farming and animal welfare are outside the scope of this book: our interest here is the language used. In the first paragraph the language is strong, emotive, even violent: there is little doubt here what the author's views are on the subject. The second paragraph is more measured: it could be read as either neutral, or perhaps slightly favourable – your own views on the subject might affect your opinion here.

Emotive language has its place, but should not be used as a substitute for reasoned argument: it is unlikely to persuade those who do not already share your point of view, and it may actually put off those who are still neutral on the issue.

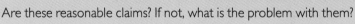

All nurses know that tried and trusted methods are preferable to constant change.

Nurses are constantly being asked to take on aspects of the medical role.

Are these reasonable claims? If not, what is the problem with them?

In both cases, the question must be: 'How do you know?' Have you actually asked any nurses? How many? Where and when?

Avoid the rash, universal statement in your writing: 'Everybody knows that . . .' Consider also: even if everybody does believe something, and you can prove they believe it, does that necessarily mean that it is true? After all, 500 years ago most people believed the world to be flat and that the Earth was the centre of the Universe. (On the other hand, beware the modernist assumption that any beliefs and opinions held by our ancestors are automatically wrong.)

> Read the following statements: how does the writer attempt to persuade you to his point of view?
>
> Surely it must be acknowledged that many people abuse the welfare system.
>
> It is perfectly obvious that nurses have a role in the operating department.

Did you notice the words 'surely' and 'perfectly obvious' are used? These may be called **persuader words** and this kind of false logic, 'the Emperor's new clothes argument'.

There are various other types of argument surrogate, but those illustrated above are the most common, and you should avoid them in your writing. Always ask yourself of any statement which you read or hear: 'why should I believe this to be true?'

HOW ARGUMENTS WORK

We have considered some of the substitutes for rational argument which you may encounter in your reading. Sometimes these argument surrogates are easy to spot, but they can also be well concealed. You may read something which appears to present a valid argument, but which leaves you with an uneasy feeling that the author is pulling a fast one on you. In these cases it can be helpful to break the argument down and examine it more closely. In doing this, you will also begin to see how arguments work, and how to go about constructing your own.

> Read the passage below. Can you spot any flaws in the argument? (If you are not familiar with the two studies cited, accept for the purposes of the exercise that they do demonstrate what the paragraph claims that they do. Pre-operative visiting is the term used for a system in which surgical patients are seen on the ward by a theatre nurse in the afternoon or evening before surgery and are given the opportunity to discuss what will happen to them – what they will see, hear, feel, where they will be when they wake up etc. – and to ask questions.)

Studies by Boore (1978) and Hayward (1975) have demonstrated that if patents receive information about their treatment in advance, they recover more quickly, require less analgesia and are discharged earlier than those who do not receive this information. The information could be conveyed by means of a pre-operative visit from a member of the theatre team, who because of their specialist knowledge is well placed to describe what the patient will experience and answer any questions. Pre-operative visiting therefore would bring benefits to the patients, and it is theatre nurses who should be carrying out such visits.

The first thing to establish is what the subject of the discussion is: in this case, it is pre-operative visiting by nurses who work in the operating department.

The next thing to establish is the position which the author appears to take up, the claim which is to be defended. Sometimes this is obvious, at other times less so, but you need to be clear about the claim made before you can judge the quality of the evidence provided in support.

What is the claim made in the passage above?

The author actually appears to make two claims, firstly that 'pre-operative visiting . . . would bring benefits to the patient' and secondly that 'theatre nurses should [carry out pre-operative visits]'. This is a mistake in itself: claims should be made singly, not bunched together.

Claims need to be supported in some way.

What is the evidence presented in support of each claim?

Let us consider the first claim, that pre-operative visiting benefits the patient. The author starts by citing two research studies which have demonstrated benefits to patients from pre-operative information giving: the first sentence thus offers facts, the accuracy of which may be easily checked. The second sentence then puts forward a suggestion, namely that theatre staff could give this information during a pre-operative visit. It therefore seems reasonable to conclude that, on the face of it, patients will benefit from pre-operative visits.

Note though that this makes the presumption that patients prefer on the whole to recover quickly and have short stays in hospital. Watch out for this kind of presumption and ask yourself 'is it reasonable to presume this?' For example the argument that 'regular exercise makes you fit, slim and healthy: everybody should exercise' presumes that everybody wants to be these things: is this the case?

Let us turn to the second claim, that theatre nurses should be doing pre-operative visits. Here the support offered for the claim is less obvious, but seems to be that theatre nurses have specialist knowledge. The chain of inference is therefore:

Patients need information (because it improves the outcome of surgery)

↓

Theatre nurses have the information (because they are specialists with specialist knowledge)

↓

Pre-operative visits are a means of passing on this information

↓

Theatre nurses should do pre-operative visits

 There are, however, a number of presumptions here. Can you spot what they are?

Firstly, is it reasonable to claim that theatre nurses have specialist knowledge? Some might well do, but not all. It might be better to say 'an experienced member of the theatre team' or 'a specially trained member of the team'. Secondly, is the theatre nurse well placed to answer *any* questions? How about those which relate to the proposed surgery, or the anaesthetic to be used? Thirdly, is a pre-operative visit necessarily the best way of conveying the information which the patient might need?

Does the conclusion therefore follow from the evidence put forward? Should we accept that theatre nurses should be the ones to provide information? It would be perfectly possible to argue that ward-based nurses have more opportunity to develop the necessary rapport than a theatre nurse during a brief visit.

There is one final point to note, and that is how the two claims are put together at the end in a way which suggests that the one implies the other, when they are, as we have seen, two separate ideas. This type of argument surrogate is **conflation**.

CONSTRUCTING AN ARGUMENT

The construction of an argument involves broadly the same elements as the analysis, namely:

- finding a suitable subject;
- identifying a question for discussion;
- considering the evidence on each side of the question;
- deciding which side to support.

The Subject

As a student, you may be given an essay title which is quite specific about the subject you are to write about and even the claim you are to defend or attack. However, you may only be given broad guidelines, in which case you are expected to develop your own title. Your first task will therefore be to identify the subject for your essay.

How might you go about identifying a subject?

Possible sources are:

- your own experience of clinical practice: are there issues which interest or concern you?
- colleagues and managers: what are the current issues in your speciality, and in nursing in general?
- professional and specialist journals: what are the subjects being written about?

The Question

The subject is the broad topic under discussion; the question is the specific issue which your argument will address, e.g. given the subject 'nurse education', you might come up with the question 'Does nurse education contain too much theory and not enough practice?' Any subject will contain potential for lots of questions, and since you will always be writing essays to a word limit, be it 2000 or 20 000 words, the more specific you can make your question the better.

 When thinking about subjects and questions, use a brainstorming approach. Write down anything and everything you can think of which might be used to develop an argument. Don't be critical or selective at this stage: you could lose valuable ideas.

The Evidence

Chapters 4 and 9 looked at practical aspects of gathering information on a chosen subject

Having found your information, you then need to analyse it in order to see if it contains evidence which relates to either side of the question. Note that we say *either* side. Although you may start off with a strong hunch, or with views already well developed in one direction, it is important to keep an open mind and consider all the evidence, not just that which supports your point of view.

Types of Evidence

Evidence may take various forms. The simplest, most direct form is fact.

- There are over 100 000 nurses in the United Kingdom.
- The UKCC was created by the Nurses, Midwives and Health Visitors Act (1979).

Both these facts could be checked and verified.

Certain statements of value are also admissible evidence in argument.

- Human life is intrinsically valuable.
- Nursing is a caring profession.

Neither of these statements could be proven objectively, but both express ideas which are almost universal, and could thus be used to support an argument. (This is not the same as the mistaken universal belief about the flatness of the world mentioned earlier in the chapter, because this was later disproven by observation and experiment. No scientific enquiry could prove or disprove either of the above statements.)

The third form of evidence is opinion. By this is meant not prejudice or unconsidered points of view, but opinions arrived at by a logical thought process. An argument consists of a claim (the conclusion), supported by evidence (the premise or premises). By convention, the premises are given first, followed by the conclusion.

■ Premise 1: to intentionally kill an innocent human being is both illegal and immoral in all cultures.

■ Premise 2: active euthanasia involves the intentional killing of another human being by lethal injection or other means.

■ Conclusion: active euthanasia is therefore morally wrong.

The conclusion, that euthanasia is morally wrong, could then be used to support an argument in favour of greater efforts to improve palliative care.

Included in this type of evidence may be the expert opinions of specialists in the topic under discussion: these usually come from books and journal articles, and if you quote from these, you must remember to acknowledge your sources using an accepted reference and citation system.

See
Appendix A

Note that this kind of argument is never completely watertight: you can pick holes in any argument you come across, but this doesn't matter. One of the things which an essay tests is your ability to marshall facts in support of an argument.

STRUCTURING THE ARGUMENT

Like a lawyer in court, your task in an essay is to convince the jury (your reader) that your point of view is the correct one (or at least, one that is worth considering). As the lawyer uses evidence and statements by witnesses to build up the case, so you have to show how your evidence supports your argument.

The above example demonstrates one basic argument which could be used against euthanasia, but is open to attack by anyone who believes that there is a moral distinction between murder as such and the use of active methods to end the life of the terminally ill. As a general rule it is a good idea to support your overall argument (that active euthanasia should not be permitted) with as many supporting arguments as you can develop in the time and space allowed.

What other arguments could be used to support the view that active euthanasia should not be permitted?

You could approach the argument as follows.

- Premise: the deliberate taking of life is wrong.
- Supporting evidence: the law and customs of all cultures, the intrinsic value of human life.

- Premise: the possibility of euthanasia would undermine the basic relationship of trust and confidence which should exist between patient and nurse or doctor.
- Supporting evidence: medical and nursing ethical codes, Hippocratic oath, statements by professional bodies (BMA, UKCC).

- Premise: the availability of euthanasia would reduce the drive to improve standards of palliative care.
- Supporting evidence: expert testimony, publications by specialists in palliative care.

- Premise: it would be impossible to legislate effectively and safely for euthanasia.
- Supporting evidence: the history of attempts to legislate, the impossibility of legislating to cover all circumstances, analogy with misuse of other laws and their extension in ways not envisaged by their creators.

- Conclusion: active euthanasia should not be permitted.

Note how each of the premises which supports the main conclusion is in a sense the conclusion of supporting argument.

HOW ARGUMENTS GO WRONG

We looked above at some of the things which pretend to be arguments but are not. This section will look at the ways in which arguments go wrong. A mistake in the reasoning process that invalidates an argument is called a **fallacy**. There are many fallacies: we will look at some of the most common ones.

An argument can go wrong in one of two ways: either the premises are faulty, and therefore the conclusion does not follow (for example, if a witness in court tells a lie, their statement cannot be used in evidence), or the premises are true, but do

ot support the conclusion. These are known respectively as
errors of content and errors of form.

What is wrong with the argument below?

All nurses are female.
  Chris is a nurse.
  Therefore Chris is female.

t can easily be shown that some nurses are male, therefore the
first premise is untrue, and the conclusion does not follow. Note
though that the **form** of the argument is perfectly valid. Were is
true that all nurses are female, the conclusion would follow.

What is wrong with this argument?

All nurses are female.
  Chris is female.
  Therefore Chris is a nurse.

n this case the problem is with the form of argument. Even if it
vere true that all nurses are female, and that Chris is female, it
does not follow that Chris is a nurse: she might be an engineer, or
n airline pilot, or anything else. She might even be a nurse, but
his argument doesn't prove it.

Consider the following statements/arguments, and try to identify
the problems with them: don't worry about trying to think of the
technical terms – these will be provided later (sometimes the older
Latin terms will also be given as a useful shorthand). The important
thing is to be able to spot when and where an argument is going
wrong.

1) Mr Lister married his sister.
2) You will meet a dark stranger, and your financial affairs will be
   affected.

These statements are **ambiguous**. In 1) the word sister can be
understood in two or three different ways, as can the word
married. Did Mr. Lister marry his biological sister and commit
incest? Was Mr. Lister the clergyman who officiated at his sister's

wedding? (In fact, neither interpretation is correct. Joseph Lister an eminent Victorian surgeon, married his theatre sister, in the best tradition of nurse–doctor romances!) In example 2), which might be found in the horoscope pages of a magazine, the whole statement could mean any number of different things.

3) Eight out of ten cats prefer Kat Din.

Here it is the information which is *not* supplied which is crucial It sounds like the results of an experiment, but how many cat were involved? Ten? 100? 10 000? What were they offered as an alternative to Kat Din? This is the **fallacy of emphasis.**

4) The argument for the use of corporal punishment as a legitimate educational tool is supported by the works of many famous authors such as Charles Dickens, and also by the Prime Minister.

You may have wondered what special knowledge of education the people referred to possess. Certainly, they are well known even famous, but are they qualified to comment on the subject o: corporal punishment and its effectiveness as a teaching tool?

This illustrates the fallacy of the **appeal to authority.** Using authorities is acceptable, but only to lend support in their area o: expertise. Advertisers who use celebrities to sell products are often using the appeal to authority.

5) Nurses and doctors are always going on about the dangers of smoking, but lots of them smoke, so it can't be that bad for you.

In this kind of fallacy the argument is directed against the failings of individuals in order to discredit the argument pu forward. However, in the example above, does the behaviour of some medical professionals discredit the idea that smoking i bad for you, or does it simply illustrate that human beings are fallible, and don't always live up to the ideals they express? The term used for this fallacy is ***argumentum ad hominem*** (meaning an argument directed against the character or behaviour of a person, rather than their ideas).

6) 'I submit, Ladies and Gentlemen of the jury, that the witness is lying when he says he saw the defendant breaking into the house. The witness is known to have a grudge against the defendant, and has also lied to the police in the past when accused of a motoring offence.'

7) It's not worth treating these people. They don't listen to advice and they won't alter their diet or their exercise habits.

These examples illustrate the same fallacy as above. The problem with *ad hominem* is that there may be occasions when it seems acceptable to direct attention to the failings of an individual. Example 7) illustrates one aspect of a debate which is beginning to be heard more often nowadays. What do you think? (And why?)

8) The majority of nurses are confident that doctors regard them as fellow professionals.

We saw an example of the fallacy, this appeal to popular belief (***argumentum ad sententiam***), above. The fact that a majority believe something to be true does not necessarily mean it is true (although, of course, it may be). For this reason, the results of the opinion polls on contentious issues should be treated with some caution.

9) I believe God exists: it has not been proved God does not exist, therefore God exists.

10) I've never known using egg white and oxygen on pressure sores do any harm, so it must be doing some good.

This is the **appeal to ignorance**, arguing that, because we don't know something is *not* true, it *is* true.

11) Fred Bloggs always tells the truth.
How do you know?
Fred Bloggs told me so.
How do you know he wasn't lying?
Because he always tells the truth.

This is the **circular argument**: the conclusion of the argument, that Fred Bloggs tells the truth, is used as one of the premises which supports the conclusion. You may have encountered this in your work (where 'it' can be changing a dressing, dealing with patients/clients, or organising the off-duty rota):
Why do we do it this way?
Because we've always done it this way.
But why have we always done it this way?
Because we always have.

12) People who drive red cars have more accidents than those who drive cars of other colours. Therefore if no cars were painted red, there would be fewer accidents.

This illustrates the *non-sequitur* (Latin, 'it does not follow'). In a sense, all fallacies are non-sequiturs, because the conclusion does not follow from the evidence presented. The argument above suggests that it is the colour of the car which causes the accident, not the behaviour of the person driving it!

CONCLUSION

In written work and discussion you need to be able to put forward your point of view clearly and effectively. This means telling your reader/audience exactly what the point you are making is, what evidence you are using in support and how that evidence supports what you are saying.

- The aim of argument is to get the other person to accept that your point of view is the correct one, or is at least worth considering.
- When you argue, you must support your claims with evidence.
- The evidence must be true, clearly stated and relevant to the argument.
- Avoid substitutes for argument such as generalisation, persuader words etc.
- Arguments go wrong either because the evidence is untrue (errors of content) or because it does not support the conclusion (errors of form).

1) Collect from magazines and newspapers advertisements and articles which contain argument surrogates of the kind discussed. Compare the styles of argument and language used in the editorial columns of 'tabloid' and 'quality' (broadsheet) newspapers.
2) In your reading, analyse some of the arguments you encounter. Identify the subject, the question under discussion, the evidence presented and the conclusion.
3) If you read something, and find that you disagree with the author, think about why this is. Do you think they have got their facts wrong, or that the conclusion doesn't follow from the premises?

BOORE J (1978) *Prescription for Recovery*. RCN Research Series. London, RCN.

HAYWARD J (1975) *Information – A Prescription Against Pain*. RCN Research Series. London, RCN.

MOORE KD (1993) *Reasoning and Writing*. New York, Macmillan.

UNITED KINGDOM CENTRAL COUNCIL FOR NURSING, MIDWIFERY AND HEALTH VISITING (1986) *Project 2000 – A New Preparation for Practice*. London, UKCC.

FURTHER READING

FAIRBAIRN G J and WINCH C (1991) *Reading, Writing and Reasoning*. Buckingham, Society for Research into Higher Education/Open University.

Advanced Writing Skills: Developing Skills for APL/APEL Claims

Elizabeth Anne Girot

This chapter aims to develop your understanding of how to think and write reflectively within an academic framework. Chapter 3 explored the development of thinking and writing reflectively to help you study. Once you establish your approach to thinking and writing reflectively, you may be required to translate those thoughts or writings into a format that can be accredited for academia. Many educational programmes now recognise the value of reflection for practice and encourage the use of reflective writing in the course assignments. Alternatively, you may wish to claim academic recognition for your practice through presenting a claim for accreditation for prior experiential learning (APEL), and so be required to document your practice achievements in an academic way.

Key issues
- The meaning of APL/APEL.
- The APEL process.
- Types of evidence.
- Presenting a claim.
- Academic levels of learning.
- Exemplars of writing reflectively within an academic framework

If you are unfamiliar with the APEL system, the following offers you a simple definition:

APEL simply allows you to gain academic credit for the learning that you have achieved in practice and that has not been formally assessed in any way previously.

This learning may take many forms, including professional work experience, short non-assessed courses or from general life experiences. Through the presentation of your evidence, the APEL system enables you to gain academic credit through a level and points system, based on a typical three-year degree programme at university. However, making an APEL claim is only of value if you wish to follow a particular academic programme towards a recognised award at a particular higher education establishment. Within nursing, the APEL system is fairly new and at present, each establishment has a slightly different approach.

You may also see the term – Accreditation of Prior Learning (APL) and wonder what this means: APL means the gaining of academic credit for the learning that is achieved from a formally taught course that has been assessed and certificated.

Some nursing departments have produced a Tariff List which shows how much Credit specific courses can attract.

THE APEL PROCESS

The APEL process can be divided into several distinct stages which are a guide to the practitioner when claiming credit. The following is offered as a general guide only:

Stage 1. Decide on Your Programme of Study

Firstly, you need to decide which overall programme of study you wish to follow and subsequently, which modules you are required to complete to gain your award. It is from these individual modules and their learning outcomes that you will be required to match your experience to date.

Stage 2. Identifying and Reviewing Experiences

To discover which prior experiences can be matched to specific learning outcomes within your chosen programme of study, you need to focus clearly on experiences which have led to valuable learning. Whilst a claim for academic credit will consist of prior learning within the past 5 years, experience prior to this will be considered as long as you show how you have updated older learning and applied it to your practice.

Stage 3. Identifying Learning Achievements

You are required to reflect on your experience in order to identify the learning which has taken place. Learning from both personal and professional achievement can be considered as long as the learning has relevance to the specific learning outcomes identified. It may be helpful to group together achievements under common headings, so you can compile your evidence in a comprehensive and coherent way.

Stage 4: Matching the Learning Achievements Against the Modular Learning Outcomes

To be considered for accreditation, your APEL claim must contain prior learning that meets the following requirements.

- **Relevance:** its must be relevant to the learning outcomes contained within the module(s).
- **Current:** it must show you have kept abreast of recent developments in the area in which you are seeking credit.
- **Quality:** it must be at the right level of learning for the identified module (e.g. level 2, diploma level).
- **Sufficient:** there needs to be enough to satisfy the requirements of the module. The amount varies within the different universities.
- **Direct:** the focus needs to be sharp and clear. You need to show that there is clear evidence of your learning.
- **Authentic:** you may be asked to have your work verified by a clinical expert to provide evidence that you have completed the work you claim.

TYPES OF EVIDENCE THAT YOU MAY LIKE TO CONSIDER

Presentation of your learning achievements may be made in a variety of ways.

- Teaching package: implemented and evaluated.
- Innovations in practice: e.g. introduction of a change in practice, standard setting.
- Practical evidence: care plans, information leaflets.

- Analysis of a clinical incident.
- Case studies.
- Reports.
- Budgets.
- Audio/video tapes.
- Essay/project.
- Interview.
- Alternatively, if you have recently completed a programme of study that has not been academically accredited, it may be appropriate to complete the actual module assignments.

Stage 5: Summarising the APEL Claim

Once you have developed your portfolio and presented your evidence to claim accreditation against a particular module of study, you need to summarise your claim and submit this summary along with the main body of your claim. This acts as an aid to assessment of the APEL claim and demonstrates clearly how these learning experiences have led to a coherent learning achievement. The actual layout will again vary according to the different institutions. You must be guided by your APEL advisor, who is someone to whom you will be assigned for guidance.

LEVELS OF LEARNING

The process of learning within academic programmes in institutions of higher education progresses through different levels of learning. Bloom *et al.* (1956) formulated a hierarchy of levels in each of the three areas of learning as follows:

- knowledge domain (cognitive);
- skills domain (psychomotor);
- attitudes (affective).

Most academic programmes are loosely based on Bloom's cognitive hierarchy:

1) Knowledge.
2) Interpretation, understanding.
3) Application.
4) Analysis.
5) Synthesis.
6) Evaluation.

For example, Year 1, Level 1 might require you to achieve Bloom's levels 1–3 with some element of level 4, as above. Year 2, Level 2 would require all that is required at level 1 plus a greater depth of analysis (Bloom's levels 1–4). Year 3, Level 3 would require all the above plus greater depth of critical thought with synthesis and evaluation (Bloom's levels 1–6).

This is of course a very rough guide to what is expected of you. You are urged to find out what your educational establishment asks of you at the different levels, as you will find that expectations vary somewhat from institution to institution and between different assignments.

WRITING REFLECTIVELY FOR ACADEMIA

Whatever the reason, if you need to translate your reflective writing and thought processes into the rigour of an academic assignment, similar rules apply to both first person reflective writings and third person academic writing. However, rather than write in the third person, as most academic programmes encourage, the reflective approach encourages you to maintain a first person reflective style of writing but at the same time support your thoughts and feelings with reference to the literature and research. For example, some of my own students have written reflective assignments to demonstrate, on reflection, how they went about planning and justifying a particular approach to the organisation of a teaching session.

I would like to share excerpts from two students' reflective writing. Both were undertaking a post-registration course on teaching and assessing in clinical practice, academic level 3.

Case Study

One student, Marcia, sought to justify teaching away from her practice area, for her formal assessment of the course.

When considering planning this session, I actively rejected the notion of undertaking it within my own area of clinical practice. I am a staff nurse working within ophthalmic trauma in a teaching hospital, where all nursing staff are qualified and the majority also hold a post-basic qualification . . . I felt threatened about practising the skill of formal teaching, which is new to me, with colleagues whose speciality knowledge base is high. Quinn (1988) suggests that by taking on the role of teacher you may be inferring that you have more knowledge than your learner. On reflection I feel that the view of the teacher in adult learning as more of a guide and facilitator is more appropriate (Knowles, 1990), as this acknowledges the value of the learner's experience.

As you can see from this example, the student openly expresses her feelings about the situation and begins to analyse it and support her thoughts with current literature. The process is no less rigorous than that used in the third person, impersonal academic style of writing, yet it comes alive and has meaning for the individual concerned and direct relevance to her own practice. Those reading it also gain by recognising similar feelings and justification for moving in different directions.

I contacted the sister prior to the session to ask what topic area they would like me to cover. In consultation with her staff she identified assessment and record keeping . . . I felt this was important as the idea of androgogy, which will be discussed in more depth later, places the learners as central in identifying learning needs (Nielson, 1992). It was interesting that I would have selected a topic related to disease or trauma of the eye. Kenworthy and Nicklin (1989) counsel against selecting pet topics that may not be of value. In my experience both of these points proved relevant as feedback from both the group and facilitator confirmed that the subject had met their learning needs and I would certainly use this strategy for a similar session.

Here again the student enters into dialogue with herself. She recognises the need as teacher to enable the students to identify their own learning needs. She also recognises that if given the choice herself, she would have picked her own pet subject, quite different from that chosen by the student group and which would not have been so appropriate. She analyses the issues, and examines alternatives, supporting her choices with current literature.

The student continues in her reflective evaluation of her teaching.

The use of lectures is suggested to be the antithesis of student-centred learning, and certainly Harvey and Vaughan (1990) found in a study that student nurses did not have a positive reaction to them, although I would suggest that this may be a reflection of their operational definition of a lecture as solely a one-way communication. I felt that the lecture/discussion was of value and had a place in an androgogical approach, a view shared by Jones (1990); not as O'Kell (1988) infers, due to nurses adopting a passive role, but as an appropriate way of introducing new information (Knowles, 1990). I also acknowledge that I selected a lecture as a strategy in part because I felt more comfortable with it as I had more control. It is interesting that Dux (1989) noted the popularity of lectures with nurse teachers, although the study does not identify why. I feel that I would use the strategy of a lecture/discussion through the fictional patient. I feel that the amount of discussion was in part due to the group rather than my teaching skill. Perhaps this could be achieved through more use of questioning (Quinn, 1988).

Here again, the student explores her own thoughts and feelings about what she did and analyses the various issues, accepting and rejecting aspects of the literature in support of her own situation. Overall, however, she consistently explores the learning she has achieved from the various activities and I suspect will continue her exploration as she develops her skills as a facilitator of learning.

Having explored the various theories of how people learn throughout her reflective account, she finally finds a way that would enable her to deliver such a session in her own practice area, the one aspect of the session she deliberately avoided:

> *I feel that by adopting the idea of the teacher as a guide (Knowles, 1990), I would be comfortable giving this session in my own area of practice.*

Case Study

This student, Margaret, a health visitor, reflects on her teaching session with a pre-registration student in the community.

> *On reflection I am pleased with the way I dealt with this session. I was able to bring the teaching material down to an appropriate level for this student by revising some basic theory before moving on to the task in hand. Looking back I realise that this was an example of 'reflection-in-action' (Schon, 1991), i.e. I was able to develop variations according to my on-the-spot understanding of the problems of this student. I would like to suggest however that while this adaption of teaching material was possible in a one-to-one teaching session, it would be far more difficult to achieve were I to try to listen and respond to the problems of individual students if I were to undertake this teaching session with a large group of students.*

As with the last case study, this student looks back on her experience and begins to link theory with practice. She actively analyses her teaching session in relation to this individual learner as well as recognising the difficulties in adapting her suggestions for a larger group of students. In addition, she refers to 'reflection-in-action' (Schon, 1991), i.e. thinking on your feet and adapting your activities as you are doing them. As a professional you will be reflecting-in-action all the time and adapting your care to suit individual needs. However, as Margaret has recognised, it is important to articulate this and identify how you are making your decisions.

As with the previous case study, this student recognises the value of Knowles' (1990) work and its application to her own teaching in the community.

Knowles (1990) suggests that the teaching–learning transaction is a mutual responsibility between teacher and student, a view which I strongly support. I feel that student responsibility is of particular relevance in the nursing profession as preparation for the ongoing learning experiences after qualification when the practitioner must ensure she is up to date with relevant research (UKCC, 1984). Self-directed learning is likely to become even more important as cash-starved Trusts coupled with a shortage of available courses place responsibility for updating knowledge squarely on the shoulders of the practitioner.

On reflection, however, the student I was teaching was very young and it may have been unreasonable to expect a student at this stage in her training to employ a way of learning that she may have had little experience of. Kenworthy and Nicklin (1989), for example, suggest that students who come into nursing straight from school, as she had, may have well-established concepts of teacher-led learning.

I cannot therefore relinquish all the responsibility for the student's lack of prior knowledge. If independent study is viewed as capability to be developed in a student (Dressel and Thompson, 1973), perhaps I did not spend enough time helping her to identify her learning needs.

Whilst overall she was pleased with the way the session had gone, she recognised a number of areas that could be improved.

On reflection immediately after the session however, I realised I had tried to cram too much material into one session. I had covered all the material but had achieved breadth at the expense of depth. In future I would certainly plan at least two sessions to cover this subject . . . In relation to this it occurred to me that I did not actually know how much the student had learned at the end of the session. We read through the objectives and agreed that we had met them but I did not actually revisit the objectives by questioning the student on her newly found knowledge. Questioning at the end of the session is suggested to enhance the retention of lecture material (Bligh, 1972), and I think in future sessions of this nature I would offer a brief quiz or self-assessment test both to enhance memory and to provide feedback.

I wonder now if one reason that I did not fully revisit the objectives as I had intended to was a 'defence mechanism' on my part. I had already felt 'let down' by her at the beginning of the session and did not wish to repeat the experience at the end, e.g. if I found she had not learned much. Why did I have this feeling of being let down? I think it was probably because I am a novice teacher and wished to perform well as I was being assessed for the ENB 998 course.

This is a painful reflection because it shows that I was, as teacher, placing my needs centrally before those of the student – a concept which is in direct contradiction to the ethos of adult learning (Knowles, 1990) that I profess to be aiming for in this teaching session. In future I shall have to ensure that I am on my guard against this in order that I can enable the student(s) to learn effectively.

The student has expressed here a truly insightful reflection. Initially, she explores the issues rather superficially. However, she then begins to express her thoughts and feelings with regard to a more in-depth analysis of the situation. She freely admits the painful experience it has been, but emerges from the reflection as having learned something positive that she can take with her to other sessions in the future.

I hope these examples will give you some idea of how to develop your reflective writing into an academic piece of work. The result offers you a truly analytical approach to your own learning. As you see, it must be supported by current literature and, where possible, current research.

However, the above case studies do not necessarily give you a feel for the whole picture in terms of structure. Overall, the structure of your assignment, or evidence presented for an APEL claim, will be the same as you are required to present for any third person academic assignment, i.e. it must have an introduction, main body and conclusion. In addition, the main body needs to be well structured and follow logically sequenced thoughts and arguments, all that you have learned in earlier chapters. However, here, you are encouraged to express your feelings, just as the major writers on reflection have identified. From the above examples, the recognition of the feelings you have experienced is a major element of the learning process. It is almost like revisiting the experience for yourself, but somehow standing outside yourself and discussing the decision-making process that you were involved in when making your decisions.

As you see from the above examples, these students thought through why they organised their teaching in the way they did, identified the advantages, recognised the different problems, but finally came to a decision about how they presented their session given the various options available. They reasoned through the decision-making process, discounting a number of options open to them. As in third person academic work, it is equally impor- tant here to develop and present your analysis of the process and not merely describe the situation. Whilst description is a part of the process, it is only one part, and it is the development of analytical thought that will represent the different academic levels. Like any academic assignment, it is important to identify what is expected from the different levels of academia in your particular institution, as they do vary slightly throughout the country.

In addition to the hierarchy of the cognitive domain as identified by Bloom (1956), Mezirow (1981, in Atkins and Murphy, 1993) offered a hierarchy of seven levels of reflectivity, ranging from a purely descriptive approach to gaining insightful learning to a sophisticated analytical process.

1) **Reflectivity:** the act of becoming aware of a specific perception, meaning or behaviour of your own or the habits you have of seeing, thinking and acting.
2) **Affective:** becoming aware of how you feel about the way your are perceiving, thinking or acting.
3) **Discriminant:** assessing the efficacy of your expectations, thoughts and actions. Recognising the reality of the contexts in which you work and identifying your relationship to the situation.
4) **Judgemental:** making and becoming aware of your value judgements about your perception, thought and actions, in terms of being positive or negative.
5) **Conceptual:** being conscious of your awareness and being critical of it (e.g. being critical of the concepts you use to evaluate a situation).
6) **Psychic:** recognising in yourself the habit of making precipitant judgements about people based on limited information.
7) **Theoretical:** becoming aware of the influence of underlying assumptions upon your judgement.

Powell (1989) adapted Mezirow's seven levels of reflectivity to six in her small study of nurses in the UK, to find out whether nurses do reflect in practice and, if so, to what level. In essence, she found that her small sample (eight nurses) demonstrated extensive but superficial levels of reflection with little critical and analytical thought. Whilst we cannot generalise from this small study, certainly translating your reflective diaries or profiles into academic assignments or evidence for an APEL claim demands that the higher levels of reflection are used. In addition, support from the literature and research is required to justify what you have done in practice.

CONCLUSION

This chapter has introduced to you the notion of thinking and writing reflectively within an academic framework. It has given you an overview of the APEL/APL process and the different levels of academic expectations. Some examples have been offered as an illustration of how to put your writing into this academic framework. Now you need to put this together with ideas from earlier chapters on the various aspects of assignment writing. Most importantly, you should recognise that whether using a third person academic style of writing or a first person reflective style, the rigour required of academia is the same.

- Reflection for academic credit must be of the appropriate quality in relation to levels of learning.
- If not already familiar with the academic system, you should seek advice regarding what is expected of you by the university you are attending.
- When writing reflection at academic level 3 (degree), then critical thought, analysis, synthesis and evaluation must be evident (two examples are given).
- As with all academic work, your reflective writing for academic purposes must follow the same rules as with third person, impersonal writing, i.e structure and logical sequencing of ideas must be evident. Support from the literature must be no less rigorous than with other academic work.

1) Next time one of your colleagues shares their reflections with you, encourage them to analyse the situation rather than simply describe it. Listen to what they have to say. Also, try to identify what, most of all, they have learned from the situation.

2) If you already have a clinical forum where you discuss incidents that occur in your workplace, try to look at the situations from different perspectives. Encourage everyone involved to put their own view forward. Try to act as devil's advocate! Afterwards write the discussion in your portfolio. Try to make sense of the discussion by examining the literature to give you some substance to the discussion.

3) Compare your work with some of the above examples. Show your work to your link tutor or to a colleague with an academic background to see if they can offer any support.

REFERENCES

ATKINS S and MURPHY K (1993) Reflection: a review of the literature. *Journal of Advanced Nursing*, 18, 1188–1192.

BLIGH D (1972) *What's the Use of Lectures?* Middlesex, Penguin Educational.

BLOOM B (1956) *Taxonomy of Educational Objectives. Handbook 1. Cognitive Domain.* New York, McKay.

DRESSEL PL and THOMPSON MM (1973) *Independent Study.* San Francisco, Jossey-Bass.

DUX CM (1989) An investigation into whether nurse teachers take into account the individual styles of their students when formulating teaching strategies. *Nurse Education Today* 9(3), 186–191.

HARVEY TJ and VAUGHAN J (1990) Student nurse attitudes towards different teaching/learning methods. *Nurse Education Today* 10(3), 181–185.

JONES RG (1990) The lecture as a teaching method in modern nurse education. *Nurse Education Today* 10(4), 290–293.

KENWORTHY N and NICKLIN P (1989) *Teaching and Assessing in Clinical Practice. An Experiential Approach.* Middlesex, Scutari Projects.

KNOWLES M (1990) *The Adult Learner: a Neglected Species.* London, Gulf Publishing.

NIELSON BB (1992) Applying androgogy in nursing continuing education. *Journal of Continuing Education in Nursing*, 23(4), 148–151.

O'KELL SP (1988) A study of the relationships between learning style, readiness for self-directed learning and teacher preference in one health district. *Nurse Education Today* 8, 197–204.

POWELL JH (1989) The reflective practitioner in nursing. *Journal of Advanced Nursing* 14, 824–832.

QUINN F (1988) *The Principles and Practice of Nurse Education.* London, Croom Helm.

SCHON D (1991) *The Reflective Practitioner: How Professionals Think in Action.* London, Maurice Temple Smith.

UNITED KINGDOM CENTRAL COUNCIL FOR NURSING, MIDWIFERY AND HEALTH VISITING (1984) Code of Professional Conduct for the Nurse, Midwife and Health Visitor. London, UKCC.

Presentation of Written Material

Sian Maslin-Prothero

INTRODUCTION

The aim of this chapter is to assist in the presentation of material. The first part of the chapter looks at different styles of writing while the remainder looks at the presentation of written material. This will provide you with a framework which you can adapt to meet your requirements.

Key issues

- Different styles of writing.
- How to prepare a project.
- Report writing.
- Presentation of written material.
- Reviewing a book/article.
- Non-discriminatory language.
- Copyright and plagiarism.
- Writing for publication.

Being asked to write something, be it an essay, a report or an article, can be a very daunting task. If you are undertaking any course of study, completing a written assignment is still the most common form of assessing student learning. How to write an essay has been covered in Chapters 8, 9 and 10; this chapter will examine other forms of presenting written material.

See Chapters 8, 9 and 10

You will already have considerable experience of writing and presenting material, for example completing assignments as part of course work in school or college; or in practice areas, writing care plans, reports either in handover to other nurses or to other colleagues in ward rounds, or individual patient plans.

With each of these scenarios you have to identify the most important information, i.e. what needs to be imparted, and what is not essential. You then provide the essential information in the most appropriate format and style. This will be different according to whether you are providing a presentation (to an audience) or a written piece of work.

DIFFERENT STYLES OF WRITING

Chapter 9 looked at essay writing. There may be other forms of writing you have to do as part of your course or as a daily activity. These may include some of the following.

See Chapter 9

- Letters to friends and family.
- Job and course applications.
- Lecture notes.
- Reports on patients and clients.
- Projects.
- Memos.
- Essays.
- Examinations
- Reviews of books or articles.

Each of the above has special features which need to be considered prior to preparation and before actually writing.

- What is it for?
- Who is going to read it?
- How long should it be?
- Should it be written in the first person or third person?

The style you adopt for writing will vary depending on the task. A letter to a member of your family or a friend will be very different to a memo sent to a colleague.

> Dear Pat
>
> How are you? I haven't heard from you since you moved into your new house. I hope the move went well. It must be a real luxury having a fridge – not having to leave your milk and butter outside the back door!

Have you been climbing recently? I still haven't been to investigate the indoor climbing centre at Nottingham. The thought of trying to find a climbing partner is a bit daunting.

The new job is going well. People have been really welcoming. Last night we were all invited round to a colleague's house for supper. They have children the same age as Jack and Charlotte. Fortunately, they all got on.

Do write soon. Send my love to Chris.
Love from

Sian

The style of a personal letter is informal and familiar. In comparison, a memorandum to a colleague will be different.

MEMORANDUM

To: Sian Maslin-Prothero
           Lecturer

From: Rachel Clarke
           Head of Department

Re: Flexible learning in the faculty.

Date: 23 November 1995

Thank you for your letter of 21 November 1995.

Would you please let me have a paper briefly outlining the achievements and how you consider the future could be planned.

HOW TO PREPARE A PROJECT

You are likely to have to undertake a project as part of a course or in your work environment. It can seem a frightening prospect; however, it can also be a satisfying experience. The key to success is preparation. This involves developing a plan. Before embarking on this you need to consider the following.

- What have I got to do? Use the assignment guidelines:
  - subject;
  - word limit;
  - date for submission.
- How much time do I have to complete the project?
  - Be realistic.
  - Structure your time.
- Plan your time and a margin for 'overrun'.
- Stick to your timetable.

This is drawing on Chapter 1, which discussed planning and organising your time. Completing a project is similar to writing an essay. Using the flow diagram in Fig. 12.1 you can organise your work effectively. Your aims and objectives will be the basis for deciding what information you require in order to complete the project.

See Chapter 1

See Chapters 8 and 9

See Chapter 1 for definition

HOW TO PREPARE A REPORT

The structure of a report is very different to that of an essay or letter. Reports are written because there is a need for specific information: usually a problem has been identified which requires investigation. Reports are written for a purpose and usually target a specific audience. They are statements of facts presented in a logical sequence leading to possible recommendations for future action. A good report is characterised by its objectivity and systematic presentation. Reports have a format which leads the reader quickly to the facts.

Content of a Report

All information contained in the report must be relevant, concise and substantiated, and it must be presented in a clear, logical sequence. The report should have an introduction where the **terms of reference** are defined. The terms of reference include: who has commissioned the report; why have they asked for the report to be written; the purpose of the report; who the report is for; and who is going to read the final report. Essential background material may be included, or you can put details of methodology in appendices. Some or all of the following may be included in the report.

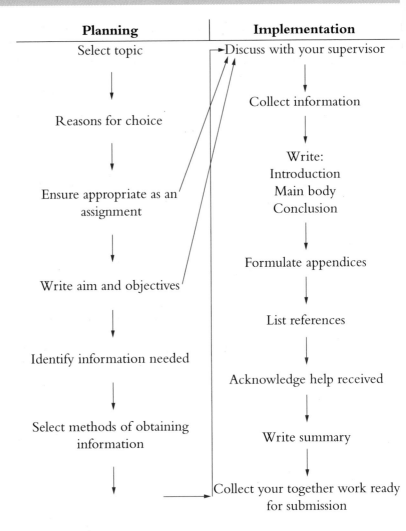

Figure 12.1   Planning and implementing project work. (Adapted from Wheatley, 1995.)

- In the **methods** you tell the reader how you went about obtaining the information, or analysing the information for the report.
- The **results** section is where you present your findings.
- The **discussion** is where you discuss the implications of your findings.
- The **summary** is where you summarise the results and make recommendations based on the report's findings.

The writing style should be clear and precise. Aim to use short and simple sentences, so that the report is clear and easily understood by the reader. The report should be non-anecdotal and coherent. All sections, sub-sections and points must have headings, and be numbered and indented. This is so that the report

---

Report

1. INTRODUCTION
   - 1.1 Style
     - 1.1.1 Ensure that the writing style, language and level is appropriate for the intended audience.
     - 1.1.2 Report writing is formal and they are usually written in the third person.
   - 1.3 Who am I writing for?
   - 1.4 What is their knowledge of the subject?

2. STRUCTURE
   - 2.1 Reports often need to be read quickly, so ensure that the reader can find their way around the document easily.
     - 2.1.1 Sections and sub-sections should be numbered appropriately.
   - 2.2 Your introduction places the report in context. The conclusion draws the argument together, and makes recommendations where appropriate.
   - 2.3 The abstract should be a précis of the introduction and conclusion.

3. MATERIAL
   - 3.1 Be selective and stick to the point.
   - 3.2 Report writing is a review of all the evidence, not a personal view.
   - 3.3 Start with the most important things first, then add the necessary detail.
   - 3.4 Avoid repeating yourself. You might find you need to reorder the material.

4. CONCLUSION

   Use clear, simple language and stick to the point. Break the report into sections and sub-sections, with headings to guide the reader. Stick to the word length (if you are given one). Your report will need an abstract, an introduction, the main body, a conclusion, recommendations and appendices.

flows logically, and information can be easily retrieved. The following example illustrates the layout of a report.

In addition, the pages must be numbered. Any diagrams must be appropriate, numbered and clearly captioned. Only include diagrams if they are relevant and referred to in the report, otherwise there is no point in including the information.

To summarise, to achieve effective communication, you should use clear, simple language. Well laid out sections and the appropriate use of headings and summaries will guide the reader through the report.

REVIEWING A BOOK OR ARTICLE

This is a valuable skill for any professional. The ability to **critically evaluate** is important for a number of reasons: preparation for any assignment or project requires the individual critically evaluating others' work in that area; not all research or reports have been reviewed by referees or peers. Critical evaluation is about being able to evaluate others' work, both positively and negatively, thus judging the quality of the work. This is a useful skill to develop, and should be used when you read papers, reports and books.

Critical evaluation is covered in more detail in Chapters 8, 9 and 10

NON-DISCRIMINATORY LANGUAGE

The aim of language is to communicate. Our use of language reflects our own attitudes, therefore if the language we use leads to misunderstanding or offends individuals, we are failing to communicate.

When using language, whether written or the spoken word, you need to be sure that you are not excluding people or discriminating against them. The way we speak and the language we use can reinforce inaccurate stereotypes. For example, the term 'mother and toddler group' insinuates that only mothers are responsible for child care. This is not the case. The term playgroup better describes what is available and includes all carers.

Non-sexist Language

The term 'man' should not be used to refer to both sexes. There are non-sexist alternatives:

Sexist	Non-sexist
mankind	people, humanity
manpower	workforce
forefathers	ancestors
fireman	firefighter
headmaster	head teacher

He/him/his are *not* universal terms for men and women.

Very few occupations or roles are exclusive to either males or females. The language used should reflect the job or task being performed.

The most important thing is to think, and to avoid discriminatory language in your written and spoken word. This is most likely to occur when using **pronouns**. A pronoun is a word used instead of a proper or other noun to indicate a person or thing already mentioned. For example, I, me, she, her, he, him, it, you, they and them are all pronouns.

There are several ways of avoiding discriminatory language.

- Avoid the pronoun. Use 'a', 'an', 'the' in place of the pronoun. For example, 'A nurse has his special patient' could be written 'A nurse has a special patient' or 'All nurses have their special patients'.
- Use 'they'. 'Once a nurse has registered to practice he knows in which area he wants to work' could be written: 'Once a nurse has registered to practice they know in which area they want to work'.
- Use both pronouns 'he/she' or 'his/her'; however this can be clumsy. For example: 'A nurse has her or his special patient'.
- Use the second-person pronoun 'you': 'As a nurse, you have your special patient'.
- Use the first-person plural 'we': 'We nurses have our special patients'.
- Use 'one' (with caution, as it also has class connotations for some people): 'As a nurse, one has a special patient'.
- Use a plural pronoun with a singular antecedent (e.g. everyone, every etc.): 'Every nurse has their special patient'; 'Everyone has their special patient'.

The use of non-discriminatory language might seem difficult, but with practice it becomes natural to use terms which do not discriminate against people because of their gender, sexuality, colour etc.

COPYRIGHT AND PLAGIARISM

It is unclear how frequently plagiarism occurs, but the aim is often to deceive, therefore many cases go undetected. It is important that you reference all material used. If you include other people's ideas or work without acknowledging their contribution then you are plagiarising, and risk failing your course or losing your job. People plagiarise for different reasons: ignorantly, innocently and deliberately.

If you copy out a quotation from a book or article, you must credit the author, i.e. reference their work including name, date of publication and page number. Referencing other people's work is very important for a number of reasons: it enables the reader to refer to the original work, and check the authenticity if they wish to; the reader might want to use the source for their own research; and the reader can distinguish between other people's ideas and your own.

The safest way of avoiding plagiarism is to acknowledge the sources you have used. When preparing an assignment and making notes, use the following guide.

See Appendix A

- Separate direct quotations from your own work by using quotation marks.
- Always cite the precise source in your reference list.
- List all sources used in the bibliography.
- When paraphrasing another's work, identify the original source including the author and date of publication.

You may refer to another person's work by paraphrasing in your own words. In this situation you must still reference the original work using the author and the date. This is referred to as the primary source. In the case where an author you are reading refers to another author and their work, and you do not access the original work, you may cite this work. This is sometimes referred to as a secondary source: for example 'Brown (1978, cited in Maslin-Prothero, 1994)'. If you are in any doubt about how to reference material, refer to Appendix A, or ask your teacher or librarian.

See Appendix A

To successfully avoid the pitfall of plagiarism consider the following points.

- Don't attempt the question until you understand it.
- Do consult your teacher and colleagues.
- Plan your time carefully.
- Reference your notes and sources as you go along. Don't wait until you have completed the essay, and then try to remember where they came from.

WRITING FOR PUBLICATION

Writing for publication provides an opportunity to share your ideas with a wider audience, and is crucial if nursing is to develop and patient care improve. For those working in academic institutions, it is a requirement of academic life. If you examine the nursing press you will find that only a small number of the total nursing workforce having submitting their work for publication. Masterson (1994) identified that the majority of papers published in nursing journals are from either nurses in management or nurse educators.

If there is to be a more representative, balanced view of nursing then you need to contribute your thoughts and ideas to the nursing press. Learning to write is straightforward as long as you prepare and follow some simple guidelines.

- Identify your audience (and journal).
- Write about what you know.
- Do background reading and preparation.
- Use the journal guidelines for contributors, and follow the 'house style'.

From personal experience it is worthwhile approaching the intended journal editor or publisher with your idea. Read a variety of journals, and decide whether what you want to write about is suitable for that particular journal. There might be a journal that is more appropriate, for example an article on the experience of part-time, mature nursing students would be more suitable in *Nurse Education Today* than the *Journal of Clinical Nursing*. Then prepare a detailed plan of what you intend to cover and write to the editor. This will save you time because the editor can express an interest (or otherwise) in the intended published work.

Having identified the journal, use the contributor guidelines when preparing the script. This will help create a favourable impression with the editor and reviewers when submitting the completed script. The guidelines for contributors include the following details: number of words, presentation issues (typed, double line spacing, width of margins, style of referencing), number of copies to be submitted, including floppy disk, copyright, payment. Proof read your work prior to submitting, or ask someone else to.

The editor will decide whether your manuscript is appropriate for their publication, and will use reviewers' comments to advise on the standard and quality of your manuscript. The referee will recommend some of the following accepting the article, that some revision required, or rejecting the article.

The journal will write to you and let you know if your work has been accepted for publication. If they recommend making some changes, and as long as it doesn't change the meaning of the work and you are willing to do the required changes, then make the changes and return the article. Be prepared for a wait of up to 1 year before seeing your work in print. Don't get despondent if your article is not accepted for publication. This chapter has been written by someone who has experienced their work being rejected, but has persevered!

It is worth noting that there is a journal specifically aimed at students who want to publish their work assignments. It is called *Assignment – Ongoing Work of Health Care Students*, and is published by the University of Wales College, Swansea.

CONCLUSION

This chapter looked at presentation of written material. The main aim was to provide you with a framework which you can use when preparing written material. This can be used in conjunction with information from other chapters for presentation of assignments. It is useful to gain feedback on any written or verbal presentations you give, to enable you to develop your skills further. You will gain in confidence and learn each time you have to submit written work.

Identify an assignment for which you received positive feedback from your assessor. Using guidelines from a nursing journal, make necessary changes and submit it for publication.

REFERENCES

MASTERSON AHR (1994) Exploring the Values of British Nursing and the Values Enshrined in UK Health Policy: A Research Proposal, MN Unpublished Thesis. Cardiff, University of Wales College of Medicine.
WHEATLY K (1995) Project development. In: Richardson A (ed.) *Preparation to Care: A Foundation NVQ Text for Health Care Assistants.* London, Baillière Tindall.

FURTHER READING

DOYLE M (1995) *The A–Z of Non-sexist Language.* London: The Women's Press.

SECTION III

APPENDICES

Appendix A: Reference and Citation Systems

is an essential requirement when researching and producing a written project that all sources used are properly acknowledged. is important that you employ and become used to a standardised reference system.

These guidelines describe the **Harvard** and the **Vancouver** systems of referencing, which are the most commonly used. You may use another system, but bear in mind that it is important to keep to a standard form throughout your written contribution.

DEFINITIONS

Reference A bibliographic description including author(s), date, title, publisher and place of publication.

Reference list Bibliographic list of items referred to or cited in the text.

Bibliography Bibliographic list of other relevant material used, but not referred to in the text.

Annotated bibliography A bibliography where each reference is accompanied by a critical or explanatory note.

BOOKS

Give the following facts in order.

) Name of the author(s), editor(s) or the institution responsible for writing the book in upper case.
) Year of publication in brackets.
) Title and subtitle, underlined.
) Volume and individual issue number (if any).
) Edition, if not the first.
) Place of publication, if known.
) Publisher.

Examples

1) With one author:
   CHANDLER T (1992) *Support Worker Training*. London, Baillière Tindall.

2) With two authors:
   IRONBAR NO and HOOPER A (1989) *Self-Instruction in Mental Health Nursing*. London, Baillière Tindall.
   ROMANINI J and DALY J (eds) (1994) *Critical Care Nursing: Australian Perspectives*. Marrickville, W.B. Saunders.

3) With three or more authors:
   KELNAR C, HARVEY D and SIMPSON C (1995) *The Sick Newborn Baby*. London, Baillière Tindall.

(In the text, it is sufficient to cite Kelnar *et al.* (1995)

REFERENCES TO CONTRIBUTIONS IN BOOKS

Enter under the name of contributing author and include relevant page numbers.

EXAMPLE

BETTS A (1995) Acquired defences. In: Hinchliff S, Montague S and Watson R (eds) *Physiology for Nursing Practice*, pp. 272–299. London, Baillière Tindall.

REFERENCES TO PART OF A BOOK YOU HAVE CONSULTED

Include page numbers or chapters.

Example

FATCHETT A (1994) *Politics, Policy and Nursing*, Chapter 4. London, Baillière Tindall.

HANDBOOKS, DIRECTORIES etc. IN SINGLE OR SEVERAL VOLUMES

Examples

CAMBRIDGE INFORMATION AND RESEARCH SERVICES LIMITED (1986) *Industrial Development Guide 1986*, 8th edn. Harlow, Longman.

THESES AND DISSERTATIONS

Include the details of level and name of awarding institution.

Example

STEPHENSON P (1995) Nursing and Race Relations. Unpublished BA (Hons) thesis, Leicester, De Montfort University.

INSTITUTIONS OR CORPORATE BODIES AS AUTHORS

Example

THE NATIONAL BOARD FOR NURSING, MIDWIFERY AND HEALTH VISITING FOR NORTHERN IRELAND (1993) *Nursing the Future*. Belfast, National Board.

JOURNAL REFERENCES

A reference to an article in a journal contains the following information in the order listed.

1) Author(s).
2) Year of publication in brackets.
3) Title of article.
4) Title of journal, underlined.
5) Volume number.
6) Issue number, in brackets
7) Specific date for a weekly journal, abbreviate the month.
8) Inclusive pages – p. is for one page, pp. for more than one page.

Example

THORNTON H (1992) The luck of the draw. *Nursing Times*
88(37), 9 Sept, p. 58

HARVARD SYSTEM OF REFERENCING

To cite a reference in the text which appears in the alphabetical'
compiled list of references at the end of the text, use the following example.

Doctors who make the diagnosis are in a powerful position. Access t
such power is controlled by professional associations with their ow
vested interests to protect (Naidoo and Wills, 1994). The 185
Medical Act established the General Medical Council which wa
authorized to regulate doctors, oversee medical education and keep
register of qualified practitioners (Hart, 1994). Medical colleges resiste
the entry of women to the profession for many years. In 1901 ther
were 36 000 medical practitioners, of whom 212 were women. Ther
is evidence that Black and Asian doctors face discrimination in thei
medical careers (Tschudin, 1994a). This implies that ability is not th
sole criterion for gaining a place to train in medicine or in subsequen
career progression. Special counselling is a good idea in such case
(Tschudin, 1994b).

REFERENCES
HART C (1994) *Behind the Mask: Nurses, their Unions an*
Nursing Policy. London, Baillière Tindall.
NAIDOO J and WILLS J (1994) *Health Promotion: Foundation*
for Practice. London, Baillière Tindall.
TSCHUDIN V (1994a) *Deciding Ethically: A Practical Approach*
to Nursing Challenges. London, Baillière Tindall.
TSCHUDIN V (1994b) *Counselling.* London, Baillière Tindall.

At every point in the text which refers to a particular document,
insert the author(s) surname(s) and year of publication. Use lower
case letters after the year if referring to more than one piece of
work published in the same year by the same author.

QUOTES

This is where you refer to an author's work. You can have direct
and indirect quotes.

Direct quote:

'Pressure groups attempt to influence policy making at both national and local levels.'

(Masterson, 1994, p. 42)

When using direct quotes, you should also include the page number. This allows the reader to find the original source.

Indirect quote:

Masterson (1994) stated that one of the aims of pressure groups was to affect policy-making decisions at both local and national levels.

In both these examples, the authors would be listed in alphabetical order in the reference list.

Secondary References

Wherever possible you should always attempt to use readily available or recent primary sources, i.e. the original publication. However, this is not always possible, and you may also want to refer to a classic piece of writing which has been quoted by another author. Use the term 'cited by' and the name of the author and the date of the text actually used.

Example

Masterson (1994) outlined the role of pressure groups
(cited by Maslin-Prothero, 1996).

or

The role of pressure groups was outlined by Masterson
(1994, cited by Maslin-Prothero, 1996).

In both of these examples only the details of Maslin-Prothero (1996) should appear in the reference list.

VANCOUVER SYSTEM OF REFERENCING

The Vancouver system of referencing is widely used in journals and some books. All references are identified in the text by numbers, in brackets or in superscript. The philosophy behind this system of referencing is that the use of numbers in the text does not distract the reader by interrupting the text.

Reference to the same author and publication uses the same number. The references are then listed in numerical order.

EXAMPLE

The World Health Organization European Region's 'Health for All – 2000 Targets' [1] and the British Government's White Paper 'The Health of the Nation' [2] both list a series of targets by which improvements in health over a specific period of time may be measured.

References
1. WORLD HEALTH ORGANIZATION (1985) *Targets for Health for All.* Copenhagen, WHO Regional Office for Europe.
2. DEPARTMENT OF HEALTH (1992) *The Health of the Nation.* London, HMSO

The style of reference, for material from a book or journal, is the same for Vancouver and Harvard referencing; the difference is the use of numbers in the Vancouver system.

CONCLUSION

There are a number of different referencing systems available. Each individual and institution has their preferred system of referencing. It is important that you identify the method preferred prior to submitting work, and use this method when compiling. Your reference list must be checked to ensure it is accurate, so that should you or anyone else want to find the original source, they can.

Appendix B: Your Personal Development and Personal Professional Profile

PERSONAL DEVELOPMENT

This section offers a few definitions and some advice about job hunting, portfolios and further education. It is aimed towards those who haven't much experience of applying for jobs or how to go about it.

Job Searching

You must look around and seek things out rather than waiting and hoping for the perfect job to be offered to you. There are various sources: local and national papers; employer's in-house publications if available to outsiders – try personnel/human resource departments; professional magazines; job centres, employment agencies; and speculative applications (i.e. applying to organisations who haven't advertised job vacancies).

Advisory material is available – articles appear regularly in all types of publications, and books/booklets are continually written, e.g. by careers or student organisations.

Application Forms

The purpose of your application form is to get you short-listed for an interview from amongst all the other applicants. Therefore it helps if you fill the application form in neatly (it impresses), the descriptive sections fully (you've made an effort), and the factual bits accurately (you might remember them when asked). Give a good account of your past and current activities, but keep it relevant. Potential employers will be looking for experiences, skills, and attitudes that meet their short-list selection criteria.

Remember to say *why* you want *this* job and what you can offer – you should use the job description as a framework, as well as any local or pertinent knowledge of the post and employing organisation.

With luck you will be invited to an interview. If you are unable to attend the interview, tell them, they might be able to rearrange another time. Various tests or weeding-out processes exist depending on the organisation and personalities, and the type and level of post for example psychological assessments, or trial by sherry/dinner.

Referees and References

The application form will ask you to include the details of at least two referees willing to give a character reference. The application will specify who they expect and it usually an individual who is your present employer, and /or your university lecturer. In some cases three references are requested, this provides you with the opportunity to use someone you may have worked with or for, such as a holiday playscheme or voluntary organisation.

Always speak to your referee before putting their name forward. Check that they are willing to provide a reference and that it will be favourable. Be enthusiastic about the post you are applying for and provide them with any necessary information including job description. Don't forget to inform them about the outcome following interview, and thank them for any reference given, you never know when you are going to need their help again.

Presentations

A fairly typical request is for you to give a presentation to the panel, as part of the actual interview, on a topic related to the job. Give it your best shot using whatever mode you are comfortable with. A high tech, super slick approach may actually intimidate the panel but it is certainly better than a half-hearted unprepared version. Avoid an interactive presentation; they might not want to participate.

See Chapter 7

Interview

Prepare for the interview, don't expect to just turn up and be naturally the best candidate. Think about the job and your thoughts and feelings about it. What would you like to tell them, and what type of questions are they most likely to ask? You should at least be able to respond to some of the latter by using the former, unless you really aren't what the panel has in mind. There is unlikely to be one correct answer to a question so as long as you've got a balanced range of responses, for example on management, practical and peripheral issues (e.g. legal aspects), then you're in with a chance.

Practice speaking the words – when the time comes you want them to flow. Some people like to rehearse with a mock interview with friends or colleagues.

Think of a few genuine questions to ask at the end. You can base them on what you have found out from the information provided by the organisation. Avoid confrontational questions or those associated with pay. You can raise those when they have offered you the job.

Don't overlook practicalities: smart clothing, travel arrangements, eating, toilet, deodorant, relaxation, presentation material, times, venue. It is advisable to take a copy of your CV and application form, to remind you what you said about yourself.

PERSONAL PROFESSIONAL PROFILES

An ordinary profile is a description of something by its key features, for example an individuals employment history. A personal professional profile (PPP) is not to be confused with an ordinary profile. A PPP is a specific document which is written by and unique to its owner.

A personal professional profile is a diary for reflecting on your professional activities and for planning your own development. Your PPP is a personal diary for:

- Recording and storing basic information for example home address, course certificates;
- Recording your reflective thoughts on your professional activities and their effects on events and outcomes;
- Setting your own professional goals and self development plan.

Your PPP is a UKCC requirement for PREP (UKCC, 1995). It is a useful and vital component of your professional career and eligibility to continue practising as a nurse. A PPP is your own document that you can use selectively in your job application and interview.

When developing your PPP you have a number of choices, your can develop your own or purchase an 'off-the shelf' copy. The pre-packaged PPPs usually come in a lever arch file with pre-printed sheets; these can be completed by you, for example the RCN profile, the ENB Professional Profile (ENB, 1991), Professional Nurse: Personal Professional Profile (Teasdale, 1993) and the Churchill Livingstone Professional Profile (Kenworthy, 1993). They look good, however they do not provide you with the flexibility to adapt and change what you choose to include in your PPP. Alternatively, you can do your own using the UKCC fact sheets (UKCC, 1995) or McGrother (1995) to create your own PPP.

A curriculum vitae (CV) records aspects of your life history that have a bearing on prospective employment: significant events; personal developments; general education; professional career; and any significant achievements or awards. A CV is an opportunity to assert your qualities, especially those qualities you think your potential employer values. Remember that they will also be used as a proxy measure of your credibility and worth (compared to other candidates), so a poor CV maybe a reason to exclude your application. They accompany an application form, even if not actually requested by employers, but can also be used prospectively if not responding to a job advert.

If you prepare a CV in advance, then you can respond instantly and without panic to a job opportunity. Don't forget to keep it updated (storage on a computer disk can be very convenient for this), and to tailor it to the specific post you're applying for.

Again, look out for advice on the style and content of CVs. Off-the-shelf ones are available if you prefer not to do it yourself (most of the nursing journals offer a CV facility, look at their back pages). Remember to get it proof read and properly typed, if at all possible, so that it is an attractive document.

CAREER ADVICE AND CHOICES

There are lots of sources available, including direct meetings with career advisors, for example at your local job centre. These are generally public organisations though private ones are also available, for which there is more likely to be a charge.

You are after, presumably, a wide range of impartial opinions and advice rather than bodies or individuals who have a vested interest in a particular option. It's not good use of time to visit agencies who are only likely to reinforce what you already think or that, for whatever reason, you are not really prepared to consider.

Don't expect miracles either, particularly if you aren't at all sure what you want to do. If this is your situation then you should think about the way you tend to act. For instance: Do you choose or drift? Do you prefer familiarity to the unknown? Do you want to work long hours or in fixed shifts? Move around or be based at a fixed location? Obviously it is more likely for you to find employment in an area that you already have experience in. Be careful though which path you take initially, because switching career paths as you get older will not be easy.

FURTHER EDUCATION

You should continue to study because, hopefully, you want to; because it maintains, develops, and complements your knowledge and skills; and because 'lifelong learning' is becoming the norm as a professional concept, and is now a UKCC requisite for nurses (PREP).

Will you study now, sooner, or later? Will this be while employed or unemployed? Will it be full time or part time? Where will you study? How will you study? What will you study? How will it be paid for?

Don't be complacent about setting yourself job and educational goals and strategies for achieving them; there is a lot of competition out there, but there are also many options and opportunities.
Good luck.

REFERENCES

ENB (1991) *ENB Professional Portfolio*. London, ENB.

KENWORTHY, N (1993) *The Churchill Livingstone Professional Portfolio*. Edinburgh, Churchill Livingstone.

McGROTHER, J (1995) *Profiles, Portfolios and How to Build Them*. London, Scutari Press.

TEASDALE, K (ed) (1993) *Professional Nurse: Personal Professional Profile*. London, Mosby Year Book.

UKCC (1995) *PREP and You*. PREP Factsheets London, UKCC.

Appendix C: Useful Addresses and Telephone Numbers

Association of Nursing Students
Royal College of Nursing
20 Cavendish Square
London W1M 0AB
Tel. 0171 872 0840

The English National Board for Nursing, Midwifery and Health Visiting
Victory House
170 Tottenham Court Road
London W1P 0HA
Tel. 0171 388 3131
Fax 0171 383 4031

The Welsh National Board for Nursing, Midwifery and Health Visiting
Floor 13
Pearl Assurance House
Greyfriars Road
Cardiff CF1 3AG
Tel. 01222 395535
Fax 01222 229366

National Board for Nursing, Midwifery and Health Visiting for Northern Ireland
RAC House
79 Chichester Street
Belfast BT1 4JE
Tel. 01232 238152
Fax 01232 333298

National Board for Nursing, Midwifery and Health Visiting for
Scotland
22 Queen Street
Edinburgh EH2 1JX
Tel. 0131 2267371
Fax 0131 2259970

United Kingdom Central Council for Nursing, Midwifery and
Health Visiting (UKCC)
23 Portland Place
London W1N 4JT
Tel. 0171 6377181
Fax 0171 4362924

Royal College of Nursing of the United Kingdom
20 Cavendish Square
London W1M 0AB
Tel. 0171 8720840
Fax 0171 3551379

National Union of Students
461 Holloway Road
London N7 6LJ
Tel: 0171 272 8900
Fax: 0171 263 5713

UCAS
PO Box 28
Cheltenham
Gloucestershire GL50 3SA
Tel: 01242 227788

Nurses & Midwives Central Clearing House
ENB
PO Box 9017
London W1A 0XA

Telephone for specific information phone the number which
corresponds with your surname.
A–F   0171 391 6291
G–L   0171 391 6305
M–Q 0171 391 6274
R–Z   0171 391 6317

Open Monday to Friday 10.00–16.00 hrs
Fax 0171 391 6252

NB From September 1997, UCAS will have an overall responsibility for both pre-registration diploma and degree applications.
Pre-registration degree courses will continue to go through the
UCAS system. However, Pre-registration diploma courses will be
administered through the Nurses and Midwives Admissions Service (NMAS) based at UCAS. Course information will be
produced in the summer (commencing in 1997) for entry into
pre-registration diploma courses in the Spring and Autumn.

Health Service Careers
PO Box 204
London SE99

Index

Numbers followed by the letter 'g' refer to glossary entries